AF477790

Human Values and Global Governance

Also edited by Björn Hettne

SUSTAINABLE DEVELOPMENT IN A GLOBALIZED WORLD

Human Values and Global Governance

Studies in Development, Security and Culture

Volume 2

Edited by

Björn Hettne

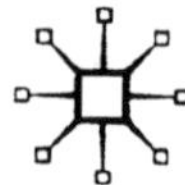

First published in 2008 by
PALGRAVE MACMILLAN
Houndmills, Basingstoke, Hampshire RG21 6XS and
175 Fifth Avenue, New York, N.Y. 10010
Companies and representatives throughout the world.

PALGRAVE MACMILLAN is the global academic imprint of the Palgrave
Macmillan division of St. Martin's Press, LLC and of Palgrave Macmillan Ltd.
Macmillan® is a registered trademark in the United States, United Kingdom
and other countries. Palgrave is a registered trademark in the European
Union and other countries.

ISBN-13: 978–0–230–55128–2 hardback
ISBN-10: 0–230–55128–9 hardback

This book is printed on paper suitable for recycling and made from fully
managed and sustained forest sources. Logging, pulping and manufacturing
processes are expected to conform to the environmental regulations of
the country of origin.

A catalogue record for this book is available from the British Library.

A catalog record for this book is available from the Library of Congress.

10 9 8 7 6 5 4 3 2 1
17 16 15 14 13 12 11 10 09 08

Printed and bound in Great Britain by
CPI Antony Rowe, Chippenham and Eastbourne

In memory of Karl Eric Knutsson

Contents

List of Tables

List of Figures

Editor's Preface: Development, Security and Culture

Björn Hettne

This book, focussing on *human values and global governance*, together with a companion volume on *sustainable development in a globalized world*, is the final outcome of six years' work of the 'Sector Committee on Culture, Security and Sustainable Social Development' within Riksbankens Jubileumsfond. This preface, providing an overall framework for the work, elaborates on the original programmatic text developed as a platform for the committee.[1] The purpose of that text was to present the genesis and scientific context of 'culture, security and development' and to discuss how the current meaning of these concepts has been influenced by what has become known as 'globalization'. Our point of departure was that the concepts should constitute an interrelated, albeit complex, research area with a focus on development and security in a cultural perspective. In the course of our work since the group was constituted in the year 2000, certain additional themes have imposed themselves through global events, in particular September 11th and the subsequent theme of terrorism, as well as intellectual encounters experienced by the group on visits in South Africa, Egypt and Brazil, actualizing issues such as reconciliation, dialogue among cultures and democratization as particular foci within the general theme. All this together, constituting the learning process of the group, forms the framework of the two books.

The ambition was thus to see how the three concepts could relate to one another, after each of them had been individually examined in the perspective of globalization. They are all good examples of 'essentially contested concepts' in the sense that there are a number of different and not always mutually consistent definitions of them, plus the fact that their meanings necessarily change over time, particularly at times of transformation.[2] This is what justifies historical specification and sensitivity to contextual discourses.[3] It is fascinating to study changes in the meaning of such contested definitions, since they reflect an underlying transformation of society about which we have but partial knowledge. That applies in particular in the case when the transformation is of a qualitative nature, that is to say, a perceived change in the fundamental social structure and the social rationality which lies behind it.

How can one know that a structural change with such dramatic ontological consequences is taking place? A reasonable method is to study what happens to the constituent principles of the system which is undergoing change. As regards the Westphalian states system and its basic unit, the nation-state, these principles comprise territorialism, sovereignty and centralized authority (based on different forms of legitimacy).[4] If these principles, albeit being social constructions, are undergoing change, we can reasonably subscribe to the view that a more fundamental structural change is actually taking place. The fact that the institutional forms of the nation-state remain in place does not imply any high degree of continuity in a situation in which the transnational context is changing and the cohesion of the nation-state is breaking up. This particular institution's historic role has changed irreversibly, but some of its functions may nevertheless remain and be taken over by other types of structures.

In the case of the nation-state, its historical efficiency has above all rested on its military capacity which was largely forgotten during the Cold War and the bilateral world order, stabilized by balance of terror (mutually assured destruction). After September 11th and the global war against terrorism, the coercive and military role of nation-states in general, and the US in particular, has again become more visible, countering previous post-sovereign tendencies linked to human rights and 'human' or 'liberal' intervention undertaken in correspondence with changing praxis of international law.[5] Whether this imperialist trend contradicts globalization or should be seen as a new, more coercive, militarized form of globalization is a matter of definition.[6]

The analysis that follows is divided into three parts: metatheoretical reflections, discursive analysis of the three concepts, and a discussion of some crucial themes and research areas suggested by the framework. To propose new research areas and facilitate organizational ways of doing interdisciplinary research were the main purposes of the committee.[7]

Metatheoretical reflections

The renaissance which has taken place over the last two decades in the theory of culture has a definite link with the equally strong interest in 'globalization'. It is thus the consequences of globalization, or what we here call 'the globalized condition', which have given the concepts a partly new meaning, which in turn justifies new research into the post-national, post-sovereign or post-Westphalian society. Therefore it is impossible to avoid a discussion also of the ontological dimension of globalization.[8]

Ontology of globalization

There is still a lack of clarity about the concept of globalization, even a debate about whether globalization really exists. This discussion does not seem very relevant however. Something has certainly happened, and then the debate is about whether this is to be called globalization or not, which in turn has to do with how the concept is defined. Communications between certain places throughout the world are virtually instantaneous (compression of the world in terms of space and time), with no significant barriers between societies previously considered as more or less separately demarcated national and local arenas. The world at large is felt to have shrunk and to be omnipresent. The world economy is integrated and the autonomy of national economies is diminished. Common ecological conditions have created a planetary existential problem for mankind. From a cultural perspective globalization is more complex, giving birth to hybrid forms. Cultural phenomena which previously were more geographically limited are now to be found throughout the world, often in new and very innovative hybrid combinations.

The question whether globalization is something new or old is also basically a matter of definition.[9] It is widely held that globalization means something more profound than internationalization, by which is meant merely an increase in the contacts between national societies, whereas globalization defines a growing transnational arena in which limited nation-state control operates and where players other than state players assert themselves. It further binds together a large number of players at different levels of society, including various sub-national levels, for example, micro-regions and local communities. It can perhaps be said that the criterion for the fact that we are faced with globalization rather than internationalization is precisely the impact on local society, as well as that local society in itself thereby coming to form part of globalization ('glocalization').

A third major debate concerns whether globalization, seen from a normative point of view, is a good or bad thing. This depends on how different individuals and groups are affected, and we can with great certainty maintain that they are affected differently. Globalization reduces the space for action by the nation-state. In consequence the state functions less and less as a protector of its 'own' population, and instead more and more as a medium for signals from the world market: structural adaptation and cutbacks on welfare.[10] This perceived 'betrayal' alienates the state from society, diminishes its legitimacy in the eyes of segments of its own population. In collapsing states the nation-state order is replaced by all kinds of local leaders, including warlords, a situation which recalls the Middle Ages. There is nothing determined by nature in a process of globalization which also unleashes anti-modern counter-movements, for example, in the form of neo-nationalism and religious fundamentalism. This, finally, implies that globalization must be thought of in the plural.[11]

Epistemological observations

This ontological transformation – the globalization of the world – suggests certain epistemological observations. The scope of the question of understanding goes wider than methodology. It is also a matter of the epistemological consequences of the globalized condition.[12] Many theorists of globalization have dwelt on the question of the compression of the world in terms of time and space. Contemporaneity in social relations and liberation from the limitations of space obviously affect identity formation and the experience of belonging, in ways which as yet can scarcely be glimpsed.[13] Epistemologically, globalization has been linked with various anti-rationalistic tendencies, which can be as dissimilar to one another as fundamentalism and post-modernism, at the same time as globalization has been seen as a consequence of modernity.[14]

In the first place, the time is now ripe to take globalization as a given point of departure, rather than to dwell on the question of what globalization actually is, as if it were a newly discovered botanical species. Globalization can instead be regarded as the new 'condition' in which all social science research must be formulated, which implies qualitatively new premises in the theory of knowledge, roughly what was earlier discussed as 'paradigm shifts'.[15] In this perspective 'normal science' no longer functions as an organizing principle for the formation of knowledge. There is a natural link between stability in a social structure, and the researcher's ability to make forecasts and to construct stringent models. If representations of society in the form of theories and models do not satisfactorily explain the course of events, it is time to strive for observing reality without preconceptions, that is to say, to try to determine its historical specificity. The focus should be on the new reality per se, rather than the relatively abstract problem of the meaning of globalization. The problem is that reality is changing faster than the scientific tools to which we have for a long time been accustomed. That applies to all three areas of research in point. There has been an upsurge in *cultural research*, directly linked with the equally rapidly increasing interest in globalization, the more complex manifestations of which are concerned precisely with the cultural sphere. In *security research* it is a question of the changed role of the nation-state and the emergence of both new identities and new threat images, that is to say, a broader concept of security and risk. In the field of *development research*, globalization implies that the traditional arena of the development expert, the national arena and the 'national development strategy' which is connected to it, is disappearing. Together these fields form part of what is often referred to as 'global studies'.

Secondly, the holistic ideal of research implied by this, the whole as something more than its parts (and parts understood in relation to the whole), deserves a revival.[16] It can, however, also be asked whether holism is really an adequate concept in the globalized social condition, characterized by networks, interaction, flows and 'hybridity'. Nowadays, the concept *complexity* is more often used in connection with analysis of globalization, but with a partly different meaning than the older concept of holism, which usually referred to territorially based and defined cultural systems, in which an analysis of the whole was considered theoretically meaningful and empirically feasible.[17] Can complexity perhaps be seen as the globalized, supra-territorial condition's counterpart to holism?[18]

Thirdly, it appears desirable, indeed necessary, that the relevant research tasks should be organized on an interdisciplinary basis, a point which is closely connected with the holistic ideal of research (or, if you wish, the ambition to take complexity seriously). It should, however, be the research problem which governs what combination of scientific specialities is appropriate. A truly interdisciplinary approach presupposes a combination of specialist and generalist competences which take a long time to acquire. Therefore it is important to give priority to cooperation between subject areas and facilitate more profound cooperation between different scientific specialities. At the same time, the increasing prevalence of collapsing societies in different parts of the world justifies greater interest in the fundamental matters of political philosophy and classical sociology (what makes society possible?), questions that were posed long before the present disciplinary specialization.

We should also, *fourthly*, encourage research at a metatheoretical level, in order better to understand the new ontology created by globalization. It is a matter not only of making the research landscape more complete, but also of being able (with the aid of appropriate methodological tools) to comprehend fundamental changes in the economic, social, political, and cultural landscapes. In addition to these two ambitions, there is the need for the analysis of society to reflect a new global reality, for which we still lack an adequate scientific language, since ontological changes have epistemological consequences. The social science language is at present far too related to a nation-state reality (methodological nationalism) and to what happens in a national arena (the container theory). The point is to change perspectives from society as contained in the nation-state to society as an emerging transnational phenomenon, which is hard to describe with the tools that current social science, confined by methodological nationalism, provides.[19]

Pluralism in research has come to stay. Post-modern theory has shown with some success how reality can be represented by symbols and models that are not immediately inter-subjective, but instead carry matters forward by means of an exchange of opinions or dialogue between observers, in which greater insight emerges in the form of a growing consensus, or at least mutual understanding. In a situation of metatheoretical uncertainty an open dialogue oriented standpoint methodology is important. In certain respects this can perhaps be compared with a multicultural dialogue between different social groups in society. The perception that disagreement on the definitions of fundamental concepts in the field of human or cultural studies is an obstacle to research and progress, rather than a natural state of affairs, builds on a false view of the formation of concepts and of their role (Åhlberg 1995). Despite this legitimate programmatic openness we cannot avoid discussions about definitions of the three concepts, but it must be made quite clear that we regard the different definitions as alternative angles of approach and not as something which is intended to lock future research into an altogether too fixed framework.

According to the post-modern view there is no given 'out there', at least, nothing that we can for certain (scientifically) know anything about. That makes it even more difficult to assert the existence of distinct researchable relations between the three concepts. We must therefore somehow relate to this dilemma. A reasonable approach has been suggested by Fredrik Barth (1987: 87):

> I assume that there is a real world out there, but that our representations of that world are constructions. People create and apply these cultural constructions in a struggle to grasp the world, relate to it, and manipulate it through concepts, knowledge, and acts. In the

process, reality impinges, and the events that occur consequently are not predicted by the cultural system of representations employed by the people, though they may largely be interpretable within it [...] The real [...] is composed of this widest compass: natural world, a human population with all its collective and statistical social features, and a set of cultural ideas in terms of which [...] people try to understand and cope with themselves and their habitat.[20]

It is important to acknowledge the simultaneous existence of different cultural concepts and a pluralistic understanding of the need for different approaches to different research requirements, which also includes normative theory as a legitimate form of knowledge-formation. On the other hand, one cannot study reality on the basis solely of normative definitions. Holism and the study of complexity presuppose pluralism, as regards both values and methodology. The conclusion is that we must take relativism seriously without allowing ourselves to become subservient to it. Scientific pluralism presupposes a programmatically open and experimental attitude to methodological alternatives.

The conceptual troika

Let us now tackle the task of delimiting and defining the field to be investigated, a field defined by the three concepts: development, security, and culture. As regards development and security, it is interesting to note that the intra-disciplinary discussion of these two fields has followed separate tracks that seldom did intersect. They constituted separate academic subcultures institutionalized in radically different ways (but equally closely linked to the modern project). Development theory was built on contributions from development economics, gradually extended through sociology, social anthropology, political science, geography, and several other disciplines. After it had been paired with ecology, the theory of sustainable development arose. Security theory emanates from political science, international relations and the more specialized discipline of strategic studies and has, as mentioned above, later also been enlarged in a fashion which has assigned an ever more subordinate role to conventional security. That has to do with the diminished likelihood of inter-state confrontations in the new geopolitical global environment.

Culture is of course of a different nature, in our approach providing the frame within which issue areas such as development and security are, consciously or unconsciously, understood. They are not only theory-dependent but also context-dependent. Each of the terms has its own complex intellectual history but will here be related to one another, as if they were a more or less coherent research area.

What difference does it make if development and security are more systematically related to culture? Security conventionally means absence from the threat of physical violence. Bring in culture, and security would also imply identity. Development could mean development of infrastructure and increased production, but with a more conscious application of the cultural dimension focus will be on human development.

Development

Development is one of the most tricky concepts to define, even in the company of security and culture. *Development studies* is generally described as an interdisciplinary field, and as such influenced by several different intra-disciplinary approaches: development economics, geography, modernization sociology, political development theory, development anthropology, etc. *Development theory* takes up elements from different theories specific to the various disciplines, but its ambition is to comprehend the totality, whether that is termed 'holistic' or 'complex'.[21]

Sustainable development takes us into the environmental sector, which makes particularly heavy demands on the interdisciplinary approach, since we are here moving between faculty boundaries.[22] We can also note a paradigm shift from nationally demarcated environmental problems, over which states were considered to have control (the Stockholm Conference 1972), to the idea of a global ecology, the problems of which can be managed only by global measures (often it is in practice a matter of local measures with global consequences) implemented by transnational players. The concept 'sustainable societal development' further broadens the sustainability dimension, from ecology to social structure, political institutions, and culture (compare with societal security). In fact, the environment can no longer be seen as an external context of human action.[23]

The concept 'sustainable development' derives from principles within the international movement for nature conservation, in which the idea was launched of a sustainable exploitation of natural resources (and later also of the environment in general).[24] It made its great breakthrough as a result of the Brundtland Commission's report entitled 'Our Common Future' in 1987 (WCDE 1987). Here sustainable development was described as 'development that meets the needs of the present generation without jeopardizing the ability of future generations to meet their own needs'. This definition, which has come to permeate debate and continued work in the United Nations, puts the concept of 'need' at the centre, and in particular the fundamental needs of the world's poor. Attention has also been drawn to the limitations that the state must impose, faced with the capacity of the environment and natural resources to satisfy human needs.[25]

Sustainable development thus deals with combining protection of the environment with global growth in which justice is applied as between the South and the North, and in a long-term perspective also for future generations. The earlier polarization between growth and environment in the debate of the 1970s could thereby be partly bridged over through the acceptance of sustainable development as a matter common to both the industrialized countries and the poor countries of the Third World. Principles of common responsibility, solidarity, and differentiated obligations have developed as important parts of the concept of sustainable development.[26]

Sustainable development, or its opposite, is strongly bound up with culturally-based patterns of behaviour ('the American way of life is not negotiable') which must first be understood if it is to be possible to change them. One of the fundamental dimensions of this concept is thus inter-generational justice, that is to say that one generation must not have the right, for the sake of its own advantage, to impair the conditions of life for future generations. The problem is that what constitutes such a development can only be determined by coming generations. A reverse problem is the dilemma involved in giving guarantees for future generations, in a situation in which human beings now living are so far from reasonable satisfaction of their needs. The definition is therefore better understood as a moral principle than as a definition of development. As argued by several contributions to this book, this principle ought also to include a children's perspective on the future.

The concept *societal* sustainable development is problematic, since the question as to which society is, in fact, meant by it is left open or, rather, is taken for granted. It is normally the 'national society' that is referred to, a society which no longer exists in its 'pure', that is to say, territorially demarcated, form. That raises intricate questions about the boundaries between societies in a globalized, deterritorialized world. These questions which affect the problem of multi-level analysis, as well as what was discussed above as the 'complexity problem', are not altogether new, but have become more and more acute as a problem of method. Is it a matter of the local society, the national society – the nation-state – a regional formation (such as the EU), or is it the world society? A decisive point when defining the meaning of 'sustainability' is thus which territorial entity does one intend to be sustainable? The ecological imperative, the absence of borders in the global condition, makes it natural to consider sustainable social development as a global process which must be governed by the insights of natural science, that is to say, a continuation of the modern project on the global scale (Eriksson 1997).

Within the subject of international relations most attention has been paid to the question of responsibility and implementation, in the case that some form of transnational measure is regarded as necessary (global governance).

Criticism of the established theory of development has come from many quarters. Latterly it has chiefly applied to 'interventionism', that is to say, the view of the state as an omnipotent director of the development process (Toye 1987). It has also been a matter of a more fundamental criticism of the 'actually existing development', which more and more violates ecological systems, or violence against the cultural pluralism which expresses itself in a growing number of politicized ethnic groups, partly as a reaction against 'development', taking violent steps against one another or against the government (Stavenhagen 1990). This fundamental critical position forms part of what is usually called 'alternative' development.[27] The alternative development theory aims to subordinate development to ecological principles, i.e. sustainable development. It is thus at root a question of an ecologically appropriate development, even if the concept has, as we have seen, been broadened to include culture and security. Feminist perspectives have further underlined the potential importance of the alternative theory (e.g. Sen and Grown 1987).

Today it has become common to talk about global development, as different from, although part of, globalization. Since development problems are globalized, and 'national development' has lost much of its meaning, development theory is necessarily merging with International Political Economy into global social theory and the new interdisciplinary field of 'Global Studies' (drawing on IR, IPE, development studies, cultural studies, the new security paradigm etc) (Björn Hettne, volume 1). Global development necessitates a further strengthening of the societal (welfare) dimension of world order – the provision of global public goods. Global development, so defined, would mean that standards applied in most (non-failed) domestic systems are increasingly taken as norms in the international system as well (Gun-Britt Andersson, volume 2). It may be said simply to refer to the quality of international relations.

Security

The conventional realist view of security emanates from the position of the individual nation-state in an anarchic international system and basically concerns the survival of the state as such, that is to say, the preservation of its sovereignty. Security policy consists, within the framework of this discourse, in warding off, above all, military threats against national sovereignty.

The perspective is historically grounded in the Westphalian era and the Westphalian political rationality. The conventional security concept therefore contains a built-in conservatism which goes together with its historical connection to balance of power, the load-bearing security principle in the Westphalian structure. The balance of power policy aims at preserving the relative strengths between states, or groups of states, if necessary by means of war. Neutrality is in practice subordinate to the balance of power policy in that it (often explicitly) pays regard to the reigning geopolitical balance.

The end of the Cold War, the collapse of the communist system, and the wave of ethno-nationalism and collapsing state formations, that is to say, internally generated security problems, have plunged the world of international relations in its conventional form into a deep crisis of confidence and opened the door to culture analysis and normative theory (Lapid and Kratochwil 1996; see also Smith 1992). None the less, militarily defined security retains a special position in the security discourse, even though threats in this area are not regarded as imminent or are overshadowed by other threat images in the global 'risk society', including terrorist threats which after September 11th reached an unprecedented scale (mega-terrorism) with the purpose of transforming world order (Falk 2004). Globalization has changed man's basic perception of security, whether that is now explicitly linked with the globalized condition or not. Such a link is made by Ulrich Beck, in his concept of the 'risk society', which is also a global society (Beck 1992; 1999).[28]

Once again, it is globalization that has changed the context, preceded by processes that were earlier described as internationalization and interdependence. The new security problem arises from internally generated disintegration within society, manifested inter alia by the decline in the power and capacity, and hence in the legitimacy of the state; by sub-national economic strategies aimed at linking parts of a country more directly with a transnational economic structure; by the disintegration of the pluralistic and inclusive community created by civil society; by a corresponding reinforcement of ethnocentric loyalties with consequent social conflicts; and by the emergence of sub-groups and subcultures, protecting what they regard as their own legitimate security interests and the right to be 'respected'.

The broader security concept is often linked with various environmental problems, but since this dimension is already covered by the concept of 'sustainability', in this connection the concept of societal security can constitute a relevant point of departure for the discussion about security (Waever et al. 1993; Buzan et al. 1998). That does not mean underrating the ecological dimension of the security problem, which would be extremely foolish: a country threatened by rising sea levels cannot defend itself by force of arms.[29] Peace (and conflict), on the one hand, and development (and underdevelopment), on the other hand, are on the concrete plane de facto very strongly related to each other, as can clearly be noted in current aid policy and the new awareness of the need to integrate aid policy and security policy. This has already gone so far that there are grounds to post a warning about the 'securitization' of the development and aid discourse.

The enlargement of the approach known as 'societal security' is thus concerned with a shift from sovereignty to identity and from state to society. But what is 'society'? The concept 'society' must not be inseparably bound to any specific historic societal entity. One may also speak of a European society, as of a world society, and nor does nation need to be the same as nation-state. There is a Kurdish nation in Turkey-Iran-Iraq and a Mohawk nation in Canada-the US. Once again we must note that globalization has made the idea of a delimited 'society' anachronistic.

A different critical line of argumentation maintains that security must be sought at the level of the individual, which likewise presupposes a break with the fixation on the state (Walker 1988). Taking it as a whole, one can evidently speak of a democratization of the concept of security, since more and more sections of society lay claim to this value. Making a question a matter of security policy is a way of putting it on the agenda. Securitization also means a risk from the point of view of democracy, since a security issue, automatically defined as 'high politics', is detached from normal democratic management (Eriksson 2001).

The UNDP's Human Development Report 1994 took up the question of *human security*, defined as 'safety from hunger, disease, and repression'. It is also of interest here to note the stark contrast between the people's and the state's need for security:

> For too long, the concept of security has been shaped by the potential for conflict between states. For too long, security has been

equated with threats to a country's borders. For too long, nations have sought arms to protect their security. For most people today, a feeling of insecurity arises more from worries about daily life than from the dread of a cataclysmic world event. Job security, income security, health security, environmental security, security from crime, these are the emerging concerns of human security all over the world. (UNDP 1994: 3)

In later UNDP reports the concept was linked to 'human development', and ultimately to the whole complex of human rights.[30] Other relevant links are 'humanitarian emergency' and 'humanitarian intervention'. One can see this contemporary focus on 'human' as part of the paradigm shift which goes together with globalization giving rise to a post-national logic. The frequent use of the concept 'human' gives associations with a transnational assumption of responsibility (the responsibility to protect), as if one could no longer rely on states to fulfil their responsibility for their citizens. It was implicit in the old state-centred paradigm that it was the task of the state to protect its citizens not only against military threat but also against other security and risk factors, as was most clearly expressed in the welfare state in which the citizen was taken care of from the cradle to the grave.

The International Commission for Global Governance spoke of 'the security of people and the planet'.[31] This line, which from the conceptual point of view is expansionist, is also supported by feminist perspectives on global security as being less directed towards dominance and sovereignty, and more towards cooperation and the construction of society (Tickner 1992).[32] All this can be summarized under the concept 'comprehensive security', expressing the complex societal connections in the globalized condition.

Culture

'Culture' is probably the most complex (according to some, 'hypercomplex') of the three concepts under discussion here. There is therefore nothing odd about the fact that there are many definitions. In this context it is obligatory to point to the classic study by Kroeber and Kluckhohn (1952), in which no less than 164 different definitions of culture were enumerated. Many definitions in this list are, of course, more or less overlapping, and can readily be reduced to a few basic perspectives on culture and society.[33] Still there remain some basic distinctions which seem to be hard to bridge.

It is customary to distinguish between an aesthetic and an anthropological/ethnological concept of culture. The former, which among other things comprises music, literature, and pictorial art, also normally includes, particularly in earlier formulations of it, a value-judgment dimension. The latter is exemplified by phenomena such as 'Swedish culture', 'immigrant culture', and 'the multicultural society'. A concept such as 'cultural landscape' falls somewhere between nature and culture. In this context it is of course highly relevant that there exist intellectual, academic cultures, such as C. P. Snow's 'two cultures' (humanities versus science), which never meet.

Culture is to do with cultivation, and 'the prerequisite for cultivation – the process – is always man as an active and thinking being' (Ek 1989). This definition in no way implies that man lives with a 'ready-made' identity.[34] From this it follows that it is complicated to choose definitions of culture. The classic definition, more than 100 years old, is probably that by E. B. Tylor: 'Culture or Civilization, taken in its wide ethnographic sense, is that complex whole which includes knowledge, belief, art, morality, law, custom, and any other capabilities and habits acquired by man as a member of society' (Tylor 1871). By virtue of its range and breadth this definition has often been taken as the point of departure for discussion of the phenomenon 'culture'. Culture is in this definition identified with civilization, which is not compatible with current usage in which the concept of civilization, based on the idea of levels of cultural aggregation, is reserved for the most aggregated cultural level, namely macro-culture. This definition emphasizes further that culture is something that the individual acquires in his/her capacity as a member of society, a perspective which, on the contrary, still seems to hold good. The result is that the cultural phenomenon is social, and vice versa.

Within the social anthropology tradition, which is less homogeneous than the above-mentioned distinctions may appear to suggest, there are according to Ulf Hannerz three ways of looking at culture, mutually quite compatible, but given different degrees of emphasis in different contexts: (1) culture is something that men learn, (2) culture is an integrated pattern of thought, (3) cultures are distinct, territorially-bound, social collectives. Of these it is the first view that in principle is valid, but the two others (that culture exists in packaged form and that there are several such packages) need to be thoroughly re-examined (something which, by the way, has largely already happened). By culture we here primarily mean the production of meaning, thus providing the prism through which the other concepts are interpreted.[35]

The post-modern turn has put culture as a coherent phenomenon in question.

In this connection we are primarily interested in the relevance of the concept of culture in relation to the globalized condition of society, where culture is manifested in 'de-territorialized' form, which in principle makes impossible a view of culture in which cultures are perceived as integrated and localized.

Globalization of culture does not imply homogenization. In fact, there is no such thing as a homogenous culture in the first place. This is what creates 'the problem of culture'. 'Culture is everywhere', as shifting as social reality itself. Culture is a way of understanding social reality. Culture can be seen as instrumental for economic growth, or as the very purpose of development, meaning ability to choose the 'good life', often culturally defined. It can be the foundation for peace as well as providing the mobilizing symbols for struggle, conflict, and violence.

Civilizational dialogue is a research area experiencing a renaissance as a consequence of the increasing importance of culture on the macroplane in the globalized condition. The concept of civilization has a long and controversial history. As far back as the eighteenth century Herder formulated the insight that the world consisted of many cultures, rather than of one civilization and many barbarians.[36] The concept of civilization in the singular was complemented by the plural understanding. Thus was laid the foundation for ethnography (and social anthropology) which took upon itself the task of describing all these cultures, a task which subsequently was made significantly more difficult by the 'Creolization' of the world (Hannerz 1996).

Totalizing tendencies

Each of the three concepts dealt with here has a built-in 'totalizing' tendency towards hegemony, in the sense that they all expand and through extension come to include each other. This is an expression of the inherent urge for holism in the subject areas covered by the concepts. The definition of *culture* in particular has become more and more inclusive. In 'Our Creative Diversity' by the World Commission for Culture and Development, a distinction is made between two ways of looking at the relationship between culture and development. In one view, culture can have an instrumental value for the achievement of economic growth.[37] In another view, with which the Commission was obviously in sympathy, it is economic growth that is the instrument for attaining what human beings attach value to, which obviously has to do with culture (Knutsson 2000). In accordance with the UNDP, *development* is seen as *human* development and defined as a process which increases mankind's opportunities to devote themselves to what they value in life. The definition was chosen on the basis of the Commission's special preoccupation that culture is a dimension of development, if not something even more comprehensive. It is asserted, for example, that culture is the basis of all development (World Commission on Culture and Development 1996: 233). It is also asserted there that culture is decisive as regards mankind's relationship with nature and the socially constructed environment, the earth, and the universe. That can be said to illustrate a totalizing culture view. As used in our framework culture is total in the sense that nothing can be conceived and understood outside a cultural prism.

The concept of *security* has also become highly expansive. To the old meaning of military security at the nation-state level have been added environmental, cultural, ethnic, economic, social, societal, individual, and other kinds of security at different levels of society. If one adds all the hitherto proposed security dimensions, one obtains a more or less complete model of society, focussed on everything that can go wrong, that is to say, which reduces security and increases uncertainty and 'risk' in a society. To define a problem as a security problem moreover implies, as discussed above, that it acquires a higher priority, thus adding to the motivation of seeing almost everything through the security prism.

Cultural identity is in itself often seen as a security issue. The importance of the culture factor in 'the new conflicts' is clear, but how is it to be understood? The new conflicts are often described as 'ethnic'. The concept 'ethnic conflicts' refers to the form and expression of the conflict, not to its inherent nature. Ethnic difference is in itself rarely or never a cause for conflict. Every ethnic conflict has its own unique features and cannot be explained by inter-civilizational division. Both the management and the solution of a conflict must therefore take its point of departure both in the underlying socio-economic problem and in the specifically ethnic way in which the distributional conflict has evolved. The state is often part of the problem – but must as a rule also be a part of the solution. In a multi-ethnic society the state is primarily an institution for conflict-resolution – or ought to be so. In a 'failed state' the protective function falls back on the primary group, defined as the smallest group bound together by a collective consciousness.

Sustainable development has gradually also come to include concerns about everything that can 'get broken' (thus being unsustainable) in the societal construction, not only the ecological balance which constituted the original problem when the concept was formulated. This extension finds expression in the concept 'sustainable societal development'. For the sake of simplicity we have used the development concept in a broad sense covering different kinds of sustainability as well, assuming that nobody wants unsustainable development. Ecology, 'ecocentrism' or 'deep ecology', has a totalizing tendency in the sense that the anthropo-centric (or cultural) perspective is subordinated to broader biological contexts.

So much for the totalizing tendency of the three concepts. If instead one wishes them to be, in a meaningful way, related to each other and to constitute a common research area, they must in some way be ana-lytically delineated in order to avoid too great an overlap. An alternative idea might be to focus on just one of the three concepts, which thus becomes the main problem, in order later to allow the other two to con-stitute dimensions of the problem chosen. The environmental question has, for example, completely decisive importance both for the develop-ment discussion (i.e. sustainable social development) and the security discussion (comprehensive security).

Notes

1. For a more detailed description, see *Culture, Security and Social Sustainable Development* (Gidlund 2003) from the sector committee, authored by Björn Hettne in dialogue with the rest of the group.
2. Gudrun Dahl discusses the concept of 'essentially contested concepts' (volume 1).
3. The contribution by Björn Hettne (volume 1) thus presents the development of development thinking in terms of historically contextualized discourses. Similarly Urban Jonsson (volume 1) describes changing paradigms in the field of nutrition, and Yudhishthir Raj Isar (volume 2) provides a discourse analysis of 'culture and development' in the UNESCO context.
4. This world order, the European dominated post-1648 world order, is often referred to as Westphalia. The post-Westphalian world order being created by globalization has certain structural similarities (the multilevel structure) with the pre-Westphalian order and sometimes therefore referred to as 'neo-medieval'.
5. In the publication *Culture, Security, and Sustainable Social Development after September 11* (Lundmark 2004) members of the group reflect over the impli-cations of September 11th. The views differed with respect to how new the post-September 11th situation actually is. It is argued by Peter Wallensteen (volume 2) that the debate now has come to circulate around certain key conceptions: the unipolar world (in practice Pax Americana), the order of the international society (what could be called the Pax Omnium Inter Omnes) and possible people-based alternatives (such as the democratic, Kantian, or enlightened peace).

6. James Mittelman (2004: 43) argues that multilateral globalization after September 11th changed into militarized globalization: from consent to coercion.
7. This contributed among other things to establishing the School of Global Studies at Göteborg University.
8. Critical central works are Ulrich Beck (1997) and Zygmunt Bauman (1998). For a systematic introduction, see Jan Art Scholte (2005), James Mittelman (2000) and David Held et al. (1999). As regards the globalization myth, see Paul Hirst and Grahame Thompson (1999). On the positive and negative effects of globalization, see Richard Falk (1999).
9. Immanuel Wallerstein (2000) says: 'Globalization is a misleading concept, since what is described as globalization has been happening for 500 years'. On the other hand, the recent dramatic spread of the concept would indicate a new underlying 'reality' (assuming that 'reality' can be known). Once upon a time (the 1780s) 'international' was also a new word (Scholte 2005: 51).
10. See Robert W. Cox and Timothy J. Sinclair (1996) *Approaches to World Order*, especially chapter 15.
11. Compare the Routledge Journal *Globalizations*.
12. Jan Art Scholte (2005: chapter 8) has made a preliminary attempt to judge what globalization means for the fundamental premises of the formation of knowledge. A similar concern may be found in James Mittelman (2004).
13. Roland Robertson (1992: 183) has defined globalization as a growth in 'the scope and depth of consciousness of the world as a single place'.
14. Anthony Giddens (1990) argues that modernity has an inherent tendency to globalization. See also Stephen Toulmin (1990) and further Ulrich Beck et al. (1995).
15. For arguments that social science must go in the direction of 'global social theory', see Björn Hettne and Frederik Söderbaum (1999).
16. Karl Erik Knutsson used the concept 'reality room': 'people live and act, not in any social, cultural, political, economic or religious sector or in any analytically constructed compartment but in a total "reality room" which has all these aspects'. In this connection one should also reiterate that, quoting Karl Eric Knutsson, synthesizing research, 'knowing what is known', is itself an important form of research.
17. This is not to say that all anthropologists were only concerned with such locally situated studies. The isolated village was never the norm but nevertheless serves as a (albeit constructed) metaphorical opposite to the globalized condition, which today is studied by what is known as global anthropology. Enrique Rodriguez Larreta (taking his departure in Karl Eric Knutsson's inaugural lecture on the 'anthropological perspective') discusses the problem of the local and the global (volume 1).
18. See Ulf Hannerz (1992 and 1996).Complexity theory is referred to by Urban Jonsson (volume 1).
19. In this context Ulrich Beck's critique of 'methodological nationalism' is highly relevant (volume 1). A similar idea lies behind methodological territorialism (Scholte 2005).
20. The quotation is taken, as abbreviated, from 'Culture and Human Development. Report on a Conference on Culture, Cultural Research and

Cultural Policy', held in Stockholm, August 1977, compiled and edited by Karl Eric Knutsson, Royal Academy of Letters, History and Antiquities.

21. Here too, it is the case that all the recent literature includes a discussion of sustainable development. See Björn Hettne (1995). The culture dimension has also received more and more attention, see Vincent Tucker (1996) and Peter Worsley (1999).

22. 'Sustainable development is so challenging, morally and intellectually, and so demanding that it will require us to organize scientific knowledge and to ask scientific questions in new ways', it is stated in the report of the Friibergh seminar (Culture and Human Development, p. 13).

23. What is 'natural' is now so thoroughly entangled with what is 'social' that there can be nothing taken for granted about it any more, see Beck et al. (1995: vii).

24. The following text dealing with the emergence of the concept of sustainability is by Katarina Eckerberg. For a background description of the evolution of the idea of sustainable development, see Michael Redclift (1987), S. Lélé (1991) and W. Adams (1990).

25. Alf Hornborg has significantly pointed out that the technology which brings about the 'time-space compression' in the centre of the world system does so at the expense of (human) time and (natural) space at the periphery, which once again brings to the fore environmental justice and risk. 'Time-space compression' is made possible by an unequal global exchange, which Hornborg has inventively called 'time-space appropriation' (volume 1).

26. Specifically, justice and the North-South problem within the concept of sustainability are discussed in detail in Adams (1990), James Meadowcroft (1997) and William Lafferty and Oluf Langhelle (1999).

27. The development concept has in the post-modernist spirit also been called an 'intellectual ruin'. Wolfgang Sachs (1992) thus speaks of an 'age of development', which begins on 20 January 1949. On that day, the American President Harry Truman attached the label 'underdeveloped areas' to a large part of the world outside Europe and the US. The lack of development appeared as a global security policy problem which must be put right in order to guarantee the stability of the new world order, and of American hegemony. Karl Eric Knutsson has described the concept of development as a 'logical invalid'.

28. Anthony Giddens talks of 'manufactured uncertainty'.

29. There is a hardly a recent textbook on international relations that does not have a chapter about the environment and sustainable development. See e.g. Dickson (1997), Booth and Smith (1995), Brown (1997) and Nicholson (1998).

30. Thorleif Pettersson provides a definition of human development (volume 2) and Urban Jonsson discusses children's human right to nutrition (volume 1).

31. See also the discussion on cultural security by Raj Isar, (volume 2).

32. See also Tickner's (1988) attempt to formulate a feminist epistemology in this field, with her reformulation of Hans Morgenthau's principles of political realism.

33. 'The mere fact that there have been so many definitions of culture [...] suggests that there is a need to discuss "the problem of culture" rather than culture "itself"' (Robertson 1992: 33).
34. 'When culture is characterized as *complex* my reading of it is that it must be understood as both *composed* of material conditions, social structures and thought patterns, and that the interplay between them is *complicated*' (Frykman 1999). See also Åhlberg (1998). In another context, Åhlberg distinguishes between the traditional (corresponding with the aesthetic) concept of culture and the anthropological-sociological concept (Åhlberg 1995).
35. This is consistent with the definition given by Raj Isar: 'Culture is the social construction, articulation and reception of meaning' (volume 2).
36. The use of the term civilization in the singular often has an ethno(euro) centric meaning, which under imperialism was described as 'the white man's burden' or 'la mission civilisatrice'.
37. From this it also follows that culture can have the opposite effect. The earlier discourse on development, which is usually summarized as the modernization paradigm, dwelt heavily on 'traditional' culture as a barrier to development that must be removed to make development possible.

References

Abiri, E. (2000) *The Securitization of Migration. Towards an Understanding of Migration Policy Changes in the 1990s. The Case of Sweden*, PhD thesis, Göteborg: Göteborg University.

Adams, W. (1990) *Green Development: Environment and Sustainability in the Third World*, London: Routledge.

Åhlberg, L-O. (1995) 'Om kulturbegreppet' [On the Concept of Culture], in Liss, P-E. and Petersson, B. (eds) (1995) *Hälsosamma tankar. 11 filosofiska uppsatser tillägnade Lennart Nordenfelt*, Nora: Nya Doxa.

Åhlberg, L-O (1998) 'Universalism, pluralism and relativism', in *Our Creative Diversity* and 'In from the Margins', *Tidskrift för kulturstudier*, no. 4.

Barth, F. (1987) *Cosmologies in the Making, A Generative Approach to Cultural Variation in Inner New Guinea*, Cambridge: Cambridge University Press.

Bauman, Z. (1998) *Globalization: The Human Consequences*, Cambridge: Polity Press.

Beck, U. (1992) *Risk Society: Towards a New Modernity*, London: Sage.

Beck, U. (1997) *Was ist Globalisierung?*, Frankfurt am Main: Suhrkamp.

Beck, U. (1999) *World Risk Society*, Cambridge: Polity Press.

Beck, U., Giddens, A. and Lash, S. (1995) *Reflexive Modernization: Politics, Tradition and Aesthetics in the Modern Social Order*, Cambridge: Polity Press.

Booth, K. and Smith, S. (eds) (1995) *International Relations Theory Today*, Cambridge: Polity Press.

Brown, C. (1997) *Understanding International Relations*, London: Macmillan.

Buzan, B., Waever, O. and de Wilde, J. (1998) *Security: a new framework for analysis*, London: Lynne Rienner.

Cox, R. W. and Sinclair, T. J. (1996) *Approaches to World Order*, Cambridge: Cambridge University Press.

Dickson, A. K. (1997) *Development and International Relations*, Cambridge: Polity Press.

Ek, S. B. (1989) *Kultur som problem*, Göteborg: Robek-Konsult.

Eriksson, J. (ed) (2001) *Threat Politics. New Perspectives on Security, Risk and Crisis Management*, Aldershot: Ashgate Publishing.

Eriksson, K-E. (1997) 'On the Roles of Science and Culture in Sustainable Development', Proceedings of the 47th Pugwash Conference on Science and World Affairs, Lillehammer, Norway, 1–7 August, 1997.

Falk, R. (1999) *Predatory Globalization. A critique*, Cambridge: Polity Press.

Falk, R. (2004) *Declining World Order. America's Imperial Geopolitics*, New York and London: Routledge.

Fornäs, J. (2001) *Advancing Cultural Studies in Sweden: An infrastructural initiative*, Norrköping: Arbetslivsinstitutet (Arbetslivsrapport 2001:1).

Frykman, B. Skarin (1999) 'Demokrati, kultur och kunskap' [Democracy, culture and knowledge], contribution to *Demokratins estetik* (Demokratiutredningens forskarvolym IV), SOU 1999:129.

Giddens, A. (1990) *The Consequences of Modernity*, Cambridge: Polity Press.

Hannerz, U. (1992) *Cultural Complexity*, New York: Columbia University Press.

Hannerz, U. (1996) *Transnational Connections. Culture, People, Places*, London and New York: Routledge.

Held, D., McGrew, A., Goldblatt, D. and Perraton, J. (1999) *Global Transformations: Politics, Economics and Culture*, Cambridge: Polity Press.

Hettne, B. (1995) *Development Theory and the Three Worlds*, London: Longman.

Hettne, B. (2003) *Culture, Security and Social Sustainable Development*, Stockholm: Gidlund.

Hettne, B. and Odén, B. (eds) (2002) *Global Governance in the 21st Century: Alternative Perspectives on World Order* (Expert Group on Development Issues, Ministry of Foreign Affairs, Sweden).

Hettne, B. and Söderbaum, F. (1999) 'Towards Global Social Theory', *Journal of International Relations and Development*, vol. 2 no. 4.

Hirst, P. and Thompson, G. (1999) *Globalization in Question*, Cambridge: Polity Press.

Huntington, S. (1993) 'The Clash of Civilizations', *Foreign Affairs*, 72:22.

Knutsson, K. E. (2000) 'Without Culture No Sustainable Development: Some reflections on the topic for the Stjernsund Seminar', September 2000.

Kroeber, A. L. and Kluckhohn, C. (1952) *Culture: A Critical Review of Concepts and Definitions*, New York: Vintage Books.

Lafferty, W. and Langhelle, O. (eds) (1999) *Towards Sustainable Development*, London: Macmillan.

Lapid, Y. and Kratochwil, F. (1996) *The Return of Culture and Identity in IR Theory*, London: Lynne Rienner.

Lélé, S. (1991) 'Sustainable Development: A Critical Review', *World Development*: 607–621.

Lundmark, F. (ed) (2004) *Culture, Security and Sustainable Social Development after September 11*, Stockholm: Gidlund.

Meadowcroft, J. (1997) 'Planning, Democracy and the Challenge of Sustainable Development', *International Political Science Review*, 20: 167–90.

Mittelman, J. (2000) *The Globalization Syndrome: Transformation and Resistance*, Princeton: Princeton University Press.

Mittelman, J. H. (2004) *Whither Globalization. The Vortex of Knowledge and Ideology*, London and New York: Routledge.

Nicholson, M. (1998) *International Relations. A Concise Introduction*, London: Macmillan.

Redclift, M. (1987) *Sustainable Development: Exploring the Contradictions*, London: Routledge.

Robertson, R. (1992) *Globalization. Social Theory and Global Culture*, London: Sage.

Sachs, W. (1992) *The Development Dictionary: A Guide to Knowledge and Power*, London: Zed Books.

Scholte, J. A. (2005) *Globalization. A Critical Introduction*, London: Palgrave.

Sen, G. and Grown, C. (1987) *Development, Crises and Alternative Visions: Third World Women's Perspectives*, New York: Monthly Review Press.

Skelton, T. and Allen, T. (eds) (1999) *Culture and Global Change*, London and New York: Routledge.

Smith, S. (1992) 'The Forty Years Retour: The Resurgence of Normative Theory in International Relations', *Millennium*, 1992, 21: 489–506.

Söderbaum, F. and Shaw, T. M. (eds) (2003) *Theories of New Regionalism. A Palgrave Reader*, Basingstoke: Palgrave.

Stavenhagen, R. (1990) *The Ethnic Question. Conflict, Development, and Human Rights*, Tokyo: United Nations University Press.

Tickner, J. A. (1992) *Gender in International Relations. Feminist Perspectives on Achieving Global Security*, New York: Columbia University Press.

Tickner, J. A. (1988) 'Hans Morgenthau's Principles of Political Realism: A Feminist Reformulation', *Millenium: Journal of International Studies*, 17(3): 429–440.

Toulmin, S. (1990) *Cosmopolis. The Hidden Agenda of Modernity*, New York: Free Press.

Toye, J. (1987) *Dilemma of Development. Reflections on the Counterrevolution in development theory*, Oxford: Basil Blackwell.

Tucker, V. (1996) 'Introduction: A Cultural Perspective on Development', *European Journal of Development Research*, 8 (2): 1–21.

Tylor, E. B. (1871) Primitive Culture, 2 vols., London: John Murray; quoted from Frykman (1999).

UNDP (1994) *Human Development Report*, New York: UNDP.

Waever, O., Buzan, B., Kesitrup, M. and Lemaitre, P. (1993) *Identity, Migration and the New Security Agenda in Europe*, London: Pinter.

Walker, R. B .J. (1988) *One World, Many Worlds: Struggles for a Just World Peace*, Colorado: Lynne Rienner.

Wallerstein, I. (2000) 'Globalization or the Age of Transition. A Long-Term View of the Trajectory of the World System', *International Sociology*, June 2000, vol. 15 (2): 249–285.

World Commission on Culture and Development (1996) *Our Creative Diversity*, Paris: UNESCO.

Worsley, P. (1999) 'Culture and Development Theory', in Skelton, T. and Allen, T. (eds) (1999) *Culture and Global Change*, London and New York: Routledge.

Foreword

Over a period of some years the Swedish research foundation Riksbankens Jubileumsfond has become ever more engaged in questions concerned with links between culture and societal development. Cultural affiliation, values, identity, and traditions have been seen to play a decisive role in many both acute and long-term problems faced by individual nations and by the world as a whole. The research community has a double task: it must analyse and understand the role of culture, but also faces a challenge to try to influence cultures in the direction of reinforcing human rights, equality and democracy, and tackling poverty, thereby encouraging development towards peace and security. In many cases the task entails creating the foundations for the translation of morally defensible actions into norms for social, cultural, and political practice. In all these contexts, cultural research has great responsibility and important tasks to perform.

In the second half of the 1990s the foundation played an active part in this field. In 1995 the World Commission on Culture and Development published its final report, 'Our Creative Diversity'. The following year the foundation decided – together with the Swedish Council for Research in the Humanities and Social Sciences and with the Royal Academy of Letters, History and Antiquities – to take part in the follow-up work on the report, by arranging a Nordic interdisciplinary conference in August 1997. A paper on the tasks and responsibilities of cultural research was published under the title 'Culture and Human Development' and given both national and international circulation during the preparations for the conference of Ministers of Culture in Stockholm in 1998.

In connection with the conference, the foundation organized three international seminars under the headings 'The Need for a New Agenda for Research', 'Shared Values in Global Governance', and 'The Role of Foundations in Cultural Research'. A report drawn up by these seminars, entitled 'Promoting Cultural Research for Human Development' has been given wide international circulation.

In cooperation with Professor Göran Bexell, Department of Theology at Lund University, and UNESCO, the foundation also arranged a Nordic conference 3–5 June 1999, on the theme 'Universal Ethics; from the Nordic Perspectives', where the relation between human rights and global ethics was examined in detail. Moreover, the foundation took the initiative in the field of research policy to reinforce, among other things, research cooperation. This work has been carried out both in Sweden and abroad in cooperation with UNESCO along with a number of European foundations. A comparative research project, entitled 'Creative Europe', about the conditions for creativity and its role in a changing Europe is in progress. The foundation has also decided to create a firmer framework for Swedish involvement in the major international project, 'World Value Survey' (WVS), which has received support both for an international secretariat in Sweden and for work at Uppsala University. This project is a long-term comparative research programme on the subject of human values, which has been in progress for 20 years and embraces more than 60 countries.

During this period we also began cooperating with the Swedish Institute of International Affairs and with STINT (The Swedish Foundation for International Cooperation in Research and Higher Education), with a view to analysing the role of the Swedish Institute of International Affairs as a strategic resource and meeting place for research and for the discussion of ideas regarding human rights, national crisis management, and security policy.

The immediate background for the formal initiation of this project was a conference on research cooperation into culture and sustainable social development, arranged together with the Royal Academy of Letters, History and Antiquities and the Swedish Council for Research in the Humanities and Social Sciences. This conference was held at Stjernsund Castle in Askersund in September 2000. The background document for the conference, written by Karl Eric Knutsson, the founding father of the project, was particularly important.

To coordinate these efforts and to promote future research efforts within the field, the management of the foundation decided in 2000 to establish a new sector committee, with responsibility for research into culture, security and sustainable development. By tradition the foundation establishes sector committees within scientific areas that are deemed important, but still not fully developed or insufficiently noticed. Their task has been to map out areas where research is needed, to initiate new research and to stimulate the dissemination of knowledge and dialogue on specific subjects. This committee held a first constituent meeting in November 2000 at which its working methods, tasks, and fields of responsibility were discussed.

At an early stage of discussion in the sector committee, the need arose to relate this research area to the societal changes inherent in what is now generally described as globalization, the consequences of which hereby will be termed 'the globalized condition'. This condition imparts to the chosen concepts a partly new content, and it is expected likewise to change the ontological, epistemological, and methodological premises for the project of studying culture, security, and sustainable social development within a reasonably coordinated conceptual framework. Professor Björn Hettne was invited to provide the sector committee with a basis for discussion, presenting the three concepts ('culture', 'security', 'sustainable social development') and their genesis in the context of the history of ideas, as well as analysing the internal relations between these concepts with a view to identifying a coherent area for research.

Three unexpected shocks have affected the work of the committee. On September 11th 2001, the twin towers of the World Trade Center in New York City collapsed after being rammed by two airplanes hijacked by Islamic terrorists. A third plane crashed into the American defence headquarters, the Pentagon, in Washington D.C., while a fourth plane, which in all probability had the White House or the US Capitol building in Washington D.C. as its target, crashed in Pennsylvania. The actual meaning of these events has been interpreted in various ways, but it is plain that world political events have taken a new course since they occurred. The previously more generalized discussion about new security threats has become much more serious and concrete. In the United States there has been talk about a 'war against terrorism' since the events took place, yet without a clearly defined enemy, explicit goal, or definable end. After having been attacked on its own territory for the first time in the modern era, the world's sole superpower no longer appeared primarily to be the force behind an economic and political globalization process, but instead mainly manifested itself as a military power. This change involved the United States simultaneously turning inwards upon itself, and outwards through its external involvement in considerable military enterprises, both in Afghanistan, which was generally accepted by the world community, and in Iraq, which provoked, and continues to provoke, considerable opposition around the world.

As a result of this, the link between culture and values on the one hand, and stringent security measures on the other, became all too clear in the general world political debate. The focus in the debate on cultural values shifted from 'Asian values' to 'militant Islam'. 'The clash of civilizations' determined much of the agenda, even if the concept itself was usually treated with scepticism. After September 11th 2001 the whole context changed, and the committee was asked to reflect on how this event impacted on its work. This resulted in a collective work: 'Culture, Security and Sustainable Social Development after September 11', edited by Fredrik Lundmark (2003).

In autumn 2002, Karl Eric Knutsson passed away after a brief period of illness. Apart from the personal loss of a friend, initiator, and inspiration, Knutsson's death had a direct impact on much of the work of the group. There had long been a plan to summarize the committee's work with a broad anthology which would incorporate Knutsson's global network of contacts, and those of other group members, and which would encompass the issues dealt with by the committee itself. Once again developmental issues became the central focus of the committee's work, and it was these issues which persuaded the group to participate in an international working meeting in Brazil in January 2006. At this time many members of the group found themselves reminded of the Latin American perspective which so strongly influenced the developmental debate during the 1970s.

The eleventh of September once again had a tragic resonance when, on September 11th 2003, Sweden's Foreign Minister, Anna Lindh, died of her injuries after having been stabbed in an attack the previous day. Her work as Foreign Minister was greatly influenced by her strong commitment to providing Sweden with an active role in the EU partnership. This was particularly the case in the area of foreign and security policy issues, but she was also highly active in emphasizing the importance of conflict prevention, and of the EU possessing the ability to handle crises. In honour of Anna Lindh, Riksbankens Jubileumsfond and the sector committee have undertaken a series of initiatives. These involve new projects dealing with conflict prevention, and European foreign and security policy issues. These projects are being sponsored together with partners in the European foundation sphere.

The present work in two volumes, produced in memory of the late Karl Eric Knutsson, is thus a result of this long work, which hereby is reaching its end. It is to be seen as a challenge to the global research community to tackle, in collaborative forms, research problems in which the focus is on global questions. The work is an outgrowth of the many discussions within the committee, first based on the original framework or platform, and later on intellectual encounters in both Swedish and international academic environments, as well as parallel dramatic changes in the world context, most importantly the September 11th horror, the subsequent war against terrorism, and the rise of inter-civilizational tensions which place the issue of culture and the need for dialogue in focus as never before.

These two volumes reflect this learning process but also, being memorial volumes, the life-work of Karl Eric Knutsson – anthropologist, international civil servant, and initiator of the committee. Necessarily, this special purpose means lack of coherence in a strict academic sense. However, we nevertheless hope that it is consistent in the sense of reflecting the work of one intellectual mind struggling to make sense of the world 'out there' – but also trying to make this world a better world in very concrete terms.

Karl Eric, an anthropologist who combined field research with development work, was instrumental in establishing social anthropology as a social science in Sweden. This also meant that social anthropology became a crucial part of the development discourse. Through the Swedish Agency for Research Cooperation with Developing Countries (SAREC), Karl Eric created the institutional framework for development research in Sweden, although the main function of the organization was to strengthen research capacity in developing countries. In 1977 he organized, as the first director of SAREC, an international seminar on development theory which initiated a broader development discourse in Sweden. Participants in that historic seminar who also appear in these volumes are from Sweden, Peter Wallensteen and Björn Hettne, and from other parts of the world, Osvaldo Sunkel from Chile, and Ponna Wignaraja from Sri Lanka, both concerned as much with development theory as with development strategy. Peter Wallensteen discusses the future of the UN and Björn Hettne provides a retrospective overview of development thinking, similar to the one he did 35 years ago in the context of the creation of SAREC. This is followed up by another student of Karl Eric, Gudrun Dahl, who explores contemporary development discourses. Penina Mlama, an old friend and colleague of Karl Eric, discusses gender and development in an African context. Gun-Britt Andersson, who worked with Karl Eric in SAREC from the start in 1975, deals with global development in the form of production and distribution of global public goods.

After SAREC, Karl Eric became involved in international development concerning the welfare of children, serving for many years in UNICEF where he worked together with Urban Jonsson who succeeded him in the South Asia office (Kathmandu). Much of their joint experience is reflected in the contribution by Urban Jonsson. Other international contacts of Karl Eric within the UN family are Raj Isar (UNESCO) and Thoraya Obaid (UNFPA) who write about the cultural dimension of development.

After his retirement from UNICEF and his position as Assistant Secretary-General of the UN, Karl Eric returned to Sweden and continued to work on his original vision for holistic social and cultural science in the framework of the Royal Academy of Letters and finally in the sector committee on Culture, Security and Sustainable Development, which was his brainchild. The rest of the contributions relate to the subsequent work of this group, some chapters written by members, others by researchers working in the same spirit and in close contact with the group.

Focussing on the key concept sustainable development, Alf Hornborg shows how unsustainability has been implied in the ecologically unequal change that has taken place over millennia. The work of the committee has been linked to the World Value Survey through Thorleif Pettersson, who contributed the chapter on 'Adolescent Education for Good Citizenship'. This project is also discussed in Hans-Dieter Klingemann and Christian Welzel's chapter on democracy. Close to this theme, and also based on the same body of data, is Göran Bexell's analysis of global ethics. Gita Sen explores the role of solidarity in creating sustainable institutions for human well-being. A distinctly European perspective is provided by Ulrich Beck who also expresses the methodological basis for both the books; the need to analyse the globalized condition in an approach liberated from what he terms methodological nationalism.

In connection with visits abroad, the group participated in crucial debates on reconciliation, cultural dialogue and democratization, for instance in Stellenbosch, Cairo, Alexandria, Egypt, and Rio de Janeiro. Ursula van Beek, who organized the South African visit, analyses the issue of reconciliation in South Africa. Saad Eddin Ibrahim, who heads the Ibn Khaldun Centre of Development in Cairo, writes about the emerging civil society and its importance for democracy and development in the Arab world. Nadia Mostafa (also from Egypt) and Assia BenSalah Alaoui (Morocco) write about civilizational dialogue with a focus on Europe and Islam, an issue that became very central during the last year of the group. Jan Niederveen Pietersee discusses cosmopolitanism in Islam.

Many of the contributors in these two volumes participated in a workshop in Rio in January 2006, generously hosted by the Candido Mendes University. The workshop which came to focus on democratization and elite-people relations, included two Brazilian contributions: by Enrique Rodriguez Larreta and Candido Mendes, both dealing with cultural identity and globalization. They illuminate the globalized condition from the point of view of cultural studies.

In the broad sense, the papers produced within the project constitute two interrelated categories, the first dealing with Sustainable Development and Globalization, and the second with Values and Global Governance, forming the two complementary volumes of the book project, with culture as the overarching perspective. The essays are different in size, reflecting the double purpose of the project to provide state-of-the-art reports on themes which were of crucial concern to Karl Eric, and smaller pieces, reflecting on various issues which belong to his field of interests. However, in essence, the books reflect the necessarily unfinished work of the Sector Committee for Culture, Security and Sustainable Social Development to come to grips with this complex but fascinating field. Hopefully others will take over from here.

*   *   *

Finally, the foundation would like to express its great gratitude to the members of the committee for their work during the past six years and to the smaller publishing group including Birgitta Skarin Frykman and Anders Mellbourn. But, above all, our thanks go to Björn Hettne, for his tremendous efforts in editing these two volumes and his invaluable contributions which have been central to the committee's work from the start, and without which we would have accomplished much less. Thanks also to Malin Hasselskog for being such an efficient assistant editor.

DAN BRÄNDSTRÖM
Chairman of the Sector Committee

FREDRIK LUNDMARK
Secretary of the Sector Committee

List of Members of the Sector Committee for Culture, Security and Sustainable Social Development

Managing Director Dan Brändström, Riksbankens Jubileumsfond, Chairperson.

Professor Göran Bexell, the Centre for Theology and Religious Studies, Lund University.

Professor Katarina Eckerberg, the Department of Political Science, Umeå University (up to and including 2002).

Ms Viola Furubjelke, MP for the Swedish Social Democratic Party, and Member of the Riksdag Committee for Foreign Affairs (as of 2002).

Mr Berndt Ekholm, MP for the Swedish Social Democratic Party.

Professor Björn Hettne, the School of Global Studies, Göteborg University.

Professor Alf Hornborg, the Department of Human Ecology, Lund University.

Professor Magnus Jerneck, the Department of Political Science, Lund University.

Professor Karl Eric Knutsson, the Royal Academy of Letters, History, and Antiquities (deceased, October 2002).

Mr Göran Lennmarker, MP for Moderaterna, and Member of the Riksdag Committee for Foreign Affairs.

Dr Jan Lundius, Ph.D., the Department for Research Co-Operation (Sarec), at the Swedish International Development Co-Operation Agency (Sida) (as of 2003); Ms. Lena Johansson, Section Head at the Division for Culture and Media, at Sida.

Director and Consulting Professor Anders Mellbourn (as of 2005 independent consultant to Riksbankens Jubileumsfond, among others).

Professor Thorleif Pettersson, the Department of Theology, Uppsala University.

Professor Birgitta Skarin Frykman, the Department of Ethnology, Göteborg University.

Professor Peter Wallensteen, the Department of Peace and Conflict Research, Uppsala University (as of 2003).

Professor Mats Widgren, the Department of Human Geography, Stockholm University.

Notes on Contributors

Assia BenSalah Alaoui, Ambassador at Large, Morocco.

Gun-Britt Andersson, Ambassador, former permanent representative of Sweden to OECD and UNESCO, former State Secretary for International Development Cooperation.

Ursula J. van Beek, Professor at the Department of Information Science, University of Stellenbosch, South Africa.

Göran Bexell, Professor of Global Ethics, Vice-Chancellor, Lund University.

Dan Brändström, Professor; former Director of the Bank of Sweden Tercentenary Foundation; Chairman of the Riksbankens Jubileumsfond's Sector Committee for Culture, Security and Sustainable Social Development.

Björn Hettne, Emeritus Professor of Peace and Development Research, School of Global Studies, Göteborg University.

Yudhishthir Raj Isar, Jean Monnet Professor of Cultural Policy Studies, the American University of Paris; President, European Forum for the Arts and Heritage (EFAH).

Hans-Dieter Klingemann, Professor of Political Science, Freie Universitaet Berlin; Director emeritus, Wissenschaftszentrum Berlin für Sozialforschung.

Fredrik Lundmark, Ph D in Sociology; Secretary of the Riksbankens Jubileumsfond's Sector Committee for Culture, Security and Sustainable Social Development.

Candido Mendes, Rector of the Candido Mendes University, Rio de Janeiro, member of the Brazilian Academy of Letters, member of the High-Level Group of the Alliance of Civilizations, United Nations, Secretary-General of the Academy of Latinity.

Nadia Mahmoud Mostafa, Professor of International Relations, Director of the Programme for Civilization Studies and Dialogue of Cultures, Faculty of Economics and Political Science, Cairo University.

Thorleif Pettersson, Professor of Sociology of Religion, Uppsala University.

Gita Sen, Professor of Economics, Institute of Management, Bangalore.

Peter Wallensteen, Professor of Peace and Conflict Research, Uppsala University.

Christian Welzel, Professor, Jacobs University Bremen.

Introduction

Björn Hettne

In this book the focus is on social relations in the global system, and values and institutions that contribute to peace: dialogue rather than clash. The global expansion of Europe, resulting in cultural clashes in the radically new context of civilizational encounters, was driven by the development of individual nation-states competing for power and wealth. Today civilizations interact in the context of globalization. The question often raised is whether this interaction will be in the form of clash or dialogue. Intercultural dialogue, which now has become a political imperative, must face the realities of this completely transformed and complex world.

Particular attention is given here to global ethics and universal human rights without neglecting cultural differences, as well as the possibilities for intercultural dialogues on different societal levels and a more institutionalized global governance. This book thus approaches the problem of development and security, here with more emphasis on the latter, from the point of view of the global system and in particular of the need for global and universal values. This is analysed as a very controversial issue in need of reflection and not as a matter of imposing values. In fact global and universal values must be a negotiated and pluralistic system of ideas, based on the fundamental value of respecting and understanding 'the other'.

The first chapters deal with the role of culture, democracy and human values in human relations. Raj Isar from UNESCO explores the ways in which people turn to cultural distinctions embodied in their traditions to resist what is perceived as a threat to their integrity and prosperity, even their very survival in terms of transmission of identities and values. This recurrent mobilization around group identity has led to a kind of cultural politics whose stakes include gaining control of (or access to) political and economic power. The standard 'development' models have paid little attention to this culturally articulated diversity, assuming that functional categories such as class and occupation are more important. The analysis is organized in three parts. First, the author traces the path through which, in UNESCO-led discourses since the late 1960s, the notion of 'culture' has made its way into the development paradigm, resulting ultimately in the binomial 'culture and development' whose high water mark came in the late 1990s. Second, he revisits the parallel lives of the two concepts, both conceptually and in public policy terms, with a view to uncovering some of the contradictions involved. Third, he explores approaches to 'cultural conflict' and 'cultural security'.

One value system with a potential of becoming universal is democracy. Between 1987 and 1996 the world has seen an unprecedented surge in the number of countries turning from autocracy to democracy. Today 119 of the world's 192 independent countries are rated electoral democracies and – considering political rights and civil liberties – 89 are evaluated free countries by Freedom House. In normative terms this is most certainly a positive development. The chapter by Hans-Dieter Klingemann and Christian Welzel, active in the World Values Survey programme, describes and compares two of the most important theoretical approaches predicting the global spread of democratic government. The first approach is called the *evolutionary resource distribution theory of democratization* and has been developed by Tatu Vanhanen. The second approach has been proposed by Inglehart and Welzel who label their approach an *emancipatory theory of democracy*. This essay tries to assess similarities and differences between these two theories. It is assumed that their major ideas can be reconciled resulting in much additional value.

Thorleif Pettersson's chapter investigates how young people's orientations towards human development are influenced by cultural and educational factors. The investigation is based on two main theoretical perspectives. The first attempts to explain how general socio-economic development leads to a growing emphasis on human autonomy and so-called self-expression values, while the second seeks to understand how young people's values and civic orientations are affected by the specific civic education they receive. The analysis is based on two different sets of data: The European/World Values Surveys and the IEA (International Association for the Evaluation of Educational Achievement) study on citizenship and education in 28 countries. It shows that young people's orientations towards citizenship and human development are open to conscious policies for positive change.

The following four papers deal with different attempts to bridge cultural differences and to create conditions for democratic dialogue within a multicultural national context as well as between cultures. Ursula van Beek analyses the issue of reconciliation in South Africa in a comparative perspective by setting the general features of the process against specifically African cultural traits. The model she discusses has often been described as a 'miracle', which might imply a low level of applicability elsewhere, but even in South Africa the 'miracle' has been questioned and found to have differing interpretations. The author suggests that although long-term prospects for reconciliation depend on the effectiveness of the overall policy of reconstruction as shaped by committed leadership, the process of dealing with a painful past cannot start without a willingness on the part of the former adversaries to be reconciled.

Nadia Mahmoud Mostafa, director of the Centre for Dialogue between Civilizations in Cairo, argues that the study of international relations is witnessing a growing methodological concern with ethical and normative dimensions. This growing concern with values is being simultaneously accompanied by a resurrecting concern with cultural dimensions, especially in light of the processes, policies, and ideologies of globalization. Following the September 11th events the contributions on the relationship between civilizations reached a climax indicating the new weight acquired by the religion-culture-civilization dimension. The author's approach reflects her experience with Arabic and Islamic trends in the field. This experience leads to three issues: the first addresses the problem of the origin of the relationship between civilizations, the second addresses the problem of the credibility of the dialogue, and the third presents a personal theoretical and political stance suggesting that the dialogue has lost its credibility. The situation requires a strategic perspective that perceives the dialogue between religions and cultures as a political issue and a tool of managing conflict, rather than an alternative to conflict.

Ambassador at Large, Assia BenSalah Alaoui, with experiences from the Barcelona process, also asks the question: What went wrong with the dialogue between cultures? She looks into various challenges: global and regional contexts, challenges inherent to culture, to increasing biased mutual images between the 'West' and the Arabs and the 'Islamic world' at large, etc., which make intercultural dialogue both a necessary and a very complex and difficult exercise. The author discusses a few noteworthy developments on the universal level, on the multilateral one and some flagship achievements by some institutions and countries, before focussing on the Euro-Mediterranean area as the main empirical example. The dialogue is necessary also in order to humanize globalization, which affects all, but whose benefits go only to a few! Intercultural dialogue is neither a panacea, nor an end in itself. Rather it is the modus operandi to make cooperation prevail over confrontation and convivi-ality over conflicts, being conscious that these contradictions are inher-ent to life itself.

In Candido Mendes' chapter it is stated that any concern with the world post September 11th not only has to face the 'civilization of fear' out of the general alert to terrorism, but the inducement of globaliza-tion into the emergent logics of hegemony. Are we just following the threat of the much promulgated idea of a 'clash of civilizations', already probably anticipated as a 'war of religions'? The crisis of the Prophet's cartoons and the condemnation of the Bushian evangelism, coming with the liberation from Saddam in Iraq are – for some – just a first example of a world torn into reciprocal fundamentalisms. We move far away from the 'culture of peace' and of a possible international détente, as shown in the 1990s, after the thaw of the Cold War. The present his-torical insertion of terrorism – in its new congenital extremist stance – leads to a new, subtle consequence, in the setting of the horizons and policies for an 'Alliance of Civilizations'. Mendes reports from the UN-established High Level Group in which he is a member and which has proposed such an alliance, in particular focussing on education, youth, migration and media.

Göran Bexell's chapter provides an analysis of global ethics as a moral voice with different expressions. The question he raises is whether it is possible to believe in globally shared, i.e. universal, values, as a basis or at least a contribution to building an international society and global governance, and, if so, how such an ethics is constructed. His starting point is that from the unique (for instance the individual experience of love) we can reach something common human, and from the common human we can reach to the individual and the unique. There is a con-verging moral voice coming from, on the one hand, the basis of ethics, and on the other hand, the international and global level, as described above. The voice is focussed on some core values and this voice can be heard in different ways, in varieties of cultural expressions. Military and economic powers are strong, but without support by the moral voice it is not possible to build a human global community.

The last papers move from moral and ethical foundations to institu-tional foundations for global peace and development. Gita Sen's chapter, focussing on India, explores the role of solidarity in creating sustainable institutions for human well-being. The author argues that 'advanced' institutions are those that are not primarily glued together by incentives or policing mechanisms but rest on shared social values. In particular, investment in such key necessities as health, education, clean water, sanitation or shelter depend particularly on how a society has been able to develop social values of solidarity. The suggested framework goes beyond traditional notions of public goods and externalities to develop a new concept of 'solidarity goods'. Traditional economics' treatment of the need for public action is based on the presence of externalities, public goods whose consumption is non-rivalrous and non-excludable, transaction costs, or incomplete information. However, much of what we would include under basic needs does not meet these criteria. While externalities certainly exist (particularly in such areas as public health and sanitation), many of the basic needs – food, curative health services, education – are rivalrous and excludable and have few associated externalities. But they are goods whose public provision often requires a degree of social solidarity.

Gun-Britt Andersson's chapter, moving to the policy implications of global solidarity, deals with what is called Global Public Goods, why they matter, why they are hard to produce and how obstacles might be overcome. Most peoples' economic, political and social lives and livelihoods are grounded in local and national contexts and conditions. Yet more and more conditions are shaped by events, decisions and politics beyond national borders. The world's promise can be realized and its perils restrained only through extensive and ambitious cooperation across borders. All peoples' health, security, and prosperity depend in part on the quality of their international cooperation, as does the health of the environment. This is widely recognized today and international cooperation has already proven to be a tangible and powerful force for progress. Many of the things which would be desirable to achieve can be described as Global Public Goods. Key among them are peace and security, control of communicable diseases, financial stability, sustainable management of global commons to e.g. mitigate climate change, an open-rule based trading system, and accessible knowledge. None of these can be achieved by countries acting alone, but, if provided, everybody would enjoy the benefits. The problem is that in most cases they will be provided only if nations accept to restrain immediate national interests and agree to institutionalize universal norms.

In his analysis of the institutionalization of world order, Peter Wallensteen discusses the future of the UN. Four trends in modern international relations provide the backdrop of this discussion on new dimensions of global governance: the growth of international cooperation, the vitalization of nation-states, the emergence of civil society, and the strengthening of global corporations. These build on intellectual developments as well as empirically observable trends. Together they create new ways in which de facto decisions are made (for instance, conference diplomacy, G8, civil society organizations, media impact). This provides challenges for the United Nations as the legally strongest international body. The reforms in the organization during the 2005–6 session have incorporated some of these dimensions but in a long-term perspective this is not enough. The author suggests different scenarios affecting the role of the UN in global governance in the next decade.

Finally, the editor wants to acknowledge the important help from the assistant editor Malin Hasselskog.

1
'Culture', Conflict and Security: Issues and Linkages

Yudhishthir Raj Isar

'Culture' has played a part in development rhetoric for several decades, contributing to the broadening and diversification of the development discourse (analysed by Björn Hettne in the first volume of this book project). In its progression, the 'culture' concept has also encountered the realms of conflict and security. I shall evoke this interface, but only after a prior detour through two other matters. First, briefly traced, the path through which, in UNESCO-led discourses since the late 1960s, 'culture' has figured in the development paradigm. Second, just as succinctly, some of the ways in which that role raises contradictions and aporiae.[1]

Before even proceeding, I should try to remove the quotation marks around the word 'culture'. As Raymond Williams famously pointed out, 'culture' is not only one of the two or three most complicated words in the lexicon but 'has now come to be used for important concepts in several distinct intellectual disciplines and in several distinct and incompatible systems of thought.' (1988: 87). Today the notion is even more commonplace than that: it has entirely escaped academic control and has entered the quotidian vocabulary of ordinary people. It has also been internationalized, taken up by people – and 'peoples' – all over the world. Because we are living through a moment of such marked cultural self-consciousness (Sahlins 1994), it has become exceedingly difficult, if not impossible, for any of us to limit ourselves to just one of the many meanings that 'culture' now enjoys. Yet the effort can be made, at least at particular moments and for particular purposes.

The working meaning of the culture concept that we have decided to use for the *Cultures and Globalization Series* (see footnote 1), for example, is the 'social construction, articulation and reception of meaning'. This involves value systems, forms of creation, enactment, presentation, and preservation as well as symbols, artefacts, and objects – a broad reading that also embraces the realms of artistic and intellectual creativity and heritage. It is what Williams (1995: 13) saw as the *'signifying system* through which necessarily (though among other means) a social order is communicated, reproduced, experienced and explored'. This working definition is much less of a grab-bag than the celebrated totalizing definition proffered by MONDIACULT, the 1982 World Conference on Cultural Policies held in Mexico, and which has become canonical, at least in the universe of the international organizations, and as regards the relationships between culture and development they have debated since the 1980s.[2] This totalizing definition has led to the kind of generalized confusion that Sahlins warned about 'when culture in the humanistic sense is not distinguished from "culture" in its anthropological senses, notably culture as the total and distinctive way of life of a people or society. From the latter point of view it is meaningless to talk of "the relation between culture and the economy", since the economy is part of a people's culture' (World Commission on Culture and Development 1995: 21).

The World Commission itself chose to side-step the so-called 'anthropological' definition and chose to confine its meaning, for the purposes of its report, to 'ways of living together'. Following Amartya Sen and the path of 'human development', it took 'development' to mean 'the widening of human opportunities and choices' and determined that the issue of 'culture and development' boils down to exploring how different ways of living together affect the enlargement of human choices.[3]

'Culture and development': the evolution of a discursive formation

Although the relationships between culture and development have by now been appropriated by many different players, the chief protagonist in twinning the two terms has been the United Nations Cultural, Scientific and Cultural Organization (UNESCO). This agency's discourse in the area began to be articulated in the late 1960s, when the notion of 'cultural policy', freshly defined in and by the Ministry of Cultural Affairs in France, was deliberately introduced to UNESCO by the French authorities. The notion was in turn based on the master concept of 'cultural development', developed by activists with the *Peuple et Culture* group based in the French resistance movement against the Nazi occupation (and, earlier still, in the left-wing *éducation populaire* movement). Cultural development was subsequently defined by UNESCO in the following terms: 'a process of development or progress in the cultural life of a community, aimed at the attainment of cultural values and related to the general conditions of economic and social development' (UNESCO 1981). Culture was clearly the dominant term here: the objective of 'cultural development' was indeed culture itself, mainly high culture – 'as a sociological dynamic in which society grows and changes; as a powerful sector of the economy; as a professional environment inhabited by skilled creators, artists, and craftspeople; as a transmitter of aesthetic expression, ideas, and values' (Epskamp and Gould 2001). Writing in 1972, Augustin Girard put it this way: 'cultural development denotes cultural life as it develops and its relations to other forms of development [...] It is given a positive colour by its combination of individual and social development, with the linear, quantitative progression that economic and scientific development implies' (Girard 1983).

Yet even within the usage of the 1960s in and around UNESCO, there was also a premonitory awareness that development itself needed to be revisited as a plural project, parsed in terms not just of the abstract universal idea of 'culture', but also and above all in terms of distinct ways of life, each with its own developmental path (Maheu 1973). This contestation of the received GNP, commodity-centred development paradigm was expressed at UNESCO by the notion of the 'cultural dimension of development' introduced in the 1970s, as UNESCO mounted a series of intergovernmental conferences on cultural policies in different world regions. No single, specific definition was ever actually provided, but language such as the following put across what was meant: 'balanced development can only be ensured by making cultural factors an integral part of the strategies designed to achieve it; consequently, these strategies should always be devised in the light of the historical, social and cultural contexts of each society' (UNESCO 1982). The policy emphasis had thus shifted from 'progress in the cultural life of the community' to the idea that culture must be made integral to the development process. Culture was no longer the leader, it was development; yet it was also assumed that the flourishing of culture would benefit development.

This newly emergent claim for voice and recognition expressed by, from and for the non-western world was largely the result of political emancipation and new nationhood, which led many newly defined 'peoples' to challenge the frame of reference in which a single system of values alone generated rules assumed to be universal. The stakes were twofold: first, the search for other kinds of modernization, as people realized that economic criteria alone could not provide a programme for human dignity and well-being and, second, the imperatives of identity and recognition.

And so, as underlined by Marshall Sahlins (1994), peoples and communities across the world found themselves replicating the process that in Europe first brought the culture concept itself into being, as the German bourgeoisie affirmed the notion of *Kultur* against the French Enlightenment concept of civilization, with Herder among others opposing ways of life to stages of development and a social mind to natural reason. *Kultur* was what truly identified and distinguished a people. Cultures came in kinds, not degrees, in the plural not the singular. This conflict between philosophic rationalism and *Kultur* anticipated the current dichotomy between development economists and the viewpoints of local peoples. In both cases, what was 'error' to the first was 'culture' to the second. In both cases, the affirmation of cultural distinctiveness emerges from a relatively underdeveloped region.

Unlike its French-inspired predecessor, the discourse of 'the cultural dimension of development' was so to speak largely endogenous to UNESCO. Yet it was also a precipitation of several coterminous attitudes, tendencies, and postures: burgeoning culturalist claims; the upsurge against the economistic dogmas of industrial society; the revolt against the priesthood of technical expertise and the world view of mainstream economics; the positions of 'Third World' ideology (*tiersmondisme*), driven as much by the neo-utopian imaginings of westerners as by the nativistic affirmations of the formerly exploited and oppressed. Its supreme moment was undoubtedly the 1982 Mexico City World Conference on Cultural Policies, whose 'Mexico City Declaration on Cultural Policies' I have already cited.

This 'cultural dimension of development' phase was clearly driven also by cultural nationalism, in which the notion of 'cultural identity' became central, at the same time as it achieved salience as a scholarly construct throughout the world. The construct was music to the ears of national governments, for it was consistent with visions of culture tied to a globally hegemonic *nationalist ideology,* a perspective in which 'nations are imagined as natural objects or things in the real world [... as] internally homogeneous in terms of what is taken to be shared cultural content – the very stuff, as it were, of identity' (Handler 1994).

The impact of the World Conference and the attraction of the 'cultural dimension of development' idea led a 'World Decade for Cultural Development' as a transnational programme of advocacy and action, voted into existence in 1987 by the United Nations General Assembly. It was as this 'World Decade' began to unfold that a notion of 'culture and development' began to emerge. Pursuing the initial suggestion of Carl-Johan Kleberg, a group of Norwegian cultural leaders decided that the time had come to do for 'culture and development' what had been achieved for 'environment and development'. They were impressed by the process which had led from the Brundtland Report to the Rio Summit and beyond: as the World Commission on Environment and Development had served notice that a marriage of economy and ecology was overdue and had set in motion a world agenda for that purpose, so the relationship between culture and development advocated by UNESCO for so long, should be clarified and reinforced, they thought, in practical and constructive ways. The public policy relevance of the cultural dimension should therefore be legitimized by an independent commission of leading thinkers and decision-makers.

A 'World Commission on Culture and Development' was as a result established jointly by UNESCO and the United Nations in 1992. What were the Commission's intellectual points of departure? To begin with, its members – a mix of social scientists, artists, and political figures – chose tactically to side-step the often recriminatory Third World rhetoric that held western capitalism wholly responsible for mis-development and all the development 'bads'. Second, they deliberated under the shadow of an incipiently recognized globalization, which had led people everywhere to assert their cultural distinctiveness while simultaneously wanting to be full-fledged members of the emerging world cultural system – two dialectically linked opposing projects which are both willed responses to globalization – to its promise as much as to its threats. The political ideals that inspired them included participatory democracy and the open society, as much as consciousness-raising and communitarian empowerment. They also recognized that the 'cultural dimension of development' was often little more than an incantatory slogan and were uncomfortable with the reifications and assumptions of 'national' homogeneity which accompanied it. As a construct, it had remained stubbornly abstract, resistant to operational application. They in fact anticipated an anthropologist's much later observations that 'complex notions such as culture inhibit an analysis of the relationships among the variables they pack together' and 'to understand culture, we must first deconstruct it. If its elements are disaggregated, it is usually not difficult to show that the parts are separately tied to specific administrative arrangements, economic pressures, biological constraints, and so forth' (Kuper 1999). 'Our Creative Diversity', the report of the World Commission, performed some of the work of disaggregation, by exploring various links between the 'cultural' and key economic, political, and societal phenomena associated with development.

The stress, therefore, was on the relationships, on parallel conceptual lives. 'Culture and development' thinking was not primarily about tinkering with a pre-established development model or about recasting the model (as in the previous phase). Instead, it was a perspective more analytical than normative, one that sought to uncover the relationships between beliefs, traditions, ways of living and development, and the extent to which they influence one another.

'Cultural development', 'the cultural dimension of development', 'culture and development': these, then, were the three principal conceptual frameworks developed, promoted and shared by UNESCO as successive master concepts for the implementation of cultural policy between the late 1960s and the beginning of the twenty-first century. 'Cultural diversity' has since taken over the reins – but that is another story.

Conceptual discontents

In our 'Cultures and Globalization Series' project, 'culture' is yoked to 'globalization', not to 'development'. This replacement of one term of the binomial by another is typical of the way in which many leading concepts and terms – or combinations of terms – so often need to give way to others as foci of interest. Certain lines of inquiry'fade away, not only because of diminishing marginal returns, but also because the phenomena themselves, as reflected on the screen of history, either lose their salience or are transformed into other events, which are more revealingly grouped under new labels' (Tambiah 1996).

Clearly, 'culture and development' is no longer the master narrative it was in the 1990s when Karl-Eric Knutsson and I were both among its champions, particularly in the follow-up to the World Commission's report, 'Our Creative Diversity', which culminated in the 1998 Intergovernmental Conference on Cultural Policies for Development held in Stockholm. As the 'Cultures and Globalization Series' project has unfolded over the last three years I have found myself standing back from and unpacking some of our ardently-shared convictions.

Both of us contributed (Knutsson far more significantly than I) to the wave of contemporary *culturalism*, or 'the conscious mobilization of cultural differences in the service of a larger national or transnational politics...' (Appadurai 1996: 15). This culturalism is spreading and diversifying as human groups at many different levels instrumentalize cultural difference in ever more complex ways, for a politics of group recognition. Today, the word 'culture' is on everybody's lips as communities everywhere mobilize a self-conscious defence and/or affirmation of their own 'culture', proclaimed as an inalienable 'right', conceived as a value in itself, and justified as an inherited 'tradition'. The values of different ways of life have risen to consciousness and have become the rallying cry of diverse claims to a space in the planetary culture. Before, culture was just lived. Now it has become a self-conscious collective project. Every struggle for life becomes the struggle of a way of life.

Cultural identity is no longer the handmaiden of national affirmation alone: it has become a more deeply, diversely and widely shared aspiration in the *zeitgeist*, as people everywhere seek to assert their cultural distinctiveness as fully fledged members of an emerging world cultural system. The latter, though, is highly incomplete, shot through with economic and political indeterminacy. There is neither providence nor government, nor an invisible hand of the market, harmonizing the actions of self-interested agents. On the contrary, multinational corporations and rapid international capital flows escape all control. Locally, the world order is experienced as uncertainty and incoherence. Even as their own traditions and relations are impacted by powerful and changeable outside forces, local peoples can find no economic or political proportion between efforts and returns. They turn to their 'culture', which offers at once some resistance to the domination of the global system and some structure to its entropy (Sahlins 1994).

And here, there is increasing evidence of the loosening of strong identifications with national cultures, and a strengthening of other ties and allegiances, 'above' and 'below' the level of the nation-state. National identities may remain strong, especially with respect to such matters as legal and citizenship rights, but local, regional and community identities have in many cases become far more significant. And above the level of the national culture, regional as well as 'global' identifications are also beginning to compete with national ones (Hall et al. 1992).

Misleading ideas on 'culture'

Despite a growing awareness of this constructed, positional and strategic nature of contemporary culturalism, a number of misleading ideas remain stubbornly in play whenever the notions of culture and 'cultural identity' are deployed.[4] First, there is the overstated assumption of *coherence*. This is not to say that cultures lack any coherence or central organizing tendencies whatsoever, but rather that: (a) the extent of such overall coherence differs from culture to culture, from historical moment to historical moment; (b) coherence is probably greatest in delimited cultural domains connected to specific social practices – hence we should speak of 'coherences' in the plural rather than in any overarching way; and (c) 'coherence' does not preclude contradiction or paradox (Avruch 1998). The inability to see cultures in this way no doubt stems from the continuing hold of the 'complex whole' view that has dominated the social sciences, including principally anthropology. Founded to deal with small, strongly integrated societies equipped with specific systems of social organization, values and religious beliefs that in fact were already beginning to be diluted in the nineteenth century by forced integration into nation-states and colonial systems, this view is based on characteristics such as 'invariance, exclusive territoriality, cultural incommensurability, cultural bias, and cognitive limitation, whose inscription into the concept of culture by way of the study of archaic societies was incidental rather than conscious...' (Wicker 1997: 36). These have lost most if not all of their relevance today. Avruch (1996) has usefully listed at least six inadequate or misleading ideas that have also tended to result from this 'complex whole' or 'billiard ball' view of culture(s):

1. *Culture is homogeneous*: an idea which makes a second inadequate idea easier to sustain, namely that:
2. *Culture is a thing*: the reification of culture – regarding it as a thing – leads to the notion that 'it' can act and have causality. A perfect contemporary illustration is the 'clash of civilizations' thesis (see below). Reification makes it easy to overlook diversity within cultures, which underpins a third inadequate idea:
3. *Culture is uniformly distributed among members of a group*: the belief that cognitive, affective and behavioural uniformity can be attributed to all members of a group. Hence the further misconception that:
4. An individual possesses but a single (generally 'national') culture: he or she is simply Brazilian, Indian, German or Swedish.
5. *Culture is custom*, in other words, tradition, something fixed and unchanging.
6. *Culture is timeless,* so when a changeless quality is attributed to culture, particularly a traditional one, we speak, for example, of the 'Arab mind', as though a unitary cognizing element has come down to us straight from Mecca of the Prophet Muhammad.

An issue of locus also encumbers the 'complex whole' perspective. Is culture 'inside' the individual? Or is it 'outside', in some super-organic structure above and beyond the individual? The latter is generally taken to be 'society', but the relationship between culture and society is neither transparent, nor unproblematic.

> Culture is conceived of in terms of objectifying philosophies with, presumably, no need for an active subject at all. In the classical concept, individuals appear mostly as carriers of culture. They exist for the sole purpose of lending expression to their culture, which, through them, is able to fulfil its true destiny. (Wicker 1997: 32)

Culture as the end and not the means?

In the light of such problems, several analysts have suggested the kinds of conceptual alignments needed. Colin Mercer (2002), for example, has underlined how important it is to capture the actual day-to-day experience of culture and the ways in which people engage what they define as 'culture' in terms of their capacities for action in a range of contexts. Once this is done, three consequences follow. First, we would find that the definitions arrived at may not necessarily coincide with the received, traditional, and official definitions and classifications of culture. Second, we do not know enough about the actual constitution, dynamics, and effects of the cultural field that lie beyond the parameters and jurisdictions of the agencies responsible for cultural policy as it is currently defined. Third, Mercer suggests, we are obliged to recognize that culture, in its day-to-day manifestations, is bound up in complex but powerful ways with the economic, the social, the environmental, the familial, and the personal. It needs thus to be a concept and field of action whose motto might be E. M. Forster's 'only connect': with social and economic policy, with industry policy, with environmental policy. Accordingly, we should break down the great abstraction that is 'culture', into four distinct *orientations*:

A *'cognitive and expressive orientation'*, or the role of culture in forming fundamental and personal value systems and forms of identity, lifestyle, expression and conduct within those systems.

A *'social reproduction orientation'*, or both the constitutive and instrumental roles of culture in forms of social organization.

A *'resource orientation'*, or the economic role of culture in both the patterns of daily life and exchanges and as a significant industry sector in its own right.

A *'political orientation'*, or the role of culture in establishing, maintaining and challenging power relations.[5]

Note, however, that three of the above orientations are instrumental in nature: they pertain to uses and advantages. Such instrumentalization is an unfortunate but integral part of the 'culture and development' discourse, which tends to envision culture not as something valuable in itself, but as a means to the ends of promoting and sustaining economic and social progress. Drawing directly on the formulations of Amartya Sen (cf. 1999), the World Commission on Culture and Development recognized the relevance of this instrumental view, yet concluded that it is

> therefore important both to acknowledge the far-reaching instrumental function of culture in development, and at the same time to recognize that this cannot be all there is to culture in judgements of development [...] Culture has to enter in a more fundamental way [...] not as a servant of ends, but as the social basis of the ends themselves. (World Commission on Culture and Development 1996: 23)

The idea here is that a constitutive view of culture would reframe 'development' by turning it into a profoundly cultural project, which reiterates a rhetorical trope generated somewhat earlier – the belief that the resources of their cultures can/will inspire every 'people' to reject and/or bypass a single (read 'western') development model in favour of a distinctive path that would prevent each from 'losing' its identity. Alas, we do not have to look far to see that this vision remains largely unrealized.[6] We continue to argue that people in the global South challenge the frame of reference in which a single system of values generated rules assumed to be universal, that they actively demand the right to forge different versions of modernization. Unfortunately, there is scant evidence that this is really the case, that visions of modernity have been or will be configured in fundamentally different ways in order to construct truly alternative ideas of progress and the good life. To what extent, despite (or perhaps even because of?) striking economic growth in East and South Asia, is it even possible to challenge the assumption that modernization is a globalizing process led by the technological and economic and political superiority of the West? To be sure, many multiple modernities are emerging (as regards Islam, see, in particular, the recent work of Nilufer Göle 2005), as people everywhere devote themselves to new forms of cultural elaboration and differentiation, as rhetorical tools, as discursive practice, and as a mode of cultural production in and for the present, for which they mobilize symbols and references from their cultural pasts (Kirshenblatt-Gimblett 1998). But where are the alternative models of development?

Clashes and alliances: difference and 'development'

It is time to turn now to the relationships between culture, 'conflict' and/or 'security' and development. Here too, it would be appropriate to define usage. In the 'Conflicts and Tensions' inaugural issue of the 'Cultures and Globalization Series', we envision conflict as a disagreement through which parties involved perceive a threat to their needs, interests, and concerns. In other words, conflict is the disagreement *plus* the perceived threat. It is socially configured, establishing a relation between parties. Parties act according to their perception of the situation, which points to the importance of values and belief systems as 'filters' as well as to information and recall (memory) of prior experience in interpreting threats. Power plays a crucial role in any conflict situation.

Our choice of theme was driven by two observed realities: (a) the ways in which the spectre of conflict within mainly national communities appear to lurk behind so much of the concern for 'culture' expressed in contemporary public debate, and (b) the need to address the untested assumptions and anxieties generated by all the various abstract predictions of 'cultural' conflict at the world level. The focus is on the first area, the ways in which identity politics generate conflicts within nations and instrumentalize the 'cultural', behind whose banner march tensions over scarce resources or over the sharing of newly acquired ones, feeding the 'narcissism of minor differences' and revealing the strength with which the 'bent twigs' of suppressed or wounded *Volksgeist* spring upright, to quote the image Isaiah Berlin, borrowing from Schiller, often used.

The idealizing 'culture and development' arguments I referred to previously invariably ignore or downplay this dark side, in particular, the ways in which this potential is exacerbated by the economic, political, and social changes that 'development' produces. The interactions between these processes and identity affirmation at the infra-national level were to a degree explored in 'Our Creative Diversity'. Citing the Human Development Report, the World Commission noted that 'of the 82 conflicts over the last three years, 79 were within nations' and that 'as populations shift and societies change, people turn to cultural distinctions embodied in their traditions to resist what is perceived as a threat to their integrity and prosperity, even their very survival in terms of transmission of identities and values'. (World Commission on Culture and Development 1995: 55).

The articulation of the boundaries between 'in-group' and 'out-group' and the relational nature of culture in social life have been topics of analysis since Simmel's seminal work on conflict. As Featherstone (1995) has remarked with regard to 'local' culture, this may have a common set of work and kinship relationships that reinforce the practical everyday lived culture which is sedimented into taken-for-granted knowledge and beliefs. Yet the articulation of these beliefs and sense of the particularity of the local place will tend to become sharpened when the locality or community becomes locked into power struggles with its neighbours and may lead it to present an oversimplified unified image of itself to outsiders. The rivalries and power struggles within such communities are likely to be forgotten when the collectivity is brought into conflict with another one. In such situations, particularity is subsumed into some larger collectivity and appropriate cultural work is done in order to develop an acceptable public face for it. This process entails the mobilization of the repertoire of communal symbols, sentiments and collective memories.

Shifts in interdependencies and power balances increase a group's consciousness of the symbolic boundary between themselves and others. This is aided by the mobilization of symbolic repertoires with which the community can formulate a unified image of its difference. What appears germane here is the capacity to shift the frame, and move between varying range of foci, the capacity to handle a range of symbolic material out of which various identities can be formed and reformed in different situations. As Featherstone (1995: 110) puts it,

> ...the contemporary world has not seen a cultural impoverishment, an attenuation of cultural resources. Rather there has been an extension of cultural repertoires and an enhancement of the resourcefulness of various groups to create new symbolic modes of affiliation and belonging, as well as struggling to rework and reshape the meaning of existing signs, to undermine existing symbolic hierarchies, for their own particular purposes in ways that become difficult for those in the dominant culture centres to ignore.

Globalization has thus generated the resurgence of the particular and the local, as communities develop strategies of negotiation and competition to cope with, counter, resist or even sometimes facilitate homogenizing forces as well as increasing levels of cultural complexity; they also have to deal with the doubts and anxieties that these phenomena often engender.

Guided in its reflections by the work of scholars such as Stanley Tambiah, the World Commission also observed how mobilizations around group identity have led to a cultural politics whose stakes include gaining control of (or access to) political and economic power. Where ethnic groups have enjoyed relatively equitable positions, tensions have arisen as soon as one or several of them have begun to feel that their own relative position is slipping. Such tensions have led to contentions over rights to land, education, the use of language, political representation, freedom of religion, the preservation of ethnic identity, autonomy or self-determination. The standard development models have paid little attention to this, assuming that functional categories such as class and occupation are more important. Yet clearly, many development failures and disasters stem from an inadequate recognition of precisely these cultural complexities and the diverse ways in which cultural dimensions such as language, race or religion have been used to distinguish the opposing players and have become determining factors in the nature and dynamic of conflict. All too frequently, one particular group has assumed state power, depriving many other groups of it. Where it is perceived that the government either favours or discriminates against groups identifiable in cultural terms, this encourages the negotiation of benefits on the basis of cultural identity and leads directly to the politicization of culture. The dynamics of this process are such that when any one group starts negotiating on the basis of its cultural identity, others are encouraged to do likewise; and it has often been cumulative.

Ethnic conflict has thus become a major reality of our time, not simply by its ubiquity alone (it occurs literally on all continents) but also by the cumulative increase in the frequency and intensity of its occurrence. These sorts of mobilizations of ethnic identity were also underlined in the 2004 Human Development Report, which agreed that 'there is little empirical evidence that cultural differences and clashes over values are in themselves a cause of violent conflict' and, after citing some of the conflicts mentioned above, considers that 'cultural identity does have a role in these conflicts – not as a cause but as a driver for political mobilization' (UNDP 2004: 3).

But neither the latter nor 'Our Creative Diversity' went into the question of *why* ethnic diversity becomes culturally articulated at particular historical junctures, and *how* culture becomes politicized as a marker of group identity, and used in struggles over resources. In search of answers to questions such as these, I have found it useful to turn to work in two areas: anthropology and political science.

Ethno-nationalism and development

Ethnicity research by anthropologists has focussed on the ways in which ethnic lines of separation were found to constitute and preserve themselves through processes of ascription – to self and other. Yet, as Wicker (1997: 35) has pointed out, following Barth,

> the origins of these processes of ethnicity, however, could not [...] be traced to the different cultural representations of the groups involved [...] Although cultural phenomena can be diacritical elements of delimitation strategies, they do not reveal sufficient information to explain the existence of ethnic borders and conflicts.

Given that nation-building has been at the core of the developmentalist project, Tambiah has traced how, in South Asia, the state has gradually, after years of escalating ethnic divisiveness and pluralistic awareness, become much more of a 'referee', adjudicating differences and enabling regional cultures and societies to attain their authentic identities and interests. He has identified two salient features in ethno-nationalism, defined as the 'generation of regional or sub-national reactions and resistances to what is seen as an over-centralized and hegemonic state, and their drive to achieve their own regional and local sociopolitical formations' (Tambiahz 1996: 16f).

First, ethnic groups qua groups demand and bargain for collective entitlements (the concepts of individual rights and individual identity are secondary here). Second, it is usually a majority group that demands affirmative action on its behalf to put right an alleged historical injustice, thereby once again giving new content to affirmative action, which is usually undertaken on behalf of depressed minorities and underclasses. Four issues have posed problems with regard to nation-state making and 'development' (or 'modernization').

First, the question of what the language or languages of education and administration ought to be, and of whether to replace English with indigenous languages, a post-colonial problem with many ramifications that has taxed countries with plural languages, such as India, Pakistan, Burma, Sri Lanka, and Malaysia, which all have their own written languages and literatures. Second, and closely related, is the 'modernization' project itself that has entailed the launching of ambitious literacy and educational programmes. The result has been an explosion of literacy in the context of a population explosion, and the creation of large numbers of educated or semi-educated youth seeking employment in economies that are slow in growth and unable to accommodate them. It is this category of unemployed youth at urban sites that has everywhere been the most visible and active participants in ethno-nationalist movements and ethnic riots. A third issue, generated by economic growth in countries of low income and high-population density and rural underemployment, is large-scale population movements and migration that cause dramatic changes in the demographic ratios of people who perceive themselves as different on the basis of ethnic origins, religion, length of residence, and so on. Tambiah cites Myron Weiner's two hypotheses concerning the social and political consequences of internal migration in a multi-ethnic low-income society: (a) 'that the process of modernization, by providing incentives and opportunity for mobility, creates the conditions for increasing internal migration'; and (b) 'that the modernization process nurtures the growth of ethnic identification and ethnic cohesions'. The second case is frequent when there is competition for control over or access to economic wealth, political power and social status, which often involves a strong concept of 'territorial ethnicity' – the notion in the zones of immigration that certain ethnic groups consider themselves rooted in space as *bhumiputra* (sons of the soil), especially when migration changes the demographic balance and the mix of ethnic groups. Migrants belonging to a particular ethnic group may come in from the periphery to work in subordinate positions to the group predominating in the core region. This situation results in a dual labour market and applies to Turkish and Greek guest workers in Germany, Moroccans in France, and Mexican labour migrants to the United States, who frequently become depressed minorities victimized by discrimination.

Quite different outcomes ensue, however, when the population flow is in the opposite direction – that is, when the migrants have skills and capacities superior to those of the locals and come to enjoy affluence and social prestige. This second situation can become particularly acrimonious and contentious, especially in post-colonial and post-independence times, when power is shifted to and exercized by the most numerous, usually the local 'sons of the soil', who then wish to displace these successful so-called 'aliens' and newcomers. Frequently, this thrust coincides with the 'indigenous' or local population producing its own educated youth, who aspire to move into occupations and enterprises held and managed by the migrants. Such moves to displace people in favoured positions are particularly acute when the avenues of employment in the modern sector cannot expand fast enough to incorporate the number of entrants among the locals into the ranks of the middle class. When such bottlenecks occur, successful migrants are viewed as obstacles to the social mobility and well-being of the indigenous majority. Well-known examples come from north-eastern India, in Assam and Tripura and elsewhere, where there are collisions between local hill tribes and incoming West Bengali Hindu and Bangladeshi Muslim migrants; in Pakistan, with the animus against the *Muhajir* who migrated to Sind after partition and became prominent in Karachi; in Uganda, Idi Amin's expulsion of Indian merchants and professionals; in Fiji, the tensions between Fijians and Indian immigrants. With the dissolution of the Soviet Union, many Russian professionals and administrators, who had been sent or migrated to the various non-Russian republics, were faced with similar displacement by 'indigenous' populations.

The fourth issue that Tambiah has analysed pertains to the viability of the secularist philosophy in the increasing number of societies, in which many people reject the relegation of religion to the private domain and believe that religious values and beliefs must necessarily inform politics and economic activities. How can this world-view be implemented in a context where multiple religions with distinctive practices, and whose followers differ in their numbers, exist together in the same political arena? India, for example, has long asserted itself as the home of a concept of secularism, different from the western one, in which the state, rather than excluding religion from politics, is even-handed in its dealings with multiple co-existing religions. And yet, in India itself, Sikh fundamentalism and the cry for *Khalistan*, together with, more recently and significantly, the Hindu version, propagated and propagandized with great effect by such organizations as the *Rashtriya Swayamsevak Sangh* (RSS) and the *Vishwa Hindu Parishad* (VHP), generating *inter alia* the Ayodhya temple dispute (the *Babri Masjid-Ram Janmabhumi* clash), have seriously challenged India's capacity to negotiate a viable compromise between a unified polity and sectarian religio-politics.

The political economy of cultural difference

More is clearly required in order to answer the 'why' and 'how' questions. The 'institutional' framework proposed by political scientists, such as Douglass North, is most helpful, interrogating the political economy of ethnic and sectarian conflict against the current discourses of economic and political liberalization and globalization. What are the links between state-fragmenting violence and globalizing forces which have weakened the capacities available to states, both political and financial, for redistributing resources? Many states have been forced to dramatically changing power relations in heterogeneous societies that were previously relatively stable.

Drawing on case studies from across the world, researchers working in this framework have demonstrated how these distributional issues and power shifts have been experienced as ethnic and religious discrimination, and are often at the root of identity politics and so-called 'cultural' conflicts (Crawford and Lipschutz 1998). Their point of departure is the opening of new markets for goods, services, capital, and people and the implementation of state-shrinking ideologies. While, with some important exceptions, prosperous market economies have experienced relatively low levels of cultural conflict, they have experienced some such conflict nonetheless, as they have begun the process of economic liberalization. The potential for conflict has been highest where economic decline, neo-liberal reforms, and institutional transformation have broken old 'social contracts' – that is, where rules and norms have been broken by which access to political and economic resources was once granted. When the ensuing power shifts are experienced as ethnic and religious discrimination (or privilege), the resulting resentment (or opportunity) provide fertile ground for modern 'political entrepreneurs' (Crawford dubs them 'cultural' entrepreneurs) to mobilize support around ethnic and sectarian identities. But changes in power do not always result in cultural discrimination. Often, for example, they result in economic oppression or discrimination along ideological lines.

When, then, do power shifts result in *cultural* conflict, these researchers ask. The answer they propose is that such conflict erupts most frequently where old social contracts permitted ethnic and religious criteria to guide the allocation of political and economic resources. That mode of resource allocation permitted the logic of identity politics to characterize and sometimes even dominate political competition. Thus, where identity politics once prevailed and when institutions upholding the old social contract are weakened, the odds of cultural conflict and even violence increase. The logic of identity politics implies that claims on resources based on ascriptive criteria are more prone to intense conflict than disputes between interest groups: while interests are malleable and multiple, cultural identity is fixed and non-negotiable. Disputes over resources among identity groups will thus prove to be particularly difficult to negotiate. But even when the logic of identity politics dominates the political game, opposing order and the institutions of central authority can help enforce those pacts. Beverly Crawford has summarized the core argument as follows:

> [...] cultural identities can be transformed into political identities when cultural groups are targeted for privilege or discrimination and when economic factors, no matter how 'impersonal', lead to disproportionate hardships among culturally defined populations. The institutions of the central state can either legitimate the political relevance of cultural identity and channel cultural conflict in ways that achieve social harmony, or they can mute the political relevance of cultural identity and construct channels of allocation without regard to cultural differences [...] If institutional legacies encourage identity politics, if economic grievances are defined in cultural terms, if political entrepreneurs are initially successful in their cultural appeals for political support, bandwagoning effects and ethnic alliances increase the odds that identity politics will escalate to violence.

It has also been found that vulnerability to cultural conflict does not automatically induce it. To be sure, the legitimation of identity politics creates incentives for political entrepreneurs to mobilize populations along exclusive cultural lines. But if states provide a legitimate arena for entrepreneurs to compete and if resources available for allocation are abundant, identity politics, like other kinds of political competition, will be legitimate and stable. It is when demographic and economic changes undermine the rules of the game as well as the legitimacy of political institutions, and thus create the perception that the balance of political power is unfair, that identity politics can become conflictual and violent.

Inability to compete in an increasingly globalized economy causes the institutions protecting social order to erode, weaken, and even collapse. Globalization means that even strong states entering global competition must give up their control over the production and distribution of goods within their territories and let the market, rather than political institutions, allocate resources. Despite the seeming impersonality of the market, when these resources are distributed in ways that privilege some cultural groups and discriminate against others, those who lose in the market will lose their loyalty to the state that may have once tried to redress the effects of discrimination. The collapse of institutions which once contained the logic of identity politics, and the consequent erosion of loyalty to the central state, may bring on violence. This may also erupt where historical legacies perpetuate the idea that cultural distinctions are politically relevant. Chronic violence appears in areas where states have practiced identity politics, and in states whose ability to allocate political and economic resources has severely declined, but whose military apparatus is strong enough to repress efforts by cultural groups to secede or capture the state for themselves.

If I have paraphrased these findings at some length, it is precisely because they offer at least tentative answers to questions that the culturalist camp, including most anthropologists, do not often pose. The approach appeared so germane, in fact, that we invited Beverly Crawford to contribute an essay to the inaugural issue of the 'Cultures and Globalization Series' in order to assess the impact of globalization on social cohesion and national political integration, including the cultural factor. Does globalization have a homogenizing influence, nourishing social and political integration and tearing down cultural barriers that divide people? Or does it hasten social disintegration and exacerbate social conflict?

The 'clash of civilizations': side-stepping a red herring

Samuel Huntington's thesis that 'the principal conflicts of global politics will occur between nations and groups of different civilizations' resonates with the current 'security' paradigm. But surely it is a red herring. As Kofi Annan has observed, 'such broad generalizations – if they ever were valid – surely cannot stand the test of modern times, when integration, migration and globalization are bringing different races, cultures and ethnicities into ever closer contact with each other'.

Yet Annan himself has also found it expedient to stand the theory on its head in order to espouse the 'dialogue among civilizations concept' (and in 2005 took a step further by creating an international 'Alliance of Civilizations'; see this volume).

Although Huntington's thesis remains largely untested empirically, the phrase 'clash of civilizations' has become a contemporary cliché, abundantly thrown around by academics, politicians, and journalists who have more often than not read neither the author nor his critics. The thesis itself is highly reductionist and abstract, starting with the monolithic 'civilizations' themselves. As Said wryly put it,

> the personification of enormous entities such as 'the West' and 'Islam' is recklessly affirmed, as if hugely complicated matters like identity and culture existed in a cartoon-like world where Popeye and Bluto bash each other mercilessly, with one always more virtuous pugilist getting the upper hand over his adversary [...] with no

> time to spare for the internal dynamics and plurality of every civilization, or for the fact that the major contest in most modern cultures concerns the definition or interpretation of each culture. (Said 2001)

In effect, the theory treats culture with little heed for the internal dynamics and plurality of every so-called 'civilization', or for the fact that the major contest in most cultures concerns the diverging definitions and interpretation of each of them, as is precisely the case of 'Islamic civilization', which has such a central place in Huntington's theory. This is particularly ironic post-September 11th for the thesis mirrors the reasoning of the chief protagonist of that horrific event, Osama Bin Laden, just as it is shared by many who have since waged latter-day 'crusades', if subsequent events in Iraq are any indication. A chimera it may be, but a powerfully influential and self-fulfilling prophecy generating one it certainly is. It is indispensable, therefore, to marshal evidence that rejects (or possibly supports) the thesis, and can help shift the debate away from its not-so-covert ideological origins and moorings.

A silver lining has emerged, however, as a result of the influence that the thesis has exerted, and thanks to the rise of Islamic terrorism and, in Europe particularly, the increasing hybridity of urban populations. These have put the tropes of the 'inter-cultural' squarely on the policy agenda. Culturalist discourse is now shot through with prefixes of the 'inter' and the 'trans'. There is both rhetorical and practical attention at the ground level to the promotion of the necessary forms of 'dialogue', 'communication' and 'competencies'. These figures of the inter-cultural are not without their own problems, however.

Abstractions such as 'culture' and 'civilization', used at such a general level, coarsen our perceptions of social reality and may obfuscate more than they enlighten. The very notion of 'cultures' in dialogue is pure reification. What is more, actual interaction takes place not between two clearly designated players on each side (by what right and at whose behest are they 'representative'?), but among many different individuals and groups; any attempt to find authoritative debating partners on either side limits the conversation to certain ideologically conspicuous groups, excluding the vast majority of the societies concerned. The paradox here, as regards the voluntaristic dedication to 'inter-cultural dialogue' on the parts of governmental institutions, is that, by its very nature, the inter-cultural project is rooted in myriad person-to-person contacts, in creative and intellectual practice, not in official policy and action. 'Multiculturalism' is indeed a definable policy challenge that governments can and do address. 'Inter-culturalism' on the other hand is a freely willed stance, taken by individuals who choose to cross existential boundaries. It is grounded, therefore, in practice between independent subjects, not in official dealings. The latter, however, as well as their societies can be guided, influenced and facilitated. For ultimately, as Alain Touraine observes, inter-cultural communication cannot be reduced to interpersonal relations; it leads to the 'construction of general forms of social and cultural life' (*elle conduit à construire des formes générales de vie sociale et culturelle*; Touraine 1997: 210).

There is a great deal more that can be – and has been – said on these recent figures of the inter-cultural (Isar 2002). It is becoming increasingly obvious that – despite the verbal inflation – these are concepts that, in terms of the cultural challenges we face, are of greater import than the notion of 'development'. For what is at stake is the incorporation of cultural difference within the public sphere. The task of finding ways to allow cultural distinctions to flourish *without* engendering conflict requires new stances and mechanisms that enable all the groups that now constitute different national communities to assume ownership of the increasingly composite cultural identity of each one. This is not simply a matter of combating intolerance and exclusion, but also of giving dignity, voice, and recognition in the public sphere to different cultural groups while constructing – negotiating – a sense of national community. It is surely not a task for governments alone. But they can and should take the lead in promoting a better understanding of the different values, practices, and interpretative frameworks that characterize societies at a time when the accent has shifted from cultural policies with a nationalist and homogenizing cast to the acceptance and even active promotion of cultural differences.

A cultural twist on 'security'

Both the 'clash of civilizations' paradigm and infra-national cultural conflict – or its inverse – as described above, have contributed in recent years to the identification of culture as a 'security' issue. Dragan Klaic (2006), for example, advocates greater governmental spending on culture (in the arts and heritage sense) in Europe, as

> it would perhaps make more sense to look at culture budgets not in terms of their economic impact [...] but rather as a security issue. An argument could be made that discrimination, exclusion and marginalization in a political, ideological and socio-economic sense nourish

a dangerous cultural insecurity; and that cultural policies aimed at inclusion and active participation of marginalized social groups nurture their sense of cultural security and belonging, and strengthen social cohesion.

And so the notion of 'cultural security' has come to enrich the culturalist vocabulary. What exactly is it? A recent formulation (Tehranian 2004) characterizes 'cultural security' as 'the security of personal and collective identity negotiations that are so characteristic of our mobile post-modern world. It includes but is not limited to freedom of thought, conscience, language, speech, life style, ethnicity, gender, association, assembly, as well as cultural and political participation'.

Many will of course at once see this list as a catalogue of cultural rights and/or, *pace* the 2004 Human Development Report, of cultural freedoms. So how pertinent is it, really, to move from the framework of rights and freedoms to the conceptual envelope of 'security'?

Most modern democratic constitutions pay lip service to such freedoms, but both pre-modern and modernist – 'republican' – prejudices impose severe constraints on them. This is where the nuance of 'security' can be brought in as a conceptual diacritical. The dual process of globalization and localization has imposed another constraint. Globalized local conflicts, such as those in Palestine-Israel, the Persian Gulf, Somalia, Rwanda-Burundi, Bosnia, and Kosovo have created increasing forced and voluntary migrations accompanied by cultural insecurities for the immigrants, refugees, and displaced persons.

This way of using the notion of cultural security is most easily grasped, as Tehranian (2004) has done, by citing cases of its opposite – cultural *insecurity*:

– A Bahaii in Iran is a non-entity. Under the Shah's regime, a Bahaii could not declare his or her faith in an application for civil service employment. Under the Islamic Republican regime, he or she is subject to arrest and execution as an apostate.
– A Kurd in Turkey is called a Mountain Turk. S/he is denied to have his or her own cultural identity, the right to speak her language and to recreate her culture.
– A girl in Afghanistan under the Taliban regime had no right to schooling let alone any other human rights.
– A woman in Saudi Arabia cannot elect or be elected to public office. She is also not allowed to drive a car or ride a bicycle.

- Females in many parts of Africa are subjected to mutilation.
- A Turkish 'guest worker' in Germany is frequently someone who has lived, worked, and been married with children for several decades. His children for the most part are more German in culture than Turkish, yet until recently they could not be German citizens.
- Many third or fourth generation Koreans in Japan continue to live there without rights of citizenship.
- The rise of anti-immigrant sentiments in Europe is creating great cultural insecurity for some 15 million foreign-born immigrants. Despite official warnings to the contrary, after September 11th and July 7th counter-terrorist measures have sometimes assumed ethnic profiling.
- Some 3.7 million people were displaced by the civil war – and ethnic cleansing – in ex-Yugoslavia.
- The genocide of half a million Tutsi civilians in Rwanda and the displacement of about 2 million, in 1994, have created cultural insecurity for both Tutsi and Hutu.

There are an estimated 27.4 million displaced persons around the world under the protection of the United Nations High Commissioner for Refugees (UNHCR), of whom 14.5 million are considered refugees. Some of these refugees have been given temporary asylum, but as UNHCR (1995) reports, 'states are increasingly taking steps to obstruct the arrival of asylum seekers, to contain displaced people within their homeland, and to return refugees to their country of origin.'

On a more positive note, UNHCR (1995) also reports that

> States have begun to respond innovatively to the causes and consequences of human displacement. It cites the creation of a 'safety zone' in northern Iraq; the deployment of human rights monitors within Rwanda; the intervention of a regional peacekeeping force in Liberia; the use of UN troops to protect the delivery of humanitarian assistance in Bosnia and Herzegovina; the introduction of 'regional safe havens' for Haitian asylum seekers; and the establishment of a war crimes tribunal for former Yugoslavia and Rwanda. The establishment of the International Criminal Court (1998) and the UN intervention in East Timor (1999) may be added.

The international human rights regime is characterized by a paradox, however. On the one hand, in the post-Cold War years, the discourse of human rights was intensified by both great and small powers. But on the other hand, in places such as Rwanda, Bosnia, Kosovo, and East Timor, massacres have not met with a timely and adequate response. While national security, both internal and external, is at the top of every state's agenda, followed perhaps by economic security, human security in general and cultural security in particular are relegated to the back burner. In point of fact, cultural security is often considered in terms that are at odds with human security. Ever since the rise of nationalism in Europe and its spread across the globe, states have tried to mould and homogenize their populations around preconceived notions of nationhood, imposing of unity of language, ethnicity, ideology, and sometimes religion.

The entire cultural rights agenda must contend therefore with the heavy legacies of the culturally homogenizing nation-state. As Bhikhu Parekh (2000) observes, the latter has taken as its basis for the idea of social unity the recognition of the individual as the sole bearer of rights; it has sought to create a homogenized legal space made up of uniform political units that are subject to the same body of laws and institutions. Requiring cultural and social homogenization as its necessary basis, it has for centuries fought to mould the wider society in that direction. As a result, we have become so accustomed to equating unity with homogeneity and equality with uniformity, that we feel morally and emotionally disturbed by the political demands of a deep and defiant diversity and are never quite sure how to accommodate it. This state of affairs is accentuated by globalization, which makes a mockery of the project of national cultural unification on which all modern states have relied for their stability and cohesion. In these circumstances, we really have to ask ourselves what 'national culture' means. What is the national narrative?

This question of the narrative is key. It requires everywhere – and thus most assuredly in 'development' too – the kind of solution advocated by Parekh (2000: 204) for the culturally diverse societies of Europe: '"We" cannot integrate "them" as long as "we" remain "we"; "we" must be loosened up to create a new common space in which "they" can be accommodated and become part of a newly constituted "we"'.

In other words, perhaps when cultural differences are at stake, the path forward depends less on harnessing them instrumentally in the service of 'development', and much more on our capacity to reshape our cultures – and our mental maps – for a radical openness that refutes all notions of closed, fixed identities and espouses a vision of planetary 'conviviality'.

Notes

1. The topics explored here are offshoots of my current reflections as Managing Editor of the Cultures and Globalization Series, whose first volume, due to appear in March 2008, is devoted to the topic 'Conflicts and Tensions'. The series will be published by Sage.
2. The MONDIACULT definition of 'culture' reads as follows: '... that in its widest sense, culture may now be said to be the whole complex of distinctive spiritual, material, intellectual and emotional features that characterize a society or social group. It includes not only the arts and letters, but also modes of life, the fundamental rights of the human being, values systems, traditions and beliefs...' (UNESCO1982).
3. The author was the Executive Secretary of the World Commission for Culture and Development 1994–5.
4. This passage reiterates concerns that academic anthropologists began raising in the 1980s. But since 'culture' and culturalist discourse are now pervasive in much broader circles and have become central in the public rhetoric of governments, intergovernmental organizations and civil society bodies alike, it seems pertinent to air the issues once again here, for the benefit of a less specialized readership.
5. This kind of breakdown also helps take us beyond the abstract, incantatory nature of the discourse and towards the disaggregation called for by Adam Kuper (1999) and which I referred to earlier.
6. This will become strikingly patent with regard to the subject matter of the next section. There is increasing evidence that much of what we consider 'cultural' conflict is not about ethnicity or religion or 'culture' as such, but rather about setting the terms of discourse in conflict over state power and control. 'Just as "democracy" and "communism" functioned as discourses in domestic struggles for power during the Cold War, so do ethnicity and religion operate today. They are instrumental means rather than ends' (Lipschutz 1998).

References

Appadurai, A. (1996) *Modernity at Large: Cultural Dimensions of Globalization*, Minneapolis: University of Minnesota Press.

Avruch, K. (1998) *Culture and Conflict Resolution*, Washington: United States Institute of Peace Press.

Bennett, T. (2001) *Differing Diversities. Cultural policy and cultural diversity*, Strasbourg: Council of Europe Publishing.

Bodo, S. and Cifarelli, R. (eds) (2006) *Quando la cultura fa la differenza*, Rome: Meltemi.

Crawford, B. (1998) 'The Causes of Cultural Conflict: An Institutional approach', in Crawford, B. and Lipschutz, R. D. (eds) (1998) *The Myth of 'Ethnic Conflict': Politics, Economics, and 'Cultural' Violence*, Berkeley: University of California.

Epskamp, K. and Gould, H. (2000) 'Outlining the Debate', in *CULTURELINK, Special issue 2000: Culture and Development vs. Cultural Development*.

Featherstone, M. (1995) *Undoing Culture. Globalization, Postmodernism and Identity*, London: Sage.

Friedman, J. and Randeria, S. (eds) (2004) *Worlds on the Move: Globalization, Migration and Cultural Security*, London: I.B. Tauris in association with The Toda Institute for Global Peace and Policy Research.

Gillis, J. R. (ed) (1994) *Commemorations. The Politics of National Identity*, Princeton: Princeton University Press.

Gilroy, P. (2004) *After Empire*, Abingdon: Routledge.

Girard, A. (1983) *Cultural development: experience and policies* (second edition). Paris: UNESCO.

Göle, N. (2005) *Interpénétrations. L'Islam et l'Europe.* Paris: Galaade Editions.

Hall, S. (1992) 'The Question of Cultural Identity', in *Modernity and its Futures*, Cambridge: Polity Press.

Hall, S., Held, D. and McGrew, T. (eds) (1992) *Modernity and its Futures*, Cambridge: Polity Press.

Handler, R. (1994) 'Is "Identity" a Useful Cross-Cultural Concept?', in Gillis, J.R. (ed) (1994) *Commemorations. The Politics of National Identity*, Princeton: Princeton University Press.

Isar, Y. R. (2002) 'The intercultural challenge: an imperative of solidarity', in *Intercultural Dialogue*, Brussels: European Communities.

Kirshenblatt-Gimblett, B. (1998) *Destination Culture: Tourism, Museums, and Heritage*, Berkeley: University of California Press.

Klaic, D. (2006) 'Thematic priorities, altered institutional typology. Cultural policies and institutions facing the challenge of multicultural societies', in Bodo, S. and Cifarelli, R. (eds) (2006) *Quando la cultura fa la differenza*, Rome: Meltemi.

Kuper, A. (1999) *Culture, the Anthropologist's Account*, Cambridge: Harvard University Press.

Lipschutz, R. D. (1998) 'Seeking a State of One's Own', in Crawford, B. and Lipschutz, R.D. (eds) (1998) *The Myth of 'Ethnic Conflict': Politics, Economics, and 'Cultural' Violence*, Berkeley: University of California.

Maheu, R. (1973) *Culture in the contemporary world. Problems and prospects*, Paris: UNESCO.

Mercer, C. (2002) *Towards Cultural Citizenship: Tools for Cultural Policy and Development*, Stockholm: The Bank of Sweden Tercentenary Foundation and Diglunds Förlag.

Parekh, B. (2000) *Rethinking Multiculturalism. Cultural Diversity and Political Theory*, London: Macmillan.

Sahlins, M. (1994) 'A Brief Cultural History of Culture', unpublished paper prepared for the World Commission on Culture and Development (UNESCO).

Said, E. (2001) 'The Clash of Ignorance', in *The Nation*, 22 October 2001.

Sen, A. (1999) *Development as Freedom*, Oxford: Oxford University Press.

Stevenson, N. (2003) *Cultural Citizenship. Cosmopolitan Questions*, Maidenhead: Open University Press.

Tambiah, S. J. (1996) *Leveling crowds. Ethnonationalist Conflicts and Collective Violence in South Asia*, Berkeley and Los Angeles: University of California Press.

Tehranian, M. (2004) 'Cultural Security and Global Governance: International Migration and Negotiations of Identity', in Friedman, J. and Randeria, S. (eds) (2004) *Worlds on the Move: Globalization, Migration and Cultural Security*,

London: I.B. Tauris in association with The Toda Institute for Global Peace and Policy Research.

Touraine, A. (1997) *Pourrons-nous vivre ensemble? Egalité et différence*, Paris: Fayard.

UNDP (2004) *Human Development Report 2004. Cultural Liberty in Today's Diverse World*, New York: UNDP.

UNESCO (1981) *International thesaurus of cultural development*, Paris: UNESCO.

UNESCO (1982) *Final Report of the World Conference on Cultural Policies* (document CLT/MD/1), Paris: UNESCO.

UNHCR (1995) *The State of the World's Refugees*, Oxford: Oxford University Press.

Werbner, P. and Modood, T. (eds) (1997) *Debating Cultural Hybridity: Multicultural Identities and the Politics of Anti-Racism*, London: Zed Books.

Wicker, H-R. (1997) 'From Complex Culture to Cultural Complexity', in Werbner, P. and Modood, T. (eds) (1997) *Debating Cultural Hybridity: Multicultural Identities and the Politics of Anti-Racism*, London: Zed Books.

Williams, R. (1988) *Keywords: A Vocabulary of Culture and Society*, London: Fontana.

Williams, R. (1995) *The Sociology of Culture* (with a new Foreword by Bruce Robbins), Chicago: The University of Chicago Press.

World Commission on Culture and Development (1996) *Our Creative Diversity*, Paris: UNESCO.

2
Theories of the Development of Democracy

Hans-Dieter Klingemann and Christian Welzel

On the Complementary Aspects of Tatu Vanhanen's Evolutionary Resource Distribution Theory of Democratization and Ronald Inglehart and Christian Welzel's Emancipative Theory of Democracy.

Introduction

Between 1987 and 1996 the world has seen an unprecedented surge in the number of countries turning from autocracy to democracy. Today 119 of the world's 192 independent countries are rated electoral democracies and – considering political rights and civil liberties – 89 are evaluated free countries by Freedom House. In normative terms this is most certainly a positive development (See Figure 2.1.).

This chapter describes and compares two of the most important theoretical approaches predicting the global spread of democratic government.The first approach is called the *evolutionary resource distribution theory of democratization* and has been developed by Tatu Vanhanen. Major results of Vanhanen's work are presented in 'The Emergence of Democracy' (1984), 'The Process of Democratization' (1990), 'Prospects of Democracy' (1997), and most recently, 'Democratization' (2003).

The second approach has been proposed by Inglehart and Welzel (2005). They label their approach an *emancipatory theory of democracy.* This theory has emerged as a confluence of congenial ideas worked out in Inglehart's 'The Silent Revolution' (1977), 'Culture Shift in Advanced Industrial Society' (1990), 'Modernization and Postmodernization' (1997), and Welzel's 'Fluchtpunkt Humanentwicklung' (2002; see also Welzel, Inglehart and Klingemann 2003).

The authors have stressed the differences between their respective approaches. Vanhanen insists that one must rely on observables when operationalizing concepts while Inglehart and Welzel are prepared to also rely on citizens' values and beliefs as well as on expert judgment.

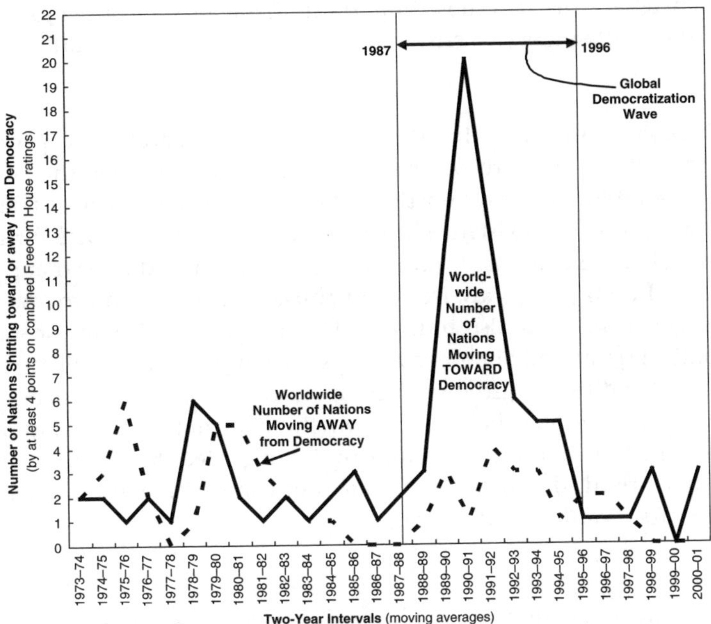

Figure 2.1   Shift to and from democracy in the world as whole.
Source: Inglehart and Welzel (2005: 176).

This essay tries to assess the similarities and differences between these two theories. It is assumed that their major ideas can be reconciled resulting in much additional value. The analysis proceeds in three steps. First, we will outline the general reasoning of the two theories. Second, we want to describe – in detail – how these two theories have operationalized their concepts. Third, and last, we want to show how these theories can be related.

Two general theories to explain the spread of democratic regimes

The evolutionary resource distribution theory of democratization

Definition of democracy

In his definition of 'democracy' Vanhanen relies on Robert Dahl (1971) who has convincingly argued that 'public contestation' and 'the right to participate' are the two most important characteristics of democracy. Vanhanen calls these two criteria 'competition' and 'participation' and goes on as follows:

> My basic argument is that they (e.g. competition and participation) represent the most crucial aspects of democracy and that, therefore, their combination may constitute the most realistic measure of democratisation. The existence of legal opportunity to compete for the control of political institutions through elections indicates that people and their groups are free to organise themselves and to oppose the government. It also indicates, indirectly, the existence of some political rights and liberties as well as certain political equality in the sense that different groups can compete for power. The degree of participation indicates the extent to which 'the people' take part in politics. [...] A political system can be regarded to be the more democratised, the higher the degrees of competition and participations are. (Vanhanen 2003: 56)

Theory

Inspired by Lipset (1959, 1960) but first and foremost by Darwin (1981), Vanhanen has developed a theoretical explanation of democratization which he calls an evolutionary resource distribution theory of democratization. Based on Darwin he argues that human politics has evolutionary roots. Without going into the details of his argument, Vanhanen hypothesizes that the degree of concentration of political power depends on the degree of the concentration of socio-economic power resources. A narrow concentration of socio-economic power resources leads to autocracy – the government of the few – while a wide dispersal of socio-economic power resources among the many leads to democracy.

Democratization takes place under conditions in which power resources have become so widely distributed that no group is any longer able to suppress its competitors or to maintain its hegemony. Vanhanen insists that this is not a new version of modernization theory, or a theory based on social class or culture. Rather, it is meant to be an evolutionary resource distribution theory of democratization which '...can be understood only on the basis of the Darwinian interpretation of politics, which explains the necessity to struggle for scarce resources and our tendency to use all available means in this struggle' (Vanhanen 2003: 29).[1]

Operationalization of major concepts

For his empirical analyses Vanhanen operationalizes competition as follows:

Competition = 100 – percentage of votes won by the largest party.

If statistical data on distribution of votes are not available, the value of this variable is calculated on the basis of the distribution of seats in parliament.

Participation is calculated as percentage of people voting in an election:

Participation = people voting as a percentage of the total population.

The reason for relying on total population as the base is a pragmatic one. More statistical data are available for a country's total population than for the adult or enfranchised population.

Vanhanen combines the two variables by multiplying them and dividing the product by 100. This index weighs the two variables equally. 'My argument is that participation is as important a dimension of democracy as competition. If only a small minority of the adult population takes part in elections, then the electoral struggle for power is restricted to the dominant stratum of the population, and the bulk of the population remains outside national politics. Power sharing is certainly more superficial in such countries compared to societies where a majority of the adult population takes part in elections' (Vanhanen 2003: 63). It seems theoretically plausible that both dimensions are necessary for democracy and that a high level of competition cannot compensate for lack of participation, or vice versa. It has been criticized that in 1993 this index was higher for Russia than for Switzerland and the United States. Subsequently Vanhanen has argued that because of the referenda the actual degree of participation in these two countries has been much higher than the participation variable indicates. In his latest studies the referenda are taken into account for these two countries and they consequently rise to the levels of the other western democracies.

However, the conceptual definitions and measurement rules do not yet answer the question of which country is a democracy and which one is an autocracy. The index ranks countries by levels of democracy. This ranking forms a continuum from very high index values to zero values. Thus, it does not tell us directly at what stage political systems cease to be democracies and begin to be autocratic systems, or vice versa.

Vanhanen sets the minimum threshold for competition at 30 per cent. This is in line with such authors as Gastil (1988) or Cutright (1963) who argue that if a group or leader regularly receives 70 per cent or more of the votes, it indicates a weak opposition, and the probable existence of undemocratic barriers in the way of its further success. For participation the threshold is set lower at 20 per cent because the percentage of electoral participation is calculated from the total population. In order to qualify as a democracy a country must cross both threshold values. Of course, this selection of threshold values is arbitrary and countries which satisfy only the minimum criteria of democracy do not necessarily satisfy more demanding standards of liberal democracy.

However, by setting threshold values Vanhanen solves two problems. First, he honours Sartori's (1987) argument that – as with pregnancy – a regime cannot be half democratic. All countries which fail to reach either one of the threshold values belong to the class of autocracies, whereas all the other countries belong to the class of democracies. Second, above the threshold the index measures levels of democracy, whereas below the threshold it measures levels of autocracy. Thus, the two criteria establish classes of democracies and autocracies, while within classes the index values represent the degree of democracy on the one hand and the degree of autocracy on the other.

Explanatory variables

How does Vanhanen measure the distribution of socio-economic power resources? He proposes an Index of Power Resources (IPR) which combines the following four explanatory variables:

1. Number of students per 100,000 inhabitants. The higher the number of students per 100,000 inhabitants, the more widely intellectual power resources are distributed and the better the chances for democracy.
2. The percentage of literates defined as the literacy rate of the population aged 15 and above. The higher the adult literacy rate, the more widely basic intellectual resources are distributed in a society and the better the chances for democracy.
3. Share of family farms on the total of agricultural holdings. The higher the share of family farms, the more widely economic resources based on ownership or control of agricultural land are distributed among the agricultural population and the better the chances for democracy.
4. The degree of decentralization of mainly non-agricultural economic power resources. This variable is based on statistical data about a

country's population below the poverty line. The higher the degree of decentralization, the more widely ownership and control of mainly non-agricultural power resources are decentralized, the better the social conditions are for democracy.

These four variables form the Index of Power Resources (IPR) as follows:

First 'students' and 'literates' are combined into a sectional index of 'Intellectual Power Resources' by calculating the mean of the two percentages.

Second 'family farms' and 'non-agricultural power resources' are combined into a sectional index of 'Economic Power Resources' by weighting both variables by percentage of agricultural population on the one hand, and percentage of non-agricultural population on the other, and after that, adding them up.

Finally, the Index of Power Resources is calculated by multiplying the values of the two sectional indices and by dividing the product by 100. It is important to note that the IPR does not use any GDP per capita measure as an element.

Empirical results

Of the many analyses Vanhanen has carried out we present the most important result. It refers to the regression of the Index of Democracy (ID) 2001 on the Index of Power Resources (IPR) in 1998 with single countries as the unit of analysis in the group of the 170 countries under investigation. The proportion of variance explained by a linear regression model amounts to 72 per cent. See Figure 2.2.

An emancipative theory of democracy

Definition of democracy

Based on Sen's (1999) notion of 'development as freedom', Welzel (2002) has elaborated an emancipative theory of human development, defining human development as people empowerment. Democracy is a central component of this perspective. It institutionalizes the opportunities that empower people to manage their own affairs and shapes collective decisions affecting their lives. In this view civil and political liberties constitute the core of democracy because it is these liberties that empower people, allowing them to make autonomous choices in private and public life.[2] As Inglehart and Welzel (2005) point out: 'Throughout history, the quest for civil and political liberties has provided a major motivation for people to struggle for democracy, seeking self-determination. Mass involvement in

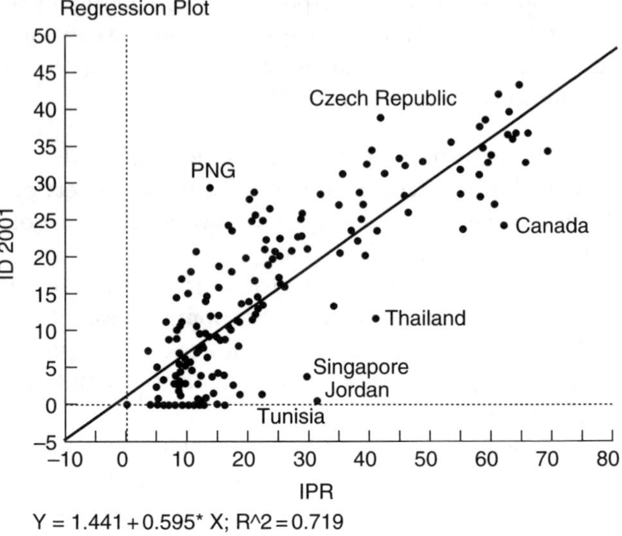

$$Y = 1.441 + 0.595{*} X; R{^\wedge}2 = 0.719$$

Figure 2.2   Results of regression analysis.
Source: Vanhanen, 2003, p. 135.

liberation movements and freedom campaigns is an essential element of democratization.'

In contrast to Vanhanen, this view considers democracy as an institutional opportunity structure. The opportunity aspect cannot be measured by election outcomes because these outcomes indicate behaviour, not opportunities, and thus miss a central element in the definition of democracy.

In the emancipative perspective of human development, democracy institutionalizes opportunities that empower people. Necessarily this involves civil and political liberties, codified as formal rights. The scope of these rights defines the extent to which democracy is formally codified. But even though formally codified rights are a necessary element of democracy, the codification alone does not make these rights effective in the sense that people can practise them. For rights to be effective requires that office holders respect them in their use of state power and comply with the rule of law. Thus Inglehart and Welzel distinguish between the *formal* presence of liberal democracy, which is the scope of institutionalized civil and political rights, and the *effective* presence of liberal democracy, which is the scope of these rights insofar as they are respected by power holders. The latter is a measure of the extent to which democratic opportunities effectively empower people. The authors use measures of effective democracy covering the years 2000–2002.

Theory

Unlike Vanhanen, Inglehart and Welzel offer a cultural explanation of the emergence and persistence of democracies. In principle they argue that pro-democratic mass values lead to the emergence and persistence of democracy. They develop this argument in the context of a revised version of modernization theory. This theory focusses on three major trajectories of societal change (Welzel, Inglehart and Klingemann 2003). The first process is economic development which includes rising levels of education and growing access to information. The second process relates to value change. Traditional conformity values give way to more emancipative values that emphasize human choice. The third process involves a society's political institutions. Autocratic regimes turn into new democracies and old democracies open up channels of direct participation in political decision-making and experience rising levels of direct civic participation. The underlying theme of the modernization process is a broadening of human choice. Socio-economic modernization reduces the external constraints on human choice by increasing people's material, cognitive, and social resources. This brings growing mass emphasis on self-expression values, which in turn leads to growing public demands for civil and political liberties, gender equality and responsive government, helping to establish and sustain the institutions best suited to maximize human choice, i.e. democracy. To underscore the normative thrust of their argument, and since they see people empowerment as the common underlying theme that integrates the whole sequence of human development, they call their theory an *emancipative theory of democracy*. See Table 2.1.

Operationalization of major concepts

In their operationalization Inglehart and Welzel rely on the summary measures of the Freedom House expert ratings of a country's political rights and civil liberties (Gastil 1988). Ratings of country experts are structured by an 11-point checklist on political rights, and a 14-point checklist on civil liberties. Details are available in the comprehensive internet appendix to the Inglehart and Welzel volume. Thus, we need not go into details. It is important to note that in operationalizing democracy Inglehart and Welzel mainly rely on expert ratings.

Vanhanen discusses the Freedom House scores, too, but dismisses the measures for his own analysis. He argues as follows: 'I agree that political rights and liberties represent essential characteristics of democracy, but I have omitted them from my measures because I think that it would not be possible to measure their existence and

Table 2.1   Welzel's concept of human development.

	Socioeconomic dimension	Cultural dimension	Institutional dimension
HD takes place when:	Individual Resources empower people *means-wise*	Self-expression values empower people *motivation-wise*	Democratic liberties empower people *rights-wise*
HD determines:	the extent to which people are able	willing	entitled
	to pursue self-chosen priorities		
HD enlarges people's:	Capabilities of self-determination	aspirations for	entitlements to
HD results in:	Human empowerment (diminishing external constraints on intrinsic human choice)		

Source: adapted from Welzel (2002: 46).

relative importance by any reliable empirical variables' (Vanhanen 2003: 61).

The index measuring the *formal* presence of liberal *democracy* is constructed by adding the inverted 7-point scores of political rights and civil liberties scales. Scale scores are expressed as a percentage of the maximum score of 12. The index of *effective democracy* is supposed to measure the degree to which given levels of formal democracy are set into effective practice by law-abiding 'honest' elite behaviour. Honest elite behaviour is measured by 'control of corruption' scores supplied by the World Bank, a measure which basically also rests on expert judgment. The 'control of corruption' or 'elite integrity' variable is used as a weight for formal democracy to produce the index of effective democracy as an index of weighted percentages. Note that this measure is constructed in a way that formal democracy cannot be upgraded by favourable scores for elite integrity. But it can be seriously downgraded by unfavourable scores for elite integrity.

Explanatory variables

Among the many independent variables Inglehart and Welzel use to explain 'effective democracy', self-expression values rank highest.

Technically the index of self-expression values is derived by factor ana-lysis. To evaluate this index it is important to know what it consists of. That is why we cite the variables Inglehart and Welzel describe in their appen-dix in some detail.

Self-expression values
The survey data by which self-expression values are measured are taken from the earliest available surveys of the second to fourth waves of the World Values Surveys. The average measurement year is 1995.

– Liberty aspirations: aggregate data measure national percentages of respondents scoring at least 2 on a 0–5 preference scale measuring priorities on civil liberties ('protecting freedom of speech') and polit-ical liberties ('seeing that people have more say about how things are done at their jobs and in their communities', 'giving people more say in important government decisions').
– Tolerance of homosexuality: aggregate data measure national per-centages of people scoring above 1 on a 1–10 scale for tolerance of homosexuality.
– Signing petitions (early 1990s; mid-1990s): aggregate data measure national percentages of people reporting to have signed a petition.
– Life satisfaction: aggregate data measure national percentages of respondents scoring at least 7 on a 1–10 scale for general life satisfaction.
– Interpersonal trust: aggregate data measure national percentages of respondents reporting that 'most people can be trusted'.

Using these five variables self-expression values are calculated as follows and aggregated to the national level:
1. A factor analysis is run over the national percentage measures of the previous five variables (ordering no specific number of fac-tors and no rotation), yielding factor loadings of 0.87 for the per-centage of people expressing liberty aspirations, 0.78 for the percentage tolerating homosexuality to some degree, 0.84 for the percentage signing petitions, 0.82 for the percentage being rela-tively satisfied with their lives, and 0.61 for the percentage trust-ing other people (only one factor extracted).
2. These factor loadings are used as weights, multiplying each per-centage variable with its factor loading.
3. The weighted percentages for each country are added.
4. The sum of this addition is divided the by the sum of the weights.

The following formula summarizes these procedures:

% emphasising self-expression values =

(0.87 * % emphasising liberty aspirations

+ 0.78 * % being somewhat tolerant to homosexuality

+ 0.84 * % signing petitions

+ 0.82 * % being satisfied with their lives

+ 0.61 * % expressing trust to other people)

/ 3.91.

This scale indicates, per country, the percentage of people emphasising self-expression values to at least some degree, measured as a mean percentage of its five factor-weighed components.

Empirical results

The relation of levels of self-expression values and level of effective democracy is shown in Figure 2.3. Linear regression explains an astonishing 82 per cent of the variance in levels of effective democracy.

Empirical results relating levels of effective democracy to a broader theory of social change and human development are convincing as shown in Figure 2.4 taken from Welzel, Inglehart and Klingemann (2003).

Relating two general theories of democracy

In the introduction we stressed that the two most influential empirically-based theories of the development of democracy as proposed by Vanhanen on the one hand, and by Inglehart and Welzel on the other, seemed to be in contradiction. Vanhanen has emphasized the relevance of objective indicators. Inglehart and Welzel, on the other hand, have argued that values and motivations of citizens must be taken into account. We wanted to show, however, that these two theories are not contradictory. Rather, they are complementary both empirically and theoretically.

If one runs a statistical horse race in which the level of effective democracy is regressed on Vanhanen's index of power resources (as measured in 1998) and Inglehart and Welzel's index of self-expression values (centred on late 1990 measures), one discovers that these two independent variables share an almost equal weight in the variance explained. A partitioning of the variance generates more detailed insights (see Figure 2.5): if we divide the variance in 'power resources' into the part which over-

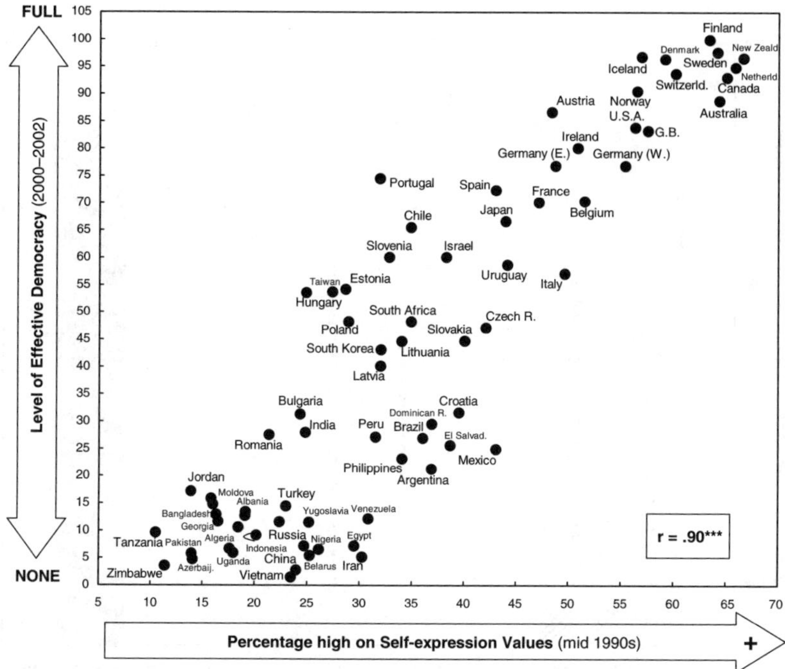

Figure 2.3 Self-expression values and effective democracy.

Note: *** denotes that significance level is at p < .001
Source: Inglehart and Welzel (2005: 155).

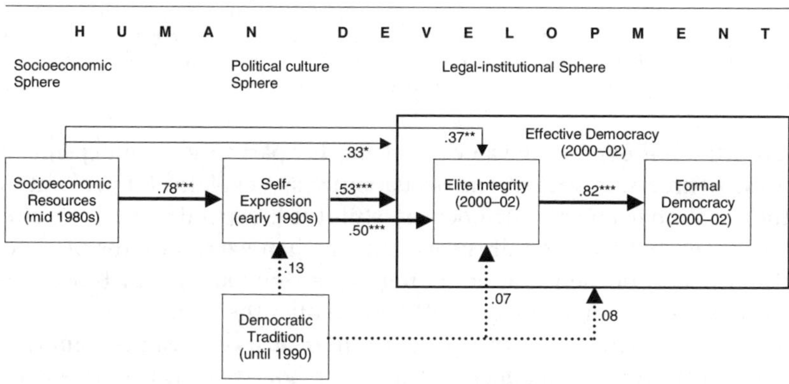

Coefficients are standardized path coefficients. Bold arrows indicate strongest effect on respective dependent variable. Interrupted arrows show insignificant effects. There is no overall fit for this fully identified model. Dropping the effects of 'Years of Democracy', the Adjusted Goodness of Fit Index is .88, showing that the impact of the democratic tradition is negligible. Number of cases: N=68.

Figure 2.4 The human development sequence; a path analysis.

Notes: * p < .10, ** p < .01, *** p < .001.
Source: Welzel, Inglehart and Klingemann (2003: 367).

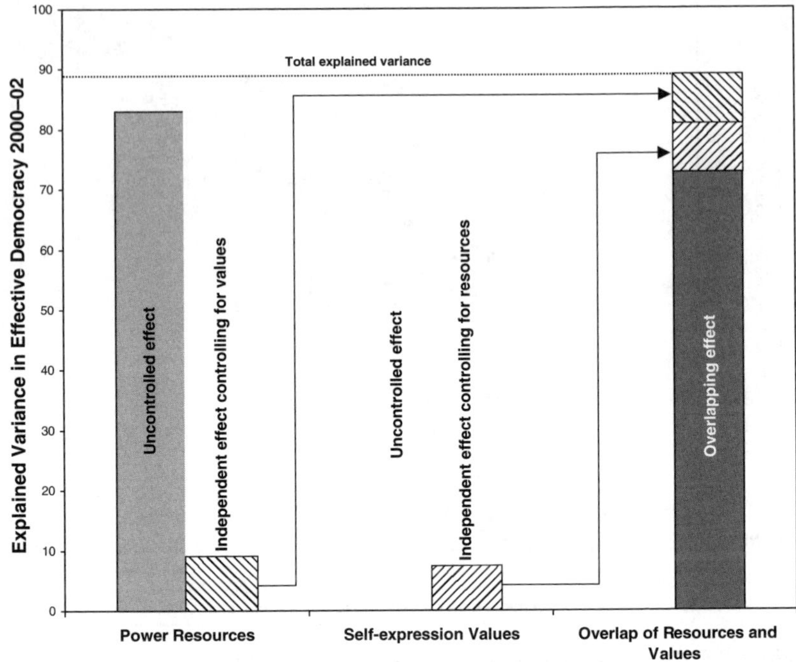

Figure 2.5   Partitioning contributions to the explained variance in effective democracy.

Notes: N=72, power resource measure for 1998 from Vanhanen (2003); self-expression values measure for late 1990s from Inglehart and Welzel (2005), effective democracy measure foe 2000–02 from Inglehart and Welzel (2005). Variance proportions calculated on the basis of two bivariate and one trivariate OLS-regression.

laps with 'self-expression values', and another part which is independent of 'self-expression values', the overlapping part explains 80 per cent of the variation in effective democracy, while the independent part explains 9 per cent, only. The result is very similar when we reverse the perspective: the part of the variation in 'self-expression values' which overlaps with 'power resources' explains 81.7 per cent of the variance in effective democracy, while the independent part just contributes another 7.3 per cent to explain effective democracy. Together the two independent effects add up to explain 16.3 per cent of the variation in effective democracy, while the overlapping effect explains 72.7 per cent.

These results make perfect sense theoretically. Self-expression values are mainly caused by power resources and in this way are expected to help explain effective democracy. Conversely, power resources help to explain effective democracy mostly because they generate self-expression values.

This reading of the evidence is plausible, if one accepts that democracy is not a machine that runs automatically given a certain structure of power resources. Instead, democracy is the product of collective action, which needs corresponding political motivations to reach this goal. Hence, power resources are relevant because they give birth to democratic attitudes. Self-expression values indicate this type of attitudes. They are not a constant so that only variations in power resources could matter – as Vanhanen assumes. Quite the contrary, motivations vary systematically with a changing structure of power resources, which is precisely the reason why these resources matter.

Although they mostly overlap in their effects, some independent contributions of both power resources and self-expression values remain when it comes to explaining effective democracy. This makes sense, too. Holding resource distribution constant, stronger self-expression values matter because an additional emphasis on self-expression provides an additional motivational push to strive for and sustain effective democracy. Conversely, holding self-expression values constant, a higher degree of equal distribution of power resources matters because they provide additional means to reach and support effective democracy.

Interestingly, these empirical findings also support two different approaches to social movement theory. First, resource mobilization theory is confirmed which emphasizes the effect of the structure of power resources for the mobilization of pro-democratic mass movements (Tilly 1978). Second, value-expectancy theory gets support which emphasizes the effect of values for the mobilization of pro-democratic mass movements (Klandermans 1984).

In any case, Vanhanen's and Inglehart and Welzel's theories of democracy have in common that they model the emergence and survival of democracy in a developmental framework. Where they differ is in the inclusiveness of their models. Vanhanen's theory focuses on the resource aspect as a condition for the democratic process, only. In contrast, Inglehart and Welzel's human development theory includes the resource aspect as well but adds to it the value-aspect, emphasizing the subjective motivation necessary for democratic action. As Welzel's human development framework suggests, the resource-aspect and the value-aspect largely overlap, since power resources and self-expression values are just different facets of human emancipation as the underlying theme. Democracy itself is the third facet of this theme, which is why it is so closely associated with both power resources and self-expression values. The crucial point seems to be that power resources, self-expression values, and democracy, are all compatible with one overarching syndrome: human development.

Notes

1. It should be noted that Vanhanen's distribution argument is not as new as he claims. The need to underline its novelty drives Vanhanen to dissociate the distribution argument from modernization theory where it has been stated repeatedly. The distribution argument is a direct corollary of the middle class thesis made by Lipset (1959) and Dahl (1971): middle class-dominated societies have a tendency to democracy *because* resources are more equally distributed in these societies. Originally, this point has already been made in Aristotle's *Politics*. The distribution argument has a much longer tradition than Vanhanen presumes. The reference to Darwin is unnecessary to come across it.
2. It should be noted that in a human empowerment perspective one would not only consider *political* liberties as part of the definition of democracy. *Civil* liberties, too, are part of the definition of democracy because they empower people in making them autonomous agents in shaping their own affairs.

References

Almond, G. A. (1980) 'The Intellectual History of the Civic Culture Concept', in Almond, G. A. and Verba, S. (eds) (1980) *The Civic Culture Revisited*, Boston: Little Brown.

Almond, G. A. and Verba, S. (eds) (1980) *The Civic Culture Revisited*, Boston: Little Brown.

Cutright, P. (1963) 'National Political Development: Measurement and Analysis', *American Sociological Review* 28: 253–264.

Dahl, R. (1971) *Polyarchy: Participation and Opposition*, New Haven: Yale University Press.

Darwin, C. (1981; originally published 1859) *The Origin of Species by Means of Natural Selection or Preservation of Favoured Races in the Struggle for Life*, Harmondsworth: Penguin Books.

Gastil, R. D. (1988) *Freedom in the World: Political Rights and Civil Liberties, 1987–88*, New York: Freedom House.

Inglehart, R. (1977) *The Silent Revolution*, Princeton: Princeton University Press.

Inglehart, R. (1990) *Culture Shift in Advanced Industrial Society*, Princeton: Princeton University Press.

Inglehart, R. (1997) *Modernization and Postmodernization*, Princeton: Princeton University Press.

Inglehart, R. and Welzel, C. (2005) *Modernization, Cultural Change and Democracy: The Human Development Sequence*, New York: Cambridge University Press.

Klandermans, B. (1984) 'Mobilization and Participation', *American Sociological Review* 49: 583–600.

Klingemann, H. (1999) 'Mapping Political Support in the 1990s: A Global Analysis', in Norris, P. (ed) (1999) *Critical Citizens. Global Support of Democratic Governance*, Oxford: Oxford University Press.

Lipset, S. M. (1959) Some Social Requisites of Democracy, Economic Development and Political Legitimacy, *American Political Science Review* 53: 69–105.

Lipset, S. M. (1960) *Political Man: The Social Basis of Politics*, New York: Doubleday.

Norris, P. (ed) (1999) *Critical Citizens. Global Support of Democratic Governance*, Oxford: Oxford University Press.

Przeworski, A. and Limongi, F. (1997) 'Modernization: Theories and Facts', *World Politics* 49: 155–183.

Sartori, G. (1987) *The Theory of Democracy Revisited*, Chatham N.J.: Chatham House.

Sen, A. (1999) *Development as Freedom*, New York: Knopf.

Tilly, C. (1978) *From Mobilization to Revolution*, Reading, MA: Addison-Wesley.

Vanhanen, T. (1984) *The Emergence of Democracy: A Comparative Study of 119 States, 1850–1979*, Commentationes Scientiarum Socialum 24. Helsinki: The Finnish Society of Sciences and Letters.

Vanhanen, T. (1990) *The Process of Democratization: A Comparative Study of 147 States, 1980–88*, New York: Crane Russack.

Vanhanen, T. (1997) *Prospects of Democracy. A Study of 172 Countries*, London: Routledge.

Vanhanen, T. (2003) *Democratization. A Comparative Study of 170 Countries*, London: Routledge.

Welzel, C. (2002) *Fluchtpunkt Humanentwicklung*, Wiesbaden: Westdeutscher Verlag.

Welzel, C., Inglehart, R. and Klingemann, H. (2003) 'The Theory of Human Development: A Cross Cultural Analysis', *European Journal of Political Research* 42: 341–379.

3
Human Values and Civic Education. Adolescent Orientations towards Gender Equality and Good Citizenship

Thorleif Pettersson

The many social and political changes which have taken place around the world in recent decades have contributed to a renewed interest in both citizenship education and how people understand citizenship and democracy (Ichilov 2003: 637; Milner 2002: 1). Likewise, human rights and human development have been given increased prominence in current world affairs, and the contemporary cultural changes are said to have affected people's orientations towards human development, citizenship, democracy, and human rights. The linkages between culture, human development, and democracy have therefore become an increasingly important research area, both to the social sciences and the arts and humanities.

This chapter will investigate how young people's orientations towards human development are influenced by cultural and educational factors. The investigation will be based on two main theoretical perspectives. The first attempts to explain how general socio-economic development leads to a growing emphasis on human autonomy and so-called self-expression values, while the second seeks to understand how young people's values and civic orientations are affected by the specific civic education they receive. These two theoretical perspectives will be shortly introduced next.

A general theory of human development

It has recently been argued that human development as the ultimate goal for social progress should be conceptualized as the 'growth of human autonomy and choice in major aspects of people's life' (Welzel 2002: 291), and as the 'capability of humans to choose the lives they want' (Welzel et al. 2003: 344). Human development is said to involve three interrelated processes: modernization which increases the available socio-economic resources, value change which gives rise to a new set of self-expression values, and democratization which secures the civil and political liberties in a society. In this sense, human development and the growth of an increasingly humanistic society is basically seen as a consequence of improved and broadened options for human choice. The broadening of human choices is assumed to take place when people have more options (resources) to choose from, when they can choose in line with their emancipative values, and when they are entitled to act according to their choices (Inglehart and Welzel 2005: 2f). Thus, human development is said to depend on the *sphere of means, the sphere of motives,* and *the sphere of rules and rights.* These three spheres are in turn related to the three main trajectories for societal change, which are processes of socio-economic development (the means), processes of value change (the motives), and processes of democratization (the rules). These three processes are said to go together, and may therefore be possible to integrate into one united theory of human development.

The linkage between on the one hand, socio-economic development and growing resources, and on the other, cultural change and rising self-expression values, is of special interest to this chapter. Obviously, the outcome of a given choice is a matter of both the available resources to choose from and the values and preferences which govern the choice. When resources are scarce, people are said to adapt their basic values to the pressing conditions under which they live. 'Aspiration adjustment leads people to aspire for the most pressing things first and to avoid wasting energy on unattainable goals' (Welzel et al. 2003: 347). Thus, in less affluent societies, people are assumed to adapt to the scarcity of resources, and be unlikely to adopt value systems which see individual self-expression and emancipative action as attractive goals. 'Striving for self-expression requires freedom and choice, and cannot unfold under pressing social constraints' (ibid.). In contrast, emancipative values are assumed to be more prevalent in more affluent societies. To mention a few examples: the more scarce the resources for female emancipation and gender equality, the weaker one should assume the demands for this kind of human development to be. Similarly, the more scarce the resources for individual self-expression, the less people are assumed to develop value orientations which put high esteem on individual efforts and choices.

Thus, three different dimensions of socio-economic development are assumed to reduce the constraints on human choice and lead to growing emphasis on human autonomy and individual self-expression (Inglehart and Welzel 2005: 24f). Economic growth is said to increase people's economic resources to the end that they become materially more secure. Rising levels of education, expanding mass communication, and increasingly knowledge-intensive work are said to widen people's intellectual resources to the end that they become cognitively more autonomous. Growing social complexity and diversification of human interactions are said to broaden people's social resources to the end that they become socially more independent. In this way, socio-economic development leads to improved human security, increased cognitive autonomy, and enhanced social independence. These three dimensions of socio-economic development are seen as general causes which lead to growing emphasis on human autonomy and self-expression values.

Yet, however plausible these linkages between socio-economic development and rising human autonomy and self-expression values may be, one may still wonder about the detailed processes which are involved in this kind of cultural change. A general assumption that a given social context more or less invariably leads to one and the same cultural effect may well hide the impact of other factors and therefore appear too simplistic (cf. Bronfenbrenner 1988: 28). Especially if one adopts the view that people's value orientations are acquired by the comprehensive primary and secondary socialization processes which they have experienced, it is of considerable interest to search for a more inclusive theoretical model for the cultural change from survival to self-expression values. To this end, some version of political socialization theory may serve.

A theory of citizenship education

As an introduction, a distinction can be made between political socialization and citizenship education. The former can be seen as 'unconscious social reproduction' and the latter as 'conscious social reproduction' (Gutman 1987: 15; Ichilov 2003: 645). With regard to citizenship education, one can furthermore distinguish between 'specific citizenship education', which refers to institutionalized forms for the acquisition of political knowledge in different educational frameworks, and 'diffuse citizenship education', which refers to educational achievements in general, even when the educational contents do not relate to specifically civic matters. This chapter is primarily focussed on the latter form of citizenship education.

In this context, it is of interest to note that during the decades following the 1960s, research on citizenship education became, if not totally out of fashion, at least a less attended field in political science. For instance, a recent comprehensive handbook of political science (Goodin and Klingemann 1994) only occasionally discusses political socialization as an important theme. However, it has also been suggested that a research agenda which would focus on socialization processes in relation to the broader field of citizenship might restore interest in the study of political socialization (Conover and Searing 1994). Such studies would focus on people's civic orientations, their loyalties, their civic virtues, their tolerance, their political self-development, and their political participation and civic behaviour (Conover and Searing 1994: 37f). Studies of how young people acquire their civic orientations should also include the impact of community characteristics, cultural values and traditions, together with the influences from social institutions like schools, families, churches, youth groups, community organizations, and the mass media. 'In effect, these social institutions represent the contexts through which other political and social factors exert an influence on the making of citizens' (Conover and Searing 1994: 43f). Along similar lines of thought, a recent comparative study of civic education for young people (Torney-Purta et al. 1999; Torney-Purta et al. 2001; Amadeo et al. 2002) has proposed a so-called 'octagon model' as the basis for research on political socialization. This model includes the effects of school characteristics (teachers, curricula, student participation, and student opportunities), family characteristics (parents, siblings, etc.), peer groups, youth social movements, mass media, etc. Thus, in order to fully grasp how young people come to adopt their value orientations and civic orientations, a number of different socialization agencies should be considered.

For instance, findings from previous research suggest that the effects of a number of school characteristics on the students' civic orientations can be divided into two groups of influences (for a review, see e.g. Ichilov 2003: 651–658). The first group includes factors such as the deliberate instruction and education programmes, while the second includes the various allocation mechanisms which come from the fact that schools also operate as a kind of 'sorting' devices. Among the influences in the first group are for instance the detailed curricula for specific courses, the specific contents of the textbooks which are used, and the detailed qualifications and competences of the teachers. However, the importance of such factors appears to be fairly moderate. By contrast, a more general factor, such as an open classroom climate, where the students can freely express themselves in a supportive school environment seems more likely to generate positive outcomes. A similar finding has suggested that school teachings in relation to controversial social issues in a closed classroom climate seem to yield negative outcomes. With regard to the second group of influences, one can note that the students tend to acquire different social networks, different stocks of cultural capital, and different political orientations depending on the kind of education they have chosen. However, since this chapter will not investigate such differences between different types and levels of education, a detailed discussion of the effects of these 'sorting' mechanisms is not needed.

In summary then, this chapter will combine two different theoretical perspectives on human values and civic education. The first assumes that socio-economic development and growing resources drive towards a stronger emphasis on human autonomy and individual self-expression values, also among young people. The second assumes that young people's values and civic orientations are affected by a number of different factors and socialization agencies in their school environments. For the analysis of these two approaches, two different sets of empirical data will be simultaneously analysed. In the following section, these two data sets will be introduced.

Two sets of data for the analysis of basic values and civic education

The European/World Values Surveys: In order to investigate the linkage between resources and motives (values), survey data from the European Values Study (EVS)/World Values Survey (WVS) will be used. This project was launched at the end of the 1970s, and aimed at investigating fundamental value orientations in western Europe. A large scale survey was conducted in all countries of the European Community (EC) in 1981, as well as in Spain, the Scandinavian countries, etc. The project aroused interest in many other countries, and about 25 countries participated in the first wave. To explore value changes, a second wave of surveys was fielded in 1990. This time, some 45 countries participated (see Ester et al. 1994; Inglehart 1997). In 1995, a third wave was conducted in about 55 countries around the world. In 1999–2000, a fourth wave was fielded in some 70 countries. This wave covered a large number of non-European countries, including for the first time some African and

Islamic ones (e.g. Tanzania, Zimbabwe, Uganda, Algeria, Egypt, Morocco, Iran, and Indonesia). In order to get comparability with the second set of data (see below), the EVS/WVS data from this wave will be used in this analysis. All in all, the EVS/WVS project covers about 80 per cent of the world population, and about 75 different countries have participated in at least one of the first four waves. A new wave of data collection started in 2005 and will last until early 2007. In each country, a representative sample of at least 1,000 respondents from the adult population, aged 18 and above, have been interviewed face-to-face for approximately one hour.[1]

The IEA study on citizenship and education in twenty-eight countries: In 1994, the International Association for the Evaluation of Educational Achievement (IEA) decided to perform a study on civic education for adolescents. The aim was to investigate similarities and differences in educational programmes and practices with regard to civic education and primarily to study the effects of these programmes and practices on student outcomes. One of the reasons for the study was the many democratic reforms which took place during the previous decades, something which called for major changes in civic education for young people. Another reason was that in many well-established democracies, young people seemed to have become detached from conventional political involvement and to demonstrate gaps in their understanding of democracy and political culture (Torney-Purta et al. 2001: 12f). A remedy for these occurrences was thought to be found in improved efforts for civic education for young people, especially with regard to students' orientations towards democracy, national identity, and social cohesion and diversity (Torney-Purta et al. 2001: 29). The project intended to establish the necessary knowledge for the implementation of such improved efforts. The project also included an additional survey of civic knowledge and engagement among 18-year-olds from 16 countries (Amadeo et al. 2002). In this chapter, data from this second part of the project will only occasionally be used.

The IEA project performed its field work during 1999, when representative samples of students in the modal grade for 14-year-olds in 28 countries completed a classroom survey. In each country, a two stage cluster sampling was used. At a first stage, schools were sampled according to school size. At a second stage, one intact classroom per school from the target grade was chosen. Where possible, the class was chosen from those studying a civic-related subject. In each country, between 112 and 185 schools were sampled, yielding sample sizes ranging from approximately 2,000 to 5,500 students per country. In addition to the questionnaire to the students, there were also surveys of teachers and headmasters from the selected schools (Torney-Purta et al. 2001: 33f). Some of the items in the quite comprehensive student questionnaire were chosen from previous comparative studies on political culture, for instance the European/World Values surveys (EVS/WVS), the International Social Survey Programme (ISSP), etc. This allows detailed analyses of similarities and differences in political attitudes among adults and adolescents.

Self-expression and traditional values

Much of the comparative research on the EVS/WVS data has focussed on two basic value orientations. The first is the 'traditional versus the secular rational value orientation', where 'the authority of God, Fatherland and Family are all closely linked' (Inglehart and Baker 2000: 25; cf. Inglehart 1997: chapter 3). The second is the 'survival versus the self-expression value orientation', which taps a syndrome of 'trust, tolerance, subjective well-being, political activism, and self-expression' (ibid). These two basic value dimensions have been shown to correlate with key macro- and micro-level characteristics (see e.g. Inglehart 1997; Inglehart and Baker 2000), for instance with economic development and the size of the industrial and the service sectors at the societal macro-level, and with age and education at the individual micro-level.

Based on findings from a previous analysis of traditional and self-expression value orientations (Halman and Pettersson 2002), this chapter will be based on two slightly modified measures for the two value orientations. For these two measures, a set of eight indicators from the EVS/WVS data will be used. Four indicators will be used to tap the self-expression values. These measure *tolerance for human diversity* (tapping tolerance for homosexuals, immigrants, and people of another ethnic origin as neighbours, respectively), *social trust* (tapping trust for others, and the importance of showing respect for other people), *liberty aspirations* (tapping preferences for giving people more to say in important decisions and protecting freedom of speech, respectively, in comparison to preferences for fighting inflation and keeping law and order, respectively), and *protest inclination* (tapping acceptance of five types of social and political protest activities). For the traditional values, four other indicators will be used. These tap *religious values* (the subjective importance of religion and confidence in religious institutions), *familism values* (the subjective importance of one's family and traditional and strict intra-family relations), *nationalism values* (national identity and national pride), and *authoritarian values* (preferences for authoritarian relations in general, in work life, and in social relations). A detailed description of these indicators is given in a previous version of this chapter (Pettersson 2003). A set of explorative and explanatory factor analyses which will not be reported in detail here, demonstrates that the eight indicators can be used to measure the two value orientations, both at the aggregated macro-level and at the individual micro-level.

The theoretical model on human development which was described above, assumed a close relation between resources and self-expression value orientation. This is also verified for the measures and data which are used in this analysis. The correlation between GDP per capita (ppp) and the aggregated factor scores for the self-expression values is as high as .78 (p < .001). Furthermore, the results from a multi-level regression analysis where the individual self-expression factors scores are regressed on age and gender, and the country level self-expression scores are regressed on GDP per capita, clearly demonstrate that the positive linkage between resources and motives remains highly significant when the effects of the age and gender composition of the respondents are controlled for (p < .001).

Adolescent civic orientations

The IEA study on civic education has reported a large set of standardized scales for the measurement of the adolescents' various civic orientations. These scales have been demonstrated to have sufficient validity for cross-cultural comparisons between the countries which participated in the study.[2] In addition to these scales, two new scales for exposure to mass media news programmes and social movement involvement, respectively, have been developed for this analysis (see Pettersson 2003).

In this chapter, the 14-year-olds' support for women's rights and good citizenship, respectively, will be analysed as examples of their orientations towards human development in a broad sense. At the individual level, each of these two orientations will be regressed on gender, socio-economic background (the IEA study measured this by the number of books in the respondents' homes), civic knowledge, classroom climate, media use, peer involvement, and involvement in social movements. The assumption is that the latter variables which tap different dimensions of the adolescents' socialization experiences (cf. the discussion in the introductory part of this chapter) will have an impact on the adolescents' orientations towards gender equality and good citizenship.

The adolescents' attitudes towards women's political and economical rights is measured by six items saying that e.g. 'women should run for public office and take part in the government just as men do', 'men are better qualified to be political leaders than women', and 'when jobs are scarce, men have more right to jobs than women'. For each of these items, a four-point response scale was used, ranging from 'strongly disagree' to 'strongly agree'. The 14-year-olds' attitudes towards social movement-based good citizenship were measured by five items, asking e.g. how important it is for an adult who is a good citizen 'to participate in a peaceful protest against a law believed to be unjust', to 'participate in activities to benefit people in the community', and 'to take part in activities to promote human rights'. The responses were given on a four-point response scale, ranging from 'not important' to 'very important'.

Content analyses of the items which are used to measure the adolescents' orientations towards gender equality and good citizenship, respectively, demonstrate that these two orientations have a more or less evident relation to human development as described above. This is especially the case if one accepts that human development involves increasing opportunities for human autonomy and choice. The orientation towards gender equality refers to increased opportunities for women, while the orientation towards good citizenship refers to citizens' responsibilities for improving the opportunities for human rights to be realized, the well-being of one's community, just laws, and the protection of the environment. Thus, at least in a general sense, these two civic orientations can be used as examples of how adolescents relate to human development. However, this assumption can also be questioned. For instance, in the case of gender equality, it has been concluded that the many sub-dimensions of human development in a broad sense do not go hand-in-hand with the position of women in a society. Rather, some dimensions of human development 'expand opportunities for women, while others, such as privatization and the contraction of social protection, create new inequalities' (Inglehart and Norris 2003: 21). Thus, the assumption that adolescents' orientations towards gender equality and good citizenship can be analysed as examples of their views towards human development in a more strict sense is partly tentative.

Self-expression values, resources, and adolescents' views on human development

Of the 28 countries which participated in the IEA project on civic education in 1999, 23 also participated in the European/World Values Surveys in 1999/2000. Three countries which did not participate in the 1999/2000 wave participated in the 1995 wave. The all-in-all 26 countries represent a remarkable blend of political cultures, religious cultures, socio-economic development, self-expression values, traditional values, etc.[3] The combined data from the EVS/WVS study and the IEA study therefore offer a potentially promising opportunity to investigate the relationship between, on the one hand, self-expression values and the available resources for human development at the aggregate level and, on the other hand, the adolescents' socialization experiences and orientations towards human development.

The 26 countries differ considerably on self-expression and traditional value orientations. However, for the latter dimension, it should be noted that none of the countries scoring highest (e.g. some African and Islamic countries) participated in the IEA study. A consequence may be that it is comparatively more difficult to demonstrate a significant impact from these values as compared to the self-expression values. However, despite this difference, the response patterns for the indicators which are used to tap the two basic value dimensions differ considerably among the 26 countries which are investigated in this chapter. The conditions for investigating both the roots and the effects of these two value orientations are therefore satisfactory.

Analytical strategy

In order to investigate the hypotheses from socialization and learning theory, the adolescents' orientations towards gender equality and good citizenship will be regressed on a set of variables which measure their school environments, and also their family backgrounds, peer relations, involvement in social movements, exposure to mass media, and general civic knowledge. For each of the 26 countries, a separate regression analysis will be performed. The results from these analyses will indicate the impact of the various socialization agencies.

In order to investigate the impact of the macro-level factors (traditional culture, self-expression culture, resources for human development), the intercepts from each of the 26 individual level country analyses will be regressed on a set of macro-level characteristics. These are the country means for self-expression and traditional values, respectively, and also the countries' resources for human development. In the case of gender equality, the resources are indicated by the Gender Empowerment Measure (GEM), while in the case of good citizenship, the Human Development Index (HDI) will serve as indicator. The contents of these two macro-level factors are explained in the Human

Development Reports, published by the United Nations Development Programme (UNDP). The expectation is that higher levels of resources and self-expression culture, respectively, will be positively related to the adolescents' orientations towards human development. Thus, self-expression culture can also be seen as a resource for such development (cf. Anand and Sen 2000).

In order to combine these two kinds of regression analyses into one simultaneous analysis, a set of hierarchical multi-level regression analyses will be performed. This kind of analysis permits the estimation of the simultaneous effects of the various macro- and micro-level independent variables (see e.g. Hox 1995; Raudenbush and Bryk 2002). For these analyses, the HLM statistical programme will be used.

Adolescent orientations towards gender equality

As already mentioned, the IEA study investigated the adolescents' attitudes towards women's political and economical rights by a six-item scale (see above). The scale had a reliability score of .79 (Chronbach alpha).

Figure 3.1 presents the national means for the adolescents' support for gender equality and the Gender Empowerment Measure (UNDP 2001). The results demonstrate a close relationship between the adolescents' orientations and the actual level of gender equality in the country where they live. As a matter of fact, the correlation coefficient for the 26 countries between these two measures is as high as .80 ($p < .001$). This is obviously in agreement with the theory of aspiration adjustment. Where the actual opportunities for gender equality are poorer, young people's normative support for such equality is also weaker.

However, the adolescents' orientations towards gender equality do not only reflect the actual level of gender equality in the countries where they live. It can be shown that their orientations are explained by their socialization experiences as well. In order to clarify this, Table 3.1 presents the results from the hierarchical multi-level regression analysis described above. This analysis investigates the simultaneous effects of three macro-level predictors (the national levels of self-expression and traditional values, respectively, and the Gender Empowerment Measure), and of a set of measures of the adolescents' socialization experiences (the parents' socio-economic background, the adolescents' exposure to mass media, their involvement in social movements, their peer relations, characteristics of their schools (an open or closed classroom

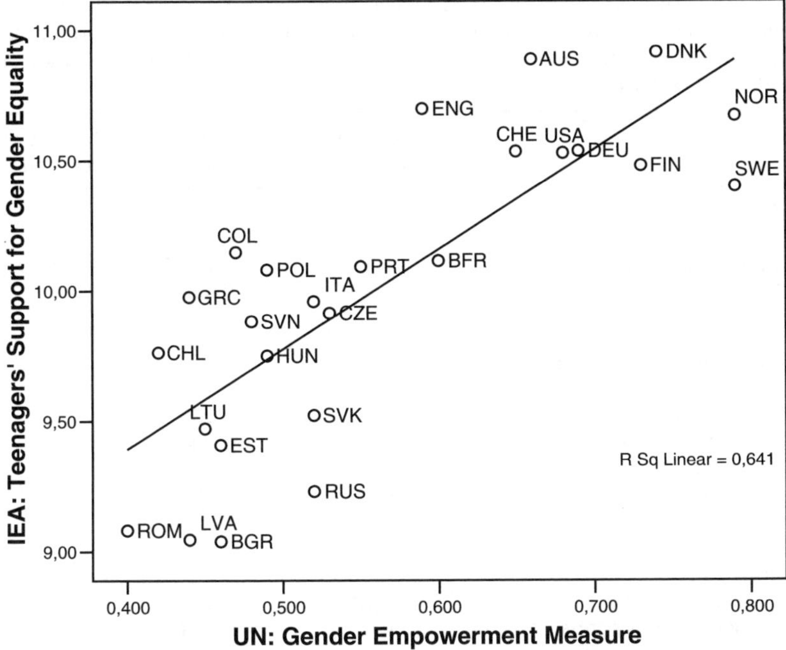

Figure 3.1   Gender empowerment measure and teenagers' support for gender equality in 26 countries.

climate), their achievements in general civic knowledge, and their gender).

The results from the hierarchical multi-level regression analysis demonstrate that the higher the levels of actual gender empowerment, the more positive the adolescents' views on gender equality. As already mentioned, this is in line with the assumption of aspiration adjustment. However, in addition to this, the results also demonstrate that the 14-year-olds' views on gender equality are affected by their socialization experiences. Not surprisingly, the female students appear to be more positive than the male ones. The results also show that this difference is larger, the higher the national level of self-expression culture. Thus, the self-expression culture seems to be more beneficial for young women than for young men. Further, the more open the classroom climate, the more positive the teenagers' attitudes towards gender equality. This effect of the school system is stronger, the more self-expressive the culture. The results also demonstrate that the more the

Table 3.1 Results from a hierarchical multi-level regression analysis of adolescents' orientations towards women's political and economic rights as dependent variable, and a set of macro- and micro-level characteristics as independent variables.

	Regression coefficients	Standard error	Degrees of freedom
Macro-level factors			
Self-expression values	0.06	0.198	22
Traditional values	−0.11	0.182	22
Gender empowerment measure	1.29[**]	0.484	22
Social-environment factors			
Parents' SES (books)	0.06[***]	0.009	23
Peer involvement	−0.02	0.008	23
Social movement involvement	0.01	0.006	23
Interaction self-expression values	0.01[**]	0.006	23
Exposure media news programmes	0.16[***]	0.026	23
Open class room climate	0.10[***]	0.005	23
Interaction self-expression values	0.02[***]	0.004	23
Student characteristics			
Female gender	1.18[***]	0.097	23
Interaction self-expression values	0.25[**]	0.074	23
Civic skills and knowledge	0.03[***]	0.002	23

Notes: * $p < .05$; ** $p < .01$; *** $p < .001$.
Entries are unstandardized multi-level regression coefficients, standard errors for these, and the degrees of freedom.

students are exposed to mass media news programmes, the more *positive* they are towards gender equality. In contrast, the more the students engage with their peers, the less positive their orientations towards women's rights. It finally deserves attention that the students with higher levels of cognitive civic skills are more positive towards gender equality. Thus, the more the students understand of democracy and social issues, the more favourable they are towards gender equality. Furthermore, this effect is stronger, the more self-expressive the culture.

In summary, the results have demonstrated that the adolescents' orientations towards gender equality are related to existing gender relations (the degree of gender empowerment) in the countries where they live. Where the opportunities for gender equality are poorer, the students are less favourable. This result is in accordance with the assumption of aspiration adjustment. In addition, the results have also demonstrated that the adolescents' orientations towards gender equality are significantly related to their socialization experiences, for instance the degree of an open classroom climate in the schools where they study, and the amount of their exposure to mass media news programmes. The impact of these socialization experiences also showed to depend on the degree of self-expression culture. Such a culture seemed to facilitate the effects of an open classroom climate and the involvement in social movements, etc.

In order to demonstrate the influences of two of the most influential socialization experiences (an open classroom climate and a frequent exposure to mass media news programmes, respectively), Table 3.2 displays the combined effects of these two factors. These effects are obtained from the following calculations: In the entire sample, the students are divided into three categories of exposure to mass media news (low, medium, and high, respectively) and three categories of classroom climate (strict, medium, and open, respectively). These categories are then combined as seen in Table 3.2. For each of the resulting nine categories, the percentages for those students who strongly agree to each of the three positively phrased items for gender equality and who also strongly disagree to each of the three negatively phrased items, are calculated. This is done in such a way that the impact of self-expression culture and gender empowerment at the macro-level, as well as the effect of gender, civic knowledge, social movements, peer relations, and

Table 3.2 Percentages of those who 'strongly agree' or 'strongly disagree' to each of six items for gender equality in nine categories with different classroom climates and levels of media exposure.

| | Classroom climate | | | |
	Strict	Medium	Open	All
Media exposure				
Low	40.3%	45.4%	57.4%	46.3%
Medium	42.1%	47.3%	59.7%	49.8%
High	47.3%	50.5%	60.9%	54.1%
All	43.2%	48.0%	59.8%	50.6%

Notes: Values after controls for the impact of nationality, gender, civic knowledge, social movements, peer relations, and home SES. The number of students in each category ranges between 4,500 and 10,600.

social background at the micro-level are controlled for. Thus, the percentages shown in Table 3.2 demonstrate the 'net effect' of classroom climate and exposure to media news programmes.

Table 3.2 demonstrates that half of the students (50.6 per cent) from the 26 countries hold very favourable attitudes towards gender equality (they agree strongly with each of the three positive statements and disagree strongly with each of the three negative statements). In the group with the least favourable socialization condition for gender equality (a strict classroom climate and a low exposure to media news), the corresponding percentage is 40.3 per cent. In the group with the most favourable socialization condition (an open classroom climate and a high exposure to media news) this percentage has increased substantially to 60.9 per cent. Thus, the difference between the least favourable and the most favourable socialization experience with regard to only these two socialization factors is quite substantial. A change in classroom climate from strict to open together with more frequent exposure to mass media news programmes from low to high, increases the number of students who strongly endorse gender equality by as much as 50 per cent! The effect of each of these two socialization factors is highly significant ($p < .001$ for each of them). This clearly demonstrates that young people's orientations towards gender equality are not only an effect of aspiration adjustment. Rather, their views on gender equality are also significantly related to such socialization agencies as mass media news programmes and the social climate they are met with in their school environments.

Adolescent orientations towards good citizenship

As already mentioned, the IEA scale which measures orientations towards good citizenship is based on four items (see above). The scale had a reliability score of .63 (Chronbach alpha). In a general way, the four items can be said to tap concerns for improved opportunities for human development. Figure 3.2 shows the national averages for the adolescents' orientations towards good citizenship and the national scores for human development as measured by the Human Development Index.

As is seen in Figure 3.2, there is a *negative* relation between the teenagers' support for good citizenship and the Human Development Index (correlation coefficient: $-.42$; $p < .05$). This is clearly *not* expected from the hypothesis of aspiration adjustment. Rather, in countries with poorer opportunities for human development (a lower Human

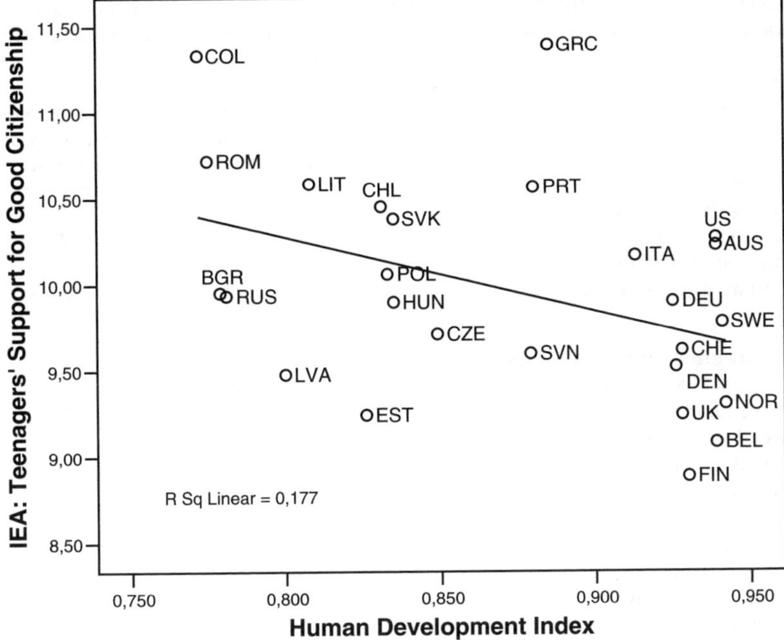

Figure 3.2   The human development index and teenagers' support for good citizenship in 26 countries.

Development Index), the adolescents tend to attach higher importance to the virtue of good citizenship. One explanation for this might be that countries with poorer resources for human development deliberately make greater efforts, for instance in the educational system, to install value orientations which may promote human development. Another explanation can simply be that the theory of aspiration adjustment does not apply in this case (cf. the discussion below).

In order to demonstrate the impact of the same kind of socialization agencies which were investigated in the case of gender equality, Table 3.3 demonstrates the results from a hierarchical multi-level regression analysis. The results show that the negative relationship between favourable attitudes towards good citizenship and the Human Development Index remains, even after controls for the various country-specific socialization experiences, while the two value orientations at the aggregated level appear to be insignificant. Among the individual level factors, the socio-economic status of the parents is negatively related to the

Table 3.3 Results from a hierarchical multi-level regression analysis of adolescents' orientations towards good citizenship for human development as dependent variable, and a set of macro- and micro-level as independent variables.

	Regression coefficients	Standard error	Degrees of freedom
Macro-level factors			
Self-expression values	−0.13	0.151	22
Traditional values	−0.11	0.145	22
Human development index	−5.52***	1.575	22
Social-environment factors			
Parents' SES (books)	−0.04*	0.012	23
Peer involvement	−0.03*	0.007	23
Social movement involvement	0.03**	0.008	23
Interact effect self-express values	0.02*	0.008	23
Exposure media news programmes	0.23***	0.042	23
Open class room climate	0.14***	0.009	23
Interact effect traditional values	0.03**	0.012	23
Student characteristics			
Gender (female)	0.06	0.037	23
Interact effect self-expression values	0.10***	0.025	23
Civic skills and knowledge	0.01*	0.003	23

Notes: $p < .05$; ** $p < .01$; *** $p < .001$.
Entries are unstandardized multi-level regression coefficients.

measure of good citizenship. Thus, both at the aggregate level and at the individual level, the better the resources, the *less* the adolescents favour adults' responsibility for the betterment of one's society. Furthermore, and similar to the case of gender equality, the more the students engage in peer relations, the lesser they favour good citizenship. In accordance with the findings for gender equality, an open classroom climate and frequent exposure to mass media news programmes are associated with increased preferences for good citizenship. Like the case of gender equality, the female students appear more in favour of good citizenship than the male ones. Finally, and not very surprising, there is also a link to the students' cognitive civic skills. Those with higher levels of civic

Table 3.4   Percentages of those who 'strongly agree' to each of four items for good citizenship in nine categories with different classroom climates and levels of exposure to mass media news programmes.

| | Classroom climate | | | |
	Strict	Medium	Open	All
Media exposure				
Low	31.8%	35.0%	41.4%	35.2%
Medium	36.2%	32.1%	34.6%	42.0%
High	35.0%	37.1%	42.9%	39.0%
All	32.9%	35.7%	42.3%	37.1%

Notes: Values after controls for the impact of nationality, gender, civic knowledge, social movements, peer relations, and home SES. The number of students in each category ranges between 4,500 and 10,600.

knowledge, including a better understanding of democracy, are more in favour of good citizenship.

In order to demonstrate the net effect of an open classroom climate and frequent exposure to mass media news programmes, the results from the same kind of analysis which was reported for gender equality are displayed in Table 3.4. In the category with the least favourable socialization experiences (low exposure to mass media news programmes and a strict classroom climate, respectively), almost one third (31.8 per cent) say that each of the four indicators of good citizenship is very important. In the group with the most favourable socialization experiences (frequent exposure to mass media news, an open classroom climate), this portion has increased significantly to two fifths (42.9 per cent). The increase is somewhat lower as compared to the case of gender equality. Nevertheless, each of the two socialization agencies demonstrates a significant impact ($p <$ .001). Finally, the results also show that in the entire sample of adolescents from the 26 countries, fewer than two out of five (37.1 per cent) agree strongly with each of the four indicators for good citizenship. In general terms, this level of support does not appear overwhelmingly strong.

Conclusion

This analysis is built on two different theoretical frameworks. One is a general theory of human development. This framework assumes that growing resources yield rising self-expression values, and that these in turn favour democratization and the extension of social and political rights. The framework also assumes that when resources are scarce, people will hold back their support for self-expression values. This tendency is explained as an example of aspiration adjustment. In this chapter, a modified measure of the self-expression values has been developed. Quite as expected, data from 71 countries showed that this measure is positively related to the Human Development Index: The better the resources, the stronger the self-expression values. It also deserves attention that a similar relationship appears for other indices of modernization, for instance GDP per capita, gender equality (the Gender Empowerment Measure), various measures of efficient government, etc. These findings are all in line with the assumption of aspiration adjustment. They also demonstrate the validity of the modified measure for self-expression values.

However, the theoretical model for human development was said to be inattentive to the mechanisms which may explain in more detail the linkage between increasing resources and the rising self-expression values. In order to identify such mechanisms, a second theoretical perspective on political socialization and learning was introduced. According to this perspective, young people's value and civic orientations are also affected by various socialization agencies which are related to school, family, peers, mass media, social movements, etc. To fully understand the growth of self-expression values and civic orientations among young people, the influences from these socialization agencies must also be taken into account.

In order to investigate the two theoretical frameworks, two different sets of data from 26 countries have been analysed. The countries were chosen since they have participated in both the 1999/2000 wave of the European/World Values Survey and in the IEA Study on Civic Education which completed its fieldwork in 1999. The combined data from these two projects allowed detailed comparative analyses of how 14-year-olds' normative orientations towards gender equality and good citizenship were related to different mixtures of resources and self-expression value profiles at the aggregated macro-level, as well as to different socialization agencies at the individual level. The analytical strategy which was developed in order to analyse these data has been fruitful and deserves further use. To combine different sets of data in this way opens new avenues for comparative research.

The teenagers showed to be less positive towards women's economic and political rights, the lower the general level of gender equality (the Gender Empowerment Measure) in the country where they live. Obviously, this finding is quite in accordance with the assumption of aspiration adjustment. When the opportunities for gender equality are poorer, the teenagers appear to be less interested in this dimension of human development. However, the results also showed that the adolescents' orientations towards gender equality were significantly affected by their socialization and learning experiences, regardless of the opportunities for gender equality in the country where they live. For instance, an open classroom climate and frequent exposure to mass media news programmes were shown to exert a substantial impact on the 14-year-olds' views, irrespective of the actual resources for gender equality (the Gender Empowerment Measure). Thus, the adolescents' orientations towards gender equality were not only an expression of aspiration adjustment to the actual resources for gender equality. They were also affected by deliberate educational efforts to influence them.

It was even more interesting to note that the teenagers in the countries with the lowest levels of human development (the lowest values on the Human Development Index) were *more positive* towards good citizenship than their counterparts from countries with higher level of human development. Thus, the more scarce the opportunities for human development, the *more* the teenagers supported (adult) efforts to improve the human rights situation, to change unjust laws, to improve community life, to better the environment, etc. In this sense, the adolescents had obviously *not* adjusted their normative aspirations for human development to the actual conditions under which they lived. This finding is clearly not in accordance with the hypothesis of aspiration adjustment. In addition, the teenagers' orientations towards good citizenship were also shown to be affected by their socialization and learning experiences. Similarly to the case of gender quality, an open classroom climate and a frequent exposure to mass media news programmes were shown to be related to a stronger endorsement of good citizenship, irrespective of the actual level of human development.

There can be many reasons for why the adolescents' orientations towards gender equality and good citizenship, respectively, were differently affected by the processes of aspiration adjustment. One explanation can be that their orientations towards gender equality are primarily affected by their immediate family patterns for the division of labour between men and women (cf. the distinction between political socialization and citizenship education). Hence, these orientations would primarily be influenced by the existing gender relations. In the case of good citizenship, however, one may assume that the formative years for this kind of civic orientation occur during later phases of the life cycle, for instance during late adolescence and early adulthood when one becomes more aware of one's obligations as a citizen. However, a set of preliminary analyses of both the EVS/WVS and the IEA data do not support this assumption. In these analyses, different age categories in the EVS/WVS data demonstrated similar patterns as the ones which have been reported for young people. Likewise, comparisons of the IEA data for the 14- and the 18-year-olds demonstrated that different civic attitudes appear to be stable across adolescence (Amadeo et al. 2002: 160). Furthermore, some additional analyses of the IEA data on the adolescents' orientations towards six different sub-dimensions of human development (social movement related good citizenship, conventional good citizenship, gender equality, the rights of ethnic minorities, expected future involvement in political and social issues, respectively) showed that orientations towards gender equality was the *only* orientation which yielded the expected pattern of aspiration adjustment.

Therefore, the conclusion from this study is that aspiration adjustment is not such a universal occurrence as assumed by the theoretical model for human development, at least not among young people. Rather, whether aspiration adjustment occurs or not may differ between different orientations towards different sub-dimensions of human development. Whether such adjustment occurs or not may also depend on which group of people one investigates. For instance, women and men, people with different levels and kinds of education, from different social classes, with different political and religious convictions, may show different patterns of aspiration adjustment. Systematic investigations of this theoretically important issue may indeed be a promising avenue for future research.

Another interesting conclusion from this investigation concerns the impact of the self-expression and traditional culture at the aggregated level. The results suggest that this impact should mainly be thought of as interaction effects, where the two basic value orientations at the aggregate level serve as moderators of the effects from the various socialization processes at lower levels. For instance, the self-expression and traditional culture seem to moderate the effects of an open classroom climate and involvement in social movements. Even if such interaction effects have not been systematically investigated by previous research on the EVS/WVS data, they have been mentioned as especially interesting for research on socialization processes in relation to human development (Bronfenbrenner 1988: 26). Furthermore, it should be noted that the two kinds of culture at the aggregated level may also display equally interesting *indirect* effects on the adolescents' orientations towards human development. In this case, they would have an impact by means of their influences on e.g. education policies, mass media coverage of the conditions for human development, social movements' programmes, etc. Such indirect patterns have not been investigated in this analysis. Investigations of this would be another interesting topic for further analyses.

Among the various socialization and learning processes, especially the classroom climate and the level of exposure to mass media news programmes have showed a positive relationship to the teenagers' orientations towards gender equality and good citizenship, respectively. As already mentioned, the positive effects of an open classroom climate are expected from previous research (Ichilov 2003: 653). However, it should also be noted that a positive statistical relationship is not sufficient evidence of a causal relationship, where an open classroom climate leads to a positive view on gender equality and good citizenship. In spite of some counter-evidence, another plausible interpretation of the positive relationship might be that it is mainly a certain category of students, for instance those with initially higher levels of efficacy, knowledge and interest in the various subject matters who are more likely to perceive the classroom climate as open (ibid.). In a similar way, the positive relationship between exposure to mass media news programmes and the teenagers' civic orientations can be differently interpreted. One may assume that the positive relationship reflects selective exposure to the mass media, e.g. by those who already hold certain views on human development, and that hence frequent exposure to mass media only has negligible effects on people's political orientations. However, this traditional view on the minimal power of the mass media has recently been questioned. A review of the research on how mass media influence how people make sense of politics (the so-called framing effect), how they decide what is important (the agenda setting effect), and how they evaluate the available alternatives (the priming effect), concluded that mass media's power appears to be 'quite impressive' (Kinder 2003: 377), although within limits. And with regard to participation in social movements, it has been proposed that people participate for a number of reasons, but that participation to a substantial extent depends on the availability of movements which fit the already existing demands of the potential participants (Klandermans 2003). But at the same time, it can also be concluded that participation in a social movement certainly 'leaves its traces in an individual's biography' (Klanderman 2003: 696). In these regards, it should also be noted that previous analyses of the IEA data from both the14- and the 18-year-olds have shown that at least three realms within schools have leverage in contributing to the civic preparation of youth. These realms are the contents of the curriculum, the classroom climate, and the school culture. The impact of these school characteristics 'maintained themselves at both age levels and in countries with very different histories' (Amadeo et al. 2002: 160).

Therefore, that young people's orientations towards two different dimensions of human development seem to depend on more or less deliberate efforts to influence them, should be regarded as a positive finding. It shows that young people's orientations towards citizenship and human development are open to conscious policies for positive change. Even if more theorizing and research is needed in order to fully 'decipher the "black box" that conceals the connection between schooling and democratic citizenship' (Ichilov 2003: 659), extended analyses of the kinds of data which have been investigated in this chapter will hopefully give better guidelines for how education on human development for young people can be improved. If one wants to develop positive orientations towards democracy, gender equality and human development, one need not passively wait until the material resources for this have improved and the tendency towards aspiration adjustment has ceased to be a contra-productive factor. Rather, the investigation which is reported in this chapter has indicated that it might be more rational to seek to expand these orientations by deliberate educational efforts.

Notes

1. For further information on issues like sampling, interview techniques, questionnaires, coverage of value domains, previous findings, and publications, etc. see e.g. Halman (2001); Inglehart and Baker (2000); see also the websites: http://evs.kub.nl and www.worldvaluessurvey.org.
2. For a closer description of these scales, see Torney-Purta et al. (2001).
3. The countries are the United States, Chile, and Colombia from the Americas, Denmark, Finland, Sweden, and Norway (1995) from northern Europe, Belgium (only the French-speaking part), the United Kingdom, Germany, Switzerland (1995), Italy, and Portugal from western Europe, Estonia, Lithuania, Latvia, and Poland from the Baltics, the Czech Republic, Slovakia, Slovenia, and Hungary from central Europe, Russia, Bulgaria, Romania, Greece from eastern Europe, and finally Australia (1995).

References

Amadeo, J., Torney-Purta, J., Lehman, R., Husfeldt, V. and Nikolova, R. (2002) *Civic knowledge and engagement. An IEA study of upper secondary students in sixteen countries*, Amsterdam: The International Association for the evaluation of educational achievement.

Anand, S. and Sen, A. (2000) 'Human Development and Economic Sustainability', *World Development* 28: 12.

Bolger, N., Caspi, A., Downey, G. and Moorehouse, M. (eds) (1988) *Persons in context. Developmental processes*, Cambridge: Cambridge University Press.

Bronfenbrenner, U. (1988) 'Interacting systems in human development. Research paradigms: present and future', in Bolger, N., Caspi, A., Downey, G. and Moorehouse, M. (eds) (1988) *Persons in context. Developmental processes*, Cambridge: Cambridge University Press.

Budge, E. and McKey, D. (eds) (1994) *Developing democracy*, London: Sage.

Conover, P. and Searing, D. (1994) 'Democracy, Citizenship and the study of political socialization', in Budge, E. and McKey, D. (eds) (1994) *Developing democracy*, London: Sage.

Ester, J., Halman, L. and de Moor R. (eds) (1994) *The Individualizing Society: Value Changes in Europe and North America*, Tilburg, Netherlands: Tilburg University Press.

Goodin, R. and Klingemann, H-D. (eds) (1994) *A new handbook in political science*, Oxford: Oxford University Press.

Gutmann, A. (1987) *Democratic education*, Princeton: Princeton University Press.

Halman, L. (2001) *The European Values Study: A Third Wave. Source book of the 1999/2000 European Values Study Surveys*, Tilburg: EVS, WORC, Tilburg University.

Halman, L. and Pettersson, T. (2002) 'A modified model for the cross-cultural measurement of two basic value orientations. Results from EVS/WVS data for 64 countries', paper presented at ISA Conference, Brisbane, Australia, July 2002.

Hox, J. (1995) *Applied Multilevel Analysis*, Amsterdam: TT-Publikaties.

Ichilov, O. (2003) 'Education and citizenship in a changing world', in Sears, D., Huddy, L. and Jervis, R. (eds) (2003) *Oxford Handbook of political psychology*, Oxford: Oxford University Press.

Inglehart, R. (1997) *Modernization and Postmodernization*. Princeton: Princeton University Press.

Inglehart, R. and Baker, W. (2000) 'Modernization, cultural change and the persistence of traditional values', *American Sociological Review*, 65: 19–51.

Inglehart, R. and Norris, P. (2003) *The rising tide. Gender equality and cultural change around the world*, Cambridge: Cambridge University Press.

Inglehart, R. and Welzel, C. (2005). *Modernization, cultural change and democratization*. Cambridge: Cambridge University Press.

Kinder, D. (2003) 'Communication and politics in the age of information', in Sears, D., Huddy, L. and Jervis, R. (eds) (2003) *Oxford Handbook of political psychology*, Oxford: Oxford University Press.

Klandermans, B. (2003) 'Collective political action', in Sears, D., Huddy, L. and Jervis, R. (eds) (2003) *Oxford Handbook of political psychology*, Oxford: Oxford University Press.

Milner, H. (2002) *Civic literacy. How informed citizens make democracy work*, London: Tufts University.

Pettersson, T. (2003) Basic values and Civic Education, Publications, http://www.worldvaluessurvey.org.

Raudenbush, S. and Bryk, A. (2002) *Linear Models. Applications and Data Analysis Methods*, London: Sage.

Sears, D., Huddy, L. and Jervis, R. (eds) (2003) *Oxford Handbook of political psychology*, Oxford: Oxford University Press.

Sears, D. and Levy, S. (2003) 'Childhood and adult political development', in Sears, D., Huddy, L. and Jervis, R. (eds) (2003) *Oxford Handbook of political psychology*, Oxford: Oxford University Press.

Torney-Purta, J., Schwille, J. and Amadeo, J. (1999) *Civic education across countries: twenty-four case studies from the IEA civic education project*, Amsterdam: The international Association for the evaluation of educational achievement.

Torney-Purta, J., Lehman, R., Oswald, O. and Schula, W. (2001) *Citizenship and education in twenty-eight countries. Civic knowledge and engagement at age fourteen*, Amsterdam: The International association for the evaluation of educational achievement.

UNDP (2001) *Human Development Report 2001. Making new technologies work for human development*, New York: UNDP.

Welzel, C. (2002) 'Effective democracy, mass culture, and the quality of elites: the human development perspective', *International journal of comparative sociology*, 43: 3–5.

Welzel, C., Inglehart, R. and Klingemann, H-D. (2003) 'The theory of human development', *European Journal of Political Research*, 42: 341–379.

4
Reflections on Reconciliation. The Case of South Africa

Ursula J. van Beek

Introduction

South Africa has emerged from a past characterized by centuries-long conflict, mass human suffering and gross social injustice. Security and sustainable social development, concepts of key interest in this book, had no place in the former reality of violence and strife. The question is whether the 'new' South Africa, having succeeded in a peaceful transition from apartheid to democracy, can overcome its troubled past and successfully carry out a project to build a new and just society.

This chapter will focus on reconciliation, assuming that it is an indispensable component of post-conflict reconstruction. It will try to contextualize the process by looking at a number of factors that jointly might have facilitated it. It will consider elements of African culture, the concepts of 'forgiveness', 'truth', and 'justice', and the role that the South African Truth and Reconciliation Commission has played in the process of reconciling former adversaries. The chapter will conclude with some empirical data on reconciliation and with the question of the applicability of the South African model to conflict resolution elsewhere in the world.

On the face of it, reconciliation is not too difficult a word to define. Among other things, it means to no longer be opposed to each other, to establish friendly relations after estrangement, or to achieve union. But a more accurate definition would have it that reconciliation means the restoration of friendship, and it is this understanding of the concept that is particularly ill-suited for South Africa, where first colonialism and later apartheid precluded any friendship between those who are now supposed to *re*-establish it. There is therefore little wonder that discussions proliferate on what reconciliation is – or should be – and whether or not it is actually taking place in South Africa.

The Truth and Reconciliation Commission (TRC)[1]

Dealing with an authoritarian past is a process that is both painful and fraught with difficulties. It consists of two main phases, the phase of knowledge, that is, of uncovering truth, and the phase of acknowledgement, that is, what happens with the knowledge once it has become officially sanctioned and entered the public domain (Kritz 1995).

The question of what happens once the truth is known, relates directly to accountability for the past, or more precisely, to whether accountability should be pursued to its logical conclusion of punishment, or whether the past should be forgiven for the sake of reconstruction, and possibly reconciliation.

The topic of accountability is particularly hotly contested in countries such as South Africa where large-scale excesses by the authoritarian regimes – augmented by politically motivated mass violence between ordinary citizens – had left behind thousands of victims, with many killings and disappearances unaccounted for at the time of transition. It is in such cases that the question posed by Huntington (1991) of 'what to do with the torturer' comes into sharpest focus. On the one hand, power-sharing negotiations by the opposition with the very perpetrators of crimes preclude harshly punitive measures if the democracy that is being negotiated for is to have any chance of survival. On the other hand, while political expediency has to take precedence, this should not happen at the expense of ascertaining the truth. Truth about the past must be uncovered and acknowledged so that healing can begin.

The body set up under the Promotion of National Unity and Reconciliation Act No. 34 of 1995 to investigate crimes committed during the apartheid era, was the Truth and Reconciliation Commission (TRC). The TRC was to a large extent fashioned on its predecessor, the Chilean Truth Commission, which at that time was considered to be a paradigmatic model.[2] The Nobel Peace Prize laureate, Archbishop Desmond Tutu, who was assisted by 16 commissioners appointed by President Nelson Mandela following a public selection process, chaired the TRC. After hearing nearly 22,000 submissions, and reviewing more than 7,500 applications for amnesty, the five-volume report was handed over to President Nelson Mandela on 29 October 1998. The report was met with mixed reactions. The ruling African National Congress (ANC) and the radically populist Pan-African Congress (PAC) rejected findings that had held those two parties accountable for gross human rights abuses. They argued that the findings ignored the distinction between the 'just cause' of the liberation struggle and the 'criminal acts' of the oppressive regime, and that it 'demonized' the liberation struggle. It was only after private discussions with Archbishop Desmond Tutu that President Nelson Mandela agreed to accept the report. However, several other parties also implicated in the report, among them the apartheid ruling party (NP, later the NNP) and the Zulu Inkatha Freedom Party (IFP), boycotted the handing-over ceremony.

Besides conducting hearings on the activities of the state security apparatus and mainstream anti-apartheid forces, the TRC also investigated and reported on the political violence during the 1980s and the first half of the 1990s between ANC and IFP supporters in the province of KwaZulu-Natal. The report concluded that, while claiming to be part of the liberation movement, the IFP had received direct financial and logistical assistance from the apartheid state to fight the ANC. Evidence in front of the TRC brought to light collaboration between the defence force and the IFP to form 'hit squads', giving substance to claims of the existence of a mysterious 'third force' in the ANC/IFP conflict. At the same time, the TRC concluded that the ANC's armed self-defence units, which committed atrocities and took the law into their own hands, had largely contributed to the spiral of violence in the province.[3]

One of the most remarkable features in the work of the South African Truth Commission was the amnesty process. No blanket amnesty was granted for fear that this would lead to shutting the door on the past and to covering up many atrocities. Instead, individual applications were submitted and then assessed with a view to establishing accountability and admission. The carrot and stick approach – the carrot of amnesty and the stick of fear of a judicial action for non-disclosure – encouraged perpetrators to apply and provide relevant information. Amnesty was granted to individuals who had made full disclosure of their activities, providing such activities were politically motivated, performed in the defence of – or the struggle against – apartheid, and carried out because of a sense of duty and respect for authority.

The Commission made recommendations to the state for the prosecution of specific individuals from both sides of the struggle, who had either not applied for or were refused amnesty. In the few criminal court cases that have followed to date, some of the accused have been found innocent. This has fuelled criticism of the Commission and given rise to opinions, voiced mainly by people associated with the apartheid regime, that the criminal justice system proved that the version of truth and history presented by the TRC was flawed.[4] The Commission was also criticized for its narrow focus on a small group of perpetrators of gross human rights violations, to the exclusion of the much bigger group of beneficiaries of apartheid, and many, both black and white, South Africans were angered by the amnesty process as they felt that too many perpetrators from both sides of the apartheid divide had walked free.

Despite its various real or perceived shortcomings, the TRC achieved its major objective as it democratized the process of dealing with the past by making it possible for thousands to tell their stories in nation-wide broadcasts. By so doing, it infused the South African psyche with facts and information that make it impossible for anyone to deny knowledge of apartheid atrocities. As opposed to the truth commission in Chile, which did not dare to hear testimony in public for fear of retaliation by the military, the TRC insisted on public testimony (in most cases) and on public interrogation of the accused by both the victims and the commissioners. In addition, it allowed for the press and television to record and broadcast the proceedings live, ensuring that the public witnessed the testimonies as they unfolded.

Archbishop Desmond Tutu handed the final TRC – report to President Thabo Mbeki on 21 March 2003. In his response to the report on 15 April 2003 in Parliament, President Thabo Mbeki stressed the importance of the work carried out by the Commission towards national reconciliation and building a united society, and he accepted the main recommendations of the report on behalf of his government. Underlining the view that no monetary value could ever be attached to a human life, the President announced a one-off grant in the current financial year of R30,000 each to some 22,000 individuals or surviving families who went through the TRC process and were designated by the TRC. In addition, the requested President's Fund was established with a call to all South Africans for voluntary contributions. The President also announced a national day of prayer and traditional sacrifice to pay tribute to those who suffered or sacrificed their lives during the period of oppression (*Sunday Times*, 27 April 2003).

The many faces of truth

Simply put, truth is the opposite of a lie. But the two seemingly contradictory concepts are somewhat linked. For Antjie Krog,[5] the moment a lie raises its head is the moment she smells blood '[B]ecause it is there, where the truth is closest' (Krog 1998). And, according to Michael

Ignatieff, there is not one truth but many truths, because 'what you believe to be true depends, in some measure, on who you believe yourself to be. And who you believe yourself to be is mostly defined in terms of who you are not' (Ignatieff 1988). Elsewhere and in reference to the aims of the TRC, expressed by Archbishop Desmond Tutu as the promotion of national unity and reconciliation for the sake of healing a traumatized, polarized and wounded people, Ignatieff has suggested that, as laudable as these aims were, they were not assumptions of epistemology, but rather 'articles of faith' about human nature, implying, as they did, that if we know the truth it will set us free (Ignatieff 1996). It would be difficult to disagree with Ignatieff and claim that truth is indivisible, fully knowable, certain and incontestable. To insist that there is such a thing as *the* truth would be to follow in the footsteps of the dogma of authoritarianism or religious orthodoxy, and to fail to recognize that the concept of truth is complex and nuanced. But the healing quality of truth belongs to a different category.

The philosopher, human rights activist, and chairman of the Chilean Commission for Truth, José Zalaquett, has made this clear, noting that what really mattered to most of the relatives of the victims was that truth was revealed as they took solace in the fact that the memory of their loved ones would not be denigrated or consigned to oblivion (Zalaquett 1992).

The same sentiment has been amply evident in South Africa. The widow of one of Eugene de Kock's[6] victims, for example, said that no one had any idea how much of a relief it was for her, and for the widows of his other victims, to hear from de Kock himself the truth about their husbands. She confided: 'Now I can mourn [my husband] properly because this has helped me retrace his steps in life in order to let him go in death'.[7]

The TRC fulfilled its mandate in that it brought to light the tyrannical excesses of the apartheid regime and the consequences of politically incited violence. This may only be a fraction of the truth and there may be scepticism as to the extent to which the Commission has cleared the way for reconciliation, but there can be no doubt that reconciliation and reconstruction can take place only when what has happened has been exposed and acknowledged.

The uncovering of truth is an onslaught on all forms of individual and collective denial and on conscious cover-ups, and as such it often invokes resistance and resentment. Seeking the truth is also a balancing act: how much truth can be uncovered without undermining the prospect of remembering and yet allowing people to come to terms with the past? Reports from Argentina, for example, indicated that there is a limit to how much the public can take. The horror stories and pictures shown in the media, instead of leading to a new consciousness of human rights, resulted in a general desire to forget. Similar cases have been recorded in Chile (Agger and Jensen 1996).

In South Africa, too, some believe that, rather than leading to reconciliation, the uncovering of the truth may have had the opposite effect as gross human right abuses have come to light, reawakening bad memories and dormant animosities (cf. Gibson 2004). The revelations of de Kock have often been evoked in this context. And yet, to suppress the truth of wrongdoing might be to forfeit the chance for a moral society to emerge, because such suppression would not only obliterate the memory of specific acts, but also allow for a general sense of past transgressions and evil to recede from collective memory (cf. Bhargava 2000). The TRC made sure that this is not the case in South Africa.

Finally, truth is important not only retrospectively to redeem the suffering, but also prospectively to send a warning that crimes committed in secret will not stay secret. However, truth is not an end in itself; it is but a part in the process of healing. To play that part it needs to be 'considered, thought about, debated and digested and metabolized by the individuals and by society'; only then can it become an 'essential component of the needed social antiseptic which could cleanse the social fabric of the systematized habit of disregard for human rights' (cf. Villa-Vicenio and Verwoerd 2000).

Perspectives on reconciliation

Justice: A nexus?

Justice might be the link between truth and reconciliation, and specifically the type of justice chosen for dealing with the unearthed truth. The choice is between past-oriented *retributive justice,* whose sole aim is to punish perpetrators, and forward-looking *restorative justice* that attempts to reconcile the perpetrators and their victims.

Historically, one of the best-known and also most widely contested examples of retributive justice is that meted out to Germany by the Treaty of Versailles after the First World War. There, the impulse to punish was dissociated from any concept of reconciliation, with the result that the seed for the Second World War may have been planted, as Germany came to nurture grievances far stronger than those that had distorted her foreign relations and domestic politics before 1914 (e.g. Lu 2002).

In another context the question was posed as to whether South African history might not have taken a different course, had the British established a truth commission after the Anglo-Boer war. However, they did not, and the death of some 26,000 Boer women and children in British concentration camps and elsewhere during the war was never officially acknowledged or condemned; at least not by the British. But the memory lived on for the Afrikaners[8] and may have led them to the determination that they should never be victimized again and to the fervent nationalism that, under the later influence of German nationalism, may have paved the way for the policy of apartheid (Krog 1998). To point this out is not to absolve the Nazi or apartheid regimes for their later deplorable actions, nor to suggest that retributive justice consistently produces negative outcomes. It is merely to stress that, as opposed to punitive justice or deliberate amnesia, restorative justice holds the potential for reconciliation and future moral regeneration.

The TRC applied this model of justice. By calling the perpetrators to account for their crimes in the same process that aimed to heal the wounds of their victims and restore their dignity, it laid the foundations for possible interaction between formerly divided peoples. The aim was moral rebirth based on mutual recognition of humanity. And in South Africa, where the past is so profoundly divisive and its legacy so utterly overwhelming, the restorative justice of truth commissions might be the only means by which to move forward.

There is, of course, no guarantee that restorative justice will lead to reconciliation or, even if it does, that it will instantly produce the right kind of reconciliation. Reconciliation ranges from 'thinner' to 'thicker' versions. At the most basic level, there is 'simple coexistence', which makes former enemies adhere to the rules of law instead of killing each other (Villa-Vicencio 1999). While this mode of reconciled co-existence is incomparably more desirable than a violent engagement with each other, it is a far cry from reconciliation based on mutual forgiveness, social solidarity, and a shared vision for the future. But this can only come gradually. What the TRC tried to do, and seemed to achieve, was to open the door for a dialogue between former adversaries.

A matter of spirit

> This thing called reconciliation [...] If I am understanding it correctly [...] if it means this perpetrator, this man who has killed Christopher Piet, if it means he becomes human again, this man, so that I, so that all of us, get our humanity back [...] then I agree, then I support it.

A mother spoke these words about the man who had killed her son.[9]

To get one's humanity back goes to the heart of the concept of *ubuntu*[10] which in African philosophy expresses one's relationship to the others in the human family. The concept, based on a fundamental respect and compassion for others, combines rules of social conduct and ethics with traditional ancestral religious beliefs, by suggesting that those who uphold the principles of *ubuntu* throughout their lives become ancestors worthy of veneration and will in death achieve unity with those still living. This inextricable bond between the living and the ancestors, who – as many Africans believe – mediate between them and God, imbues *ubuntu* with deep spirituality. It is within this context that the philosophy of *ubuntu* resonates with restorative justice, in that it gives those who have lost their humanity a chance to get it back and those who have been injured to retain theirs.

As an African and as a man of the cloth, in his role as Chairman of the TRC, Archbishop Desmond Tutu wove the threads of *ubuntu* into the fabric of the Christian spirit of forgiveness, which he put forth as the best form of self-interest. He stressed that forgiveness gives people resilience, enabling them to survive and emerge still human despite all efforts to dehumanize them.[11] One of the TRC commissioners, Wendy Orr,[12] described the Archbishop as an inspiration of Christian values and a man of genuine compassion and humility, whose approach to conflict resolution, however, was that 'we should all love each other and care of each other – just like that'. The following anecdote illustrates the man that she speaks of and his largely successful quest to turn the TRC into what it became: a spiritual forum for the redemption of the sins of apartheid.

The Archbishop, who was to chair the first Johannesburg hearing of the TRC, was discussing proceedings for that and the following days (29 April to 3 May 1996) with Dr Fazel Randera, chief of the Johannesburg office of the TRC. The discussion was quite detailed, as the next few days were expected to set the pattern for all the subsequent TRC hearings. Also, in addition to the representatives of world media, a large contingent of the diplomatic corps, politicians, and senior government officials indicated that they would attend and that former President Nelson Mandela was to make an appearance. Fazel Randera and his colleagues expressed the view that both the first hearing in East London, and the many TRC ceremonies held in the preceding weeks, were far too 'religious'. They pointed out that the TRC process was a legal proceeding and should be conducted as such; there should be no prayers or singing of hymns before or during the hearings. In short: it was a juridical hearing in Johannesburg, not a

Sunday service at St George's Cathedral in Cape Town (Tutu 1999). The Archbishop accepted the suggestion that, instead of a prayer, the example of Parliament should be followed, and the proceedings would open with a moment of silence and quiet meditation. At the stroke of 9 o'clock, the TRC procession moved into the hall. The Archbishop and his colleagues shook hands with the victims seated in the first few rows, after which the Archbishop announced: 'We will now observe half a minute's silence before we commence with our programme'. Subsequently, the first witness was duly called and asked to take the oath. The stage was set. But the Archbishop was clearly not at ease; he shifted in his seat, he ruffled the papers in front of him, he cleared his throat and eventually he said: 'No! This is not the way to do it. We cannot start without having prayed'. He then asked everyone to close their eyes and placed the hearing of the day in the hands of the Lord, asking Jesus Christ, who himself is the Truth, to guide the commission in its quest for truth, and the Holy Spirit of God to grant it the wisdom and grace needed for the task. After a resounding 'Amen', he announced with a disarming smile: 'Now we are ready to start the day's work'. With his intuitive understanding of the spiritual needs of the victims and the audience, the Archbishop had set the tone of the hearings, which from that day onwards would start – and end – in this fashion.[13]

Referring to the TRC as 'secular Eucharist', one author has pointed out how the commission suspended conventional concepts of justice, law and fairness, and instead demanded a belief in the ritual of confession and showing faith in the rite of reconciliation (Moosa 2000). Another commentator drew attention to the extraordinarily large religious component of the TRC vis-à-vis the rather small number of lawyers (except in amnesty proceedings). He concluded that 'the strongly Christian subtext of repentance and forgiveness' may have both put at ease the ordinary and humble South Africans who came before the TRC to tell their stories, and conveyed the right message of 'what reconciliation is all about' (Jorge Heine, *Sunday Independent*, 15 November 1998).

On history and symbols

An event, no matter how significant, never takes place in a vacuum, but is always the outcome of the many events that precede it. The TRC, with its mandate to uncover truth and to promote national reconciliation, was no exception. It was part of a process whose roots stretch back in history and whose ultimate aim is a shared South African nationhood.

The universal image that the outside world has had – and probably continues to have – is that of a black and white South Africa. Yet, South Africa is home to many other peoples[14] and, in terms of the political parlance of the liberation struggle, the adjective 'black' encompassed all the non-white, as well as a number of white opponents of racial discrimination. In short, it united all those who struggled against apartheid. The liberation struggle was carried out under the banner of the Freedom Charter, modelled on the Universal Declaration of Human Rights proclaimed by the United Nations on 10 December 1948. The basic message of the Freedom Charter is now enshrined in the country's progressive constitution, proclaiming that South Africa belongs to all who live in it and who should enjoy equal rights and opportunities, without distinction of colour, race, sex or creed.

Inherent in the inclusive message of shared nationhood is the idea of reconciliation and as Jakes Gerwel[15] has observed, despite its deep and multi-layered divisions, South Africa is not an un-reconciled nation, at least not in the sense of being in danger of falling apart as a result of an immediate internecine confrontation. Quite the contrary: in a world replete with unresolved disputes, it may serve as a singularly successful example of a multi-ethnic and multi-racial country that has resolved its potentially disastrous conflicts consensually and with a particular sense of historical self-definition (Gerwel 2000). The idea of reconciliation is indeed positively related to the idea of a shared nationhood, but the question is how such a united nation can emerge from a past dominated by an ideology whose overriding purpose was to keep peoples of different cultures apart. It would be foolish to assume that a negotiated transition to democracy alone could effect such a miraculous transformation. It did not, but it did represent a vital step in the process of transformation that among other things brought the TRC into being. The fact that the erstwhile foes had agreed on how the Commission would be structured and what principles would guide it, may suggest that its work would be easy and its outcome predictable. This was not to be. The TRC hearings were often a most traumatic ordeal for the victims who told their tragic stories, and a harrowing experience for the survivors who learnt how their loved ones had suffered and died. In addition, the TRC needed to come up with a workable strategy to involve as many perpetrators in its process as possible and, at the same time, defend its policy of restorative justice against the many harshly critical voices demanding that the guilty be punished. The commissioners themselves, coming from different cultural backgrounds, first had to reconcile themselves to each other, before tackling the promotion of a national reconciliation.[16]

And they had to find a way in which a tragic past would not wreck the very process that they were there to promote.

Also, even though there were historical predispositions that may have augured well for the search of a shared nationhood, these were primarily ideological in nature. In reality, the intensity of polarization of the South African society along deep ethnic and racial cleavages made many – if not most, people, both in and outside the country – doubt that such an outcome was ever possible.

The ideals of a shared nationhood were rather forgotten when the forces of the apartheid state and those of the liberation struggle engaged in what can only be described as low-intensity civil war. The two sides were locked in military combat since the declaration of armed struggle by the ANC in 1961. The declaration, and the subsequent 'Peoples' War', announced by the ANC in 1985, were met with the policy of 'Total Onslaught', formally announced by the regime in 1977. Organized civilian cells loyal to the ANC, known as Self-Defence Units, sprang up throughout the country. At the same time, the ethnically based Zulu Inkatha Freedom Party (IFP) formed its own units. Both sides drew their members largely from the ranks of urban youths. As a result, the popular culture of resistance and revolt against the apartheid state became heavily militarized. The same occurred on the side of the state. From 1968 onwards, white males were drawn into military service, mostly through compulsory conscription, and after serving an initial period of one year, later extended to two years, they were retired to regional commands where they were to remain on standby as 'civil militia' for emergency call-ups. At the same time, the regime originated many projects aiming to instil a military ethos into the cultural life of white civilians.[17] Widespread violence intensified to reach its peak in the early 1990s and, predictably, civilians were its frequent victims. It is not difficult to imagine that under such circumstances, racial attitudes, already polarized by enforced segregation and stereotyping, would have further hardened.

Jointly, the negotiations and the work of the TRC did much to set the culturally diverse peoples of South Africa on the road to becoming a nation. But, historically speaking, the process has only just begun and only time will tell to what degree it is successful. What holds promise are the words of Friedrich Meinecke who believed that it is not a common *culture* but a common *will* to be a nation that makes a nation (Meinecke 1922), or, as Ernest Renan put it, the 'desire to continue a common life' (Renan 1990). But to be maintained in later generations, this will to be a nation must not only be embodied in laws and institutions. It must also be accompanied by culture, albeit a new one. Ultimately, it is the new common culture of the nation that creates the will of its members to be a nation.

Many steps have been taken in this effort to create a common culture and a new nation. Among them, one could list the decision to embrace 11 official languages as an indication of equality in, and respect for, cultural diversity within the context of one nation. The later adoption of the libertarian and egalitarian constitution, a document that enshrines the concepts of human dignity and grants inclusive and equal citizenship to all, further stressed the point. The combination of the old and new songs of praise in one national anthem also sends its own powerful message of unity and reconciliation.

On the political scene, the role of the country's first black president, Nelson Mandela, can not be overemphasized. With his cherished vision of unity and reconciliation and his determination to promote it, with his disarming charisma, with his iconic standing in the liberation struggle – and as the very symbol of that struggle – in Nelson Mandela the South Africa nation has its founding father. His successor, President Thabo Mbeki, has a more chequered record, but his public pronouncements often contain the same theme of a shared nationhood. In his address on the occasion of the tenth anniversary of South Africa's democracy, for example, he expressed his pride that 'every day now, black and white South Africans discover that they are, after all, one another's keeper'. He underscored the visible determination of all people, regardless of colour and ethnicity, to work together to build a South Africa 'defined by a common dream'.[18] In 2005, on the Day of Reconciliation celebrated on 16 December, he drew from the 1805 poem 'The Prelude' by William Wordsworth, with its theme of overcoming divisions.

There is also the rich imagery that casts South Africa variously as the 'Rainbow Nation' of Archbishop Desmond Tutu, and as a mighty river fed by many smaller tributaries flowing majestically 'into the great ocean of humanity', as the educationalist and political activist Neville Alexander put it. Such rhetoric may seem pathetic, yet similar metaphors have been invoked by no lesser thinkers than Durkheim, Herder or Humboldt who, while differing on many other issues, shared the view that human beings are complementary and able to bond – not despite differences, but because of them.

The TRC added its own metaphor, that of the symbolic redemption. In accordance with the negotiated transition, the TRC mandate was not to open up to scrutiny apartheid as a system, with its myriad ways of discriminating and oppressing the majority of the people on a daily basis, but to focus on its most serious transgressions in terms of human rights abuses, such as abductions, torture and killings. This limitation has been frequently criticized for leaving all the beneficiaries of apartheid out of the process. However, by concentrating on – and by the public broadcast of – the most heinous crimes, the TRC in a symbolic sense carried the burden of the entire past with its conflicts, suffering and injustice.[19]

Reconciliation empirically

Given the fact that South Africa has moved from a virtual state of civil war to a state of peaceful co-existence where shared symbols of a common national life do exist, it is reasonable to assume that, generally speaking, reconciliation is taking place.[20] But what does reconciliation really mean more concretely?

Several meanings of the term have already been mentioned, and there are numerous others (e.g. Hamber and van der Merwe 1998; Villa-Vicencio and Verwoerd 2000). Rather than choosing one definition over another, it might be safer to presume that reconciliation is not a specific fixed *thing* but a dynamic entity located somewhere along the continuum ranging from a point where it is possible for former adversaries to start tolerating each other, to a point where they begin to trust each other.[21] Such an understanding of the term allows for a better fit with social reality in which the degrees of reconciliation, or its absence, not only differ between individuals and groups, but where the general feeling of reconciliation might move forwards or backwards depending on circumstances. An example of the former might be South Africa's win in the 1995 World Rugby Cup, which brought an emotional boost to reconciliation when, caught in the moment, the nation united in pride as champions. However short-lived such moments are, they do make their little unifying contribution.

For reason of limited space, it is not possible to discuss the various other elements that might play a role in bringing about reconciliation, for example, understanding and forgiveness – something that the TRC tried so actively to promote. But the use of the categories of tolerance and trust allows for quantifying social capital, the indispensable component of reconciliation and civil co-existence.

The analyses of surveys from 1995–2001 by Kotze and du Toit (2005) indicate that the low levels of generalized trust noted in South Africa in 1995 subsequently declined further. Given the relatively close proximity to the apartheid era, during which the pervasive presence of a police state in people's private lives made it inadvisable to be trustful, it is not too difficult to understand why trust on a personal level would be low in 1995. But one would have expected an increase in trust by 2001, which did not happen. One possible explanation might be the growth – or perceived growth – in crime over those years.

Tolerance, on the other hand, grew substantially over the same period, with an increase of nearly 10 per cent and a simultaneous 20 per cent decrease in 'intolerance', and with many respondents moving to the neutral category. The authors ascribed this encouraging pattern partly to the influence of the Bill of Rights in the 1996 Constitution, which – they believe – is slowly inculcating a 'rights culture' in South Africa, but also to the positive role of the Truth and Reconciliation Commission, which had created 'a climate of reconciliation'.

Kotze and du Toit conclude that, although declining levels of trust were not encouraging, increasing tolerance of diverse values and life-styles might counter this and become the crucial ingredient in the building of new networks between individuals from across social divides, created by language, religion, ethnicity, or race.

In an empirical investigation entitled 'Overcoming apartheid: Can truth reconcile a divided nation?', James Gibson (2004) draws some-what similar conclusions with regards to the climate created by the TRC, which in his opinion may have changed the way South Africans used to think about each other. He credited the TRC with successfully deconstructing stereotypes by, among other things, showing that all sides involved in the struggle – whether fighting for apartheid or against it – committed atrocities.[22] This, in his view, provided a basis for dialogue because, if people are freed from a dogmatic 'good versus evil' view of the struggle, then a space for reconciliation might be opened.

Reporting on an earlier national survey of ordinary South Africans[23] in 'Truth – yes, Reconciliation – maybe: South Africans judge the truth and reconciliation process', James Gibson and Helen MacDonald (2001) reach the overall conclusion that South Africa has indeed achieved a certain level of racial reconciliation, although the evidence of reconciliation is mixed and the exact degree difficult to determine. Nevertheless, they conclude that there is substantially more racial reconciliation than expected and that, although not exactly the con-tented 'Rainbow nation' of Archbishop Desmond Tutu, South Africans seem to have rejected the racial animosity of the past.

The report on the latest in the series of the Reconciliation Barometer Surveys of December 2005 (Fifth round report 2005) suggests, on the basis of longitudinal analyses, that there might be a narrowing of the gap in sentiments between the various population groups.[24] This attitudinal convergence is regarded as a positive development that broadens the common ground between South Africans of different backgrounds. The survey confirmed the earlier findings of low levels of trust, with 41.5 per cent of the respondents indicating that they find it hard to trust people from other groups. However, levels of tolerance, expressed as support for social integration in the private sphere (neighbourhoods and schools, cross-racial marriages), have remained high and showed increasing convergence. The report concludes that, although it might be premature to define the findings as a longer-term trend, they do bode well for 'the greater national reconciliation process' (ibid.).

Conclusions: The miracle

The emergence of a non-racial democracy in South Africa has often been described as a 'miracle', presumably because a peaceful transition took place where a bloody racial confrontation was widely expected and because forgiveness, not revenge, followed.

Describing what happened in South Africa as a 'miracle' implies a uniqueness not applicable elsewhere. And this is exactly how many have interpreted it. At a time of celebrating the country's tenth anniversary of democratic majority rule, Antjie Krog wrote a cutting article in response to the many voices that she had heard when visiting foreign journalists or scholars expressed their opinions on the TRC and the process it had initiated (Krog 2004). She first describes the outburst of an Australian academic who angrily stated that, what the whites did to the blacks by forcing them to accept this truth and reconciliation garbage, was done by conning and manipulating the black people, and was 'worse than apartheid'. She then proceeds to quote commentators who, though lauding forgiveness and reconciliation as a remarkable process, could not relate it to their own countries. A television producer from Tel Aviv felt it would never work in Israel because one needed 'Christians to make it work'; an Irish journalist believed it would fail in his country because there are 'too many Catholics'; and an American newsman opined that it is wonderful that the blacks could forgive and reconcile, but the Americans as a world power have the responsibility to uphold right and wrong. The sentiment that forgiveness and reconciliation are somewhat *wrong*, has also been voiced by noted intellectuals, who variously suggest that reconciliation might mean an embrace of evil, or agree with Nietzsche, considering forgiveness to be a primitive unhistorical act; or who, like Jacques Derrida, consider it to be mad and something that should remain exceptional and more or less impossible.[25]

Krog concludes by asking a number of questions:

> Why would people praise and support something they themselves would never dream if doing? And why would a model be hailed and admired but not claimed as a worthy alternative [to the retributive model adopted in Nuremburg] by the First World? [...] Is it because forgiveness is for the inferior, revenge for the civilized? [or] because the West is fascinated by anger, understands revenge and deeply admires hatred?

Or is it, as writer Sandile Dikeni has remarked, because it was proposed by Africans, and that which is put forward by Africans 'is treated like exotic African masks – to be hung in houses or photographed in brochures but never treated with the same respect as [...] own philosophies' (quoted by Krog ibid.). These are thought-provoking questions, which should not be dismissed lightly.

Much has been said in this book and elsewhere about globalization, but whatever definition, or set of definitions, one wishes to apply to it, one thing is beyond question: Globalization has made intercultural contact and exchange possible. But do we learn from one another?

South Africa has overcome her explosive conflict without external intervention, which, as the introduction to this book points out, is not the norm. It has since then been actively engaged in what is termed post-conflict reconstruction, so that – to refer to the Introduction again – the conflict does not recur.[26] In the course of this process, the country has been able to embrace reconciliation and to forge a collective national memory of terrible crimes. If what has happened in South Africa is a 'miracle' – which by definition is an event that breaks the law of nature – it was only in that it broke the law of *human* nature with its seemingly endless devotion to cycles of conflict and retribution.

The final question is: Is a reconciliation model 'out of Africa' of any use elsewhere, or is the rest of the world indeed bent only on revenge? Before answering this question, it might be useful to interject that a conciliatory mechanism, such as the TRC, would most likely not produce any significant results in a society that is not willing to be reconciled, and that the desire to reconcile is almost always shaped by committed leadership. This was made quite clear by the chairman of the South African Human Rights Commission, Jody Kollapen, who explained that South Africa could share the TRC – model and its legal framework with others, but cautioned that before that 'comes political and moral leadership' (quoted in Cohen 2006).

An encouraging development in that regard is that a high-level delegation from one of the currently most conflict-ridden countries in the world, Iraq, recently visited South Africa. Comprising Sunni, Shiite and Kurdish leaders, the group – by their own admission – came to learn from South Africa's reconstruction and reconciliation experience. One of its members, Iraq's national security adviser Mowaffak al-Rubaie, expressed the view that the only way forward is 'tolerance, truth and reconciliation, forgiveness and [...] living together [because] nobody can win from this violence'. Another member of the delegation, Sheikh Humam Hammoudi the chairman of Iraq's constitutional committee, expressed the hope that his country would end up the same way as South Africa, and said that he and his colleagues had come to realize that 'beautiful things can come out from very, very sad and tragic situations' (Business Day 2006). Such sentiments expressed by the leaders of a deeply troubled land might be the sign of another 'miracle' about to happen. One can only but wait and hope!

Notes

1. For a full account of the TRC, see Boraine et al. (1997). For a comparative assessments in an international context, see Beek (2005: 377–407).
2. On the subject of building on the Chilean experience, see for example Heine (1998) and Asmal and Robertson (1996).
3. Despite KwaZulu-Natal having the highest levels of political violence in the country, participation of people from that province in the TRC was inhibited by the boycott of the proceedings by the IFP. This resulted in what a provincial ANC leader later described as an 'absence of war, not an achievement of peace' (*Sunday Times*, 27 April, 2003).
4. For an example of such interpretations, see 'Oud-generaals verheug oor Basson uitspraak', *Beeld* (2002) 11 April.
5. Antjie Krog is a South African poet, journalist and writer. She is most noted for her engaged capturing of the complexity of the TRC in her award-winning book *Country of my skull* (1998).
6. South African media has described Eugene De Kock as a mass killer and a psychopath, and he has become known to the public as the 'Prime Evil'. De Kock was a former police colonel and apartheid's arch-assassin, who came to the TRC to confess and who was subsequently applauded for his honesty and help in making other perpetrators, and his former colleagues, come forward.
7. Quoted in Pumla Gobodo-Madikizela (2003) in her fascinating study of de Kock, based on her personal meetings with him in a maximum security prison in Pretoria.

8. Afrikaners are people of predominantly Dutch descent who used to be collectively referred to as the Boers. They trace their history back to the arrival in 1652 at the Cape of Good Hope of Jan van Riebeeck, who on orders from the Dutch East India Company established a fortified refreshment station in the Cape to promote Dutch trade with the East Indies.

9. Cynthia Ngewu, the mother of Christopher Piet, one of the Gugulethu Seven. On 3 March 1986, seven young black activists were ambushed in a roadblock set up by the police in the township of Gugulethu near Cape Town. The murder of the Gugulethu Seven is an example of one of the most callous acts of the apartheid security forces. Two of the police officers admitted to the TRC their involvement in the murders, explaining that they did what they did because of a suspicion that the young men were planning to attack a police van. The officers received amnesty to the frustration of many inhabitants of Gugulethu. The young men are commemorated by the Gugulethu Seven Memorial situated in Gugulethu (which means 'Our Pride'). The memorial, consisting of seven solid granite statues, was unveiled in March 2000, on Human Rights Day.

10. The word *ubuntu* is enshrined in the Zulu maxim *umuntu ngumuntu ngabantu*, meaning 'a person is a person through other persons'.

11. For Tutu's thought on the subject, see Tutu (1999).

12. In 1985, as a young district surgeon, Wendy Orr took on the entire apartheid establishment by obtaining a court order to stop prison authorities in her district of Port Elisabeth from torturing her prisoner patients. She took this action at the height of the hysterical period of the supposed Total Onslaught (by communism) and characterized by the imposition of a series of states of emergency during which – though a common occurrence in apartheid prisons, as the TRC hearings revealed – torture was vehemently denied by the regime that claimed that accusations of torture were nothing but a propaganda tool, used by various subversive agents to discredit the government.

13. The first Johannesburg TRC hearing has been described by Meiring (2000: 123–133).

14. These people include the aboriginal inhabitants of the Cape of Good Hope, the Khoisan and the Griquas (formerly Hottentots and Bushmen), who in 1999 received official recognition as a distinct cultural group, but who were earlier classified as 'Coloureds'. Apartheid attached the label 'Coloured' to a community of vastly heterogeneous people who can trace their ancestry to the Khoi, the San, the Griquas, the white Dutch settlers, the black Xhosa tribe, and the slaves from such diverse regions as Indonesia, Ceylon, China, India, and Madagascar, and include Christians and Muslims. The Indians are another distinct community in South Africa, comprising Hindi, Muslim, and Christian religions, as well as many languages, customs and political beliefs (Van Beek 2005).

15. Jakes Gerwel was Director-General in the Office of the former President Nelson Mandela.

16. For an exceptionally candid 'inside story', see Orr (2000).

17. For thorough analyses, see Kotzé and du Toit (2005).

18. Address by President Thabo Mbeki, at his inauguration and the tenth anniversary of freedom, Pretoria, 27 April 2004.

19. On national reconciliation between the sacred and the secular, see Gerwel 2000.
20. Not everyone would agree with this statement, especially in South Africa where the debate on reconciliation continues and depends largely on the definition of the term.
21. This notion is similar to the 'thinner' and 'thicker' versions of reconciliation proposed by Charles Villa-Vicnecio (1999) cited above.
22. Alongside granting blanket amnesty, equating atrocities committed in the course of the 'just war' against apartheid with those perpetrated by the oppressive regime, was the most controversial aspect of the TRC process, the contention being that in the case of the liberation struggle, the ends justified the means.
23. The survey was based of on a representative sample of adult population (over 18 years old) with a total of 3,727 interviews.
24. i.e. black, white, coloured and Indian.
25. For full quotes, see Krog (2004).
26. It goes beyond the scope of this chapter to consider such vital aspects of reconstruction as provision of housing, basic services delivery, cutting down of unemployment and crime, and other challenging problems that must continuously be tackled if reconstruction and reconciliation are to progress satisfactorily.

References

Agger, I. and Jensen, S. N. (1996) *Trauma and healing under state terrorism*, London: Zed Books.

Asmal, K. A. L. and Robertson, R. S. (1996) *Reconciliation through truth: a reckoning of apartheid's criminal governance*, Cape Town: David Philip.

Bhargava, R. (2000) 'Restoring decency to barbaric societies', in Rotberg, R. I. and Thompson, D. (eds) *Truth v. justice: the morality of truth commissions*, Princeton NJ and Oxford: Princeton University Press.

Boraine, A., Levy, J. and Scheffer, R. (1997) *Dealing with the past. Truth and reconciliation in South Africa*, Cape Town: IDASA.

Business Day (2006) 'SA to open embassy in Baghdad, Mbeki tells Iraqis', *Business Day*, 8 March.

Cohen, R. (2006) 'A South African model for reconciling in Iraq?', *International Herald Tribune*, 11 March.

Fifth round report (2005) *The SA reconciliation barometer survey*, December 2005. Rondebosch: Institute for Justice and Reconciliation.

Gerwel, J. (2000) 'National reconciliation: Holy Grail or secular pact?', pp. 277–286 in Villa-Vicencio, C. and Verwoerd, W (eds) *Looking back reaching forward*, Cape Town: University of Cape Town Press.

Gibson, J. L. (2004) *Overcoming apartheid: Can truth reconcile a divided nation?*, New York: Russell Sage Foundation.

Gibson, J. L. and MacDonald, H. (2001) *Truth – yes, Reconciliation – maybe: South Africans judge the truth and reconciliation process*, Research Report, Institute for Justice and Reconciliation, Rondebosch: Institute for Justice and Reconciliation, 11 June 2001.

Gobodo-Madikizela, P. (2003) *A human being died that night: A story of forgiveness*, Boston: Houghton Mifflin.

Hamber, B. and van der Merwe, H. (1998) 'What is this thing called reconciliation?', paper presented at a forum entitled 'After the Truth and Reconciliation Commission', Goedgedacht Farm, Cape Town, 28 March 1998.

Heine, J. (1998) 'Truth commissions in Chile and South Africa', Occasional Paper 1, Diplomatic Forum, Johannesburg: Rand Afrikaans University.

Huntington, S. P. (1991) *The third wave: democratization in the late twentieth century*, Oklahoma: University of Oklahoma Press.

Ignatieff, M. (1996) 'Articles of faith', in *Index on censorship*.

Ignatieff, M.(1998) *The warrior's honour: ethnic war and the modern conscience*, London: Vintage.

Lu, L. (2002) 'Justice and moral regeneration: Lessons from the Treaty of Versailles', *International Studies Review*, 4.

Kotzé, H. and du Toit, P. (2005) 'Civil society and democracy' pp. 243–334 in van Beek, U. J. (ed) (2005) *Democracy under construction: Patterns from four continents*, Bloomfield & Opladen: Barbara Budrich Publishers.

Kritz, N. J. (ed) (1995) *Transitional justice: how emerging democracies reckon with former regimes* (volume 1: General considerations; volume 2: Country studies; volume 3: Laws, rulings, and reports) Washington, DC: United States Institute of Peace.

Krog, A. (1998) *Country of my skull*, Johannesburg: Random House.

Krog, A. (2004) 'Embarrassed by forgiveness', *Sunday Times*, 29 February.

Meinecke, F. (1922) *Weltbürgertum und nationalstaat. Studien zur genesis des deutschen nationalstaats*, (first edition 1907) München: Oldenbourg.

Meiring, P. (2000) 'The baruti versus the layers: The role of religion in the TRC process', pp. 123–133 in Villa-Vicencio, C. and Verwoerd, W. (2000) *Looking back reaching forward*, Cape Town: University of Cape Town Press.

Moosa, I. (2000) 'Truth and reconciliation as performance: Spectres of Eucharistic redemption', pp. 113–122 in Villa-Vicencio, C. and Verwoerd, W. (2000) *Looking back reaching forward*, Cape Town: University of Cape Town Press.

Orr, W. (2000) *From Biko to Basson: Wendy Orr's search for the soul of South Africa as a commissioner of the TRC*, Saxonwold: Contra Press.

Renan, R. (1990) 'What is a nation?', in Bhabha, H. K. (ed) (1990) *Nation and narration*, London and New York: Routledge.

Rotberg, R. I. and Thompson, D. (eds) (2000) *Truth v. justice: the morality of truth commissions*, Princeton NJ and Oxford: Princeton University Press.

Tutu, D. (1999) *No future without forgiveness*, London: Rider.

Van Beek, U. J. (ed) (2005) *Democracy under construction: Patterns from four continents*, Bloomfield & Opladen: Barbara Budrich Publishers.

Villa-Vicencio, C. (1999) 'A different kind of justice: the South African truth and reconciliation commission', *Contemporary Justice Review*, 407–428.

Villa-Vicenio, C. and Verwoerd, W. (2000) 'Writing up the truth', in Rotberg, R. I. and Thompson, D. (eds) (2000) *Truth v. justice: the morality of truth commissions*, Princeton NJ and Oxford: Princeton University Press.

Villa-Vicencio, C. (2000) 'Getting on with life: a move towards reconciliation', pp.199–209 in Villa-Vicencio, C. and Verwoerd, W. (eds) (2000) *Looking back reaching forward*, Cape Town: University of Cape Town Press.

Villa-Vicencio, C. and Verwoerd, W. (eds) (2000) *Looking back reaching forward*, Cape Town: University of Cape Town Press.
Zalaquett, J. (1992) 'Balancing ethical imperatives and political constraints: The dilemma of new democracies confronting past human rights violations', *Hastings Law Journal*, 43: 1437.

5
Arab-Islamic Debates on Dialogue and Conflict between Cultures*

Nadia Mahmoud Mostafa

Towards a new normative paradigm?

Western academia have tended, until recently, to ignore religion as a source of knowledge or at least an object of analysis. When religion and culture returned to the forefront of the political scene by the end of the Cold War, that situation changed. Increasingly, scholars in these disciplines began to take the religious and cultural factors seriously.

On the other side, normative epistemological systems in general, and the Islamic one in particular, are based on the admission that religion is a major source of knowledge, values, concepts, and world vision. The Islamic perspectives on social phenomena can contribute to the actual revision of the social theory in general and the state of the arts of political science and International Relations paradigms.

The justification of this revision is based on the following reasons in particular.[1]

- The increased conviction that values have great impact on the existing reality.
- The increased critique that the absolute rationalization and the modernization philosophy have to give way to the re-emergence of values and cultural aspects.

* I would like to express my deepest thanks and gratitude to the research team who participated in translating, editing and revising the original text (40 pages) before being edited by the book editors: Amira Abou-Samra, Dr. Ahmad Ali Salem, Aliaa Wagdy, and Yasmeen Zein El-Abedeen.

– The increased consciousness that scientific and modernization values are not by themselves enough to prevent the destruction of human beings.

Therefore the need for a new humanitarian vision has developed. It admits that rationalization does not provide, by itself, the spiritual essence that human beings need.

The relationship between religion, culture, and politics is not anymore an 'internal' issue within the Arab and Muslim world. Its external and global dimensions have acquired a great importance. The actual international system provides – directly or indirectly – various external influences and interventions in the domestic affairs related to religion and culture. Influence and intervention are not new phenomena, but they have reached a peak with the process, policies, and tools of globalization.

Since the contemporary Islamic revival started in the late 1970s, new Orientalist approaches have developed and extended their interests to the study of the relation between Islam, society and politics. Moreover, 'Islam and the West' has become a dominant theme in the study of the international system and foreign policies.

After the end of the Cold War, the western world has also witnessed the impact of religion. The Balkan war, the Muslims' identity in Europe, and the Christian fundamentalism in the United States are the most illustrative examples.

To sum up, the concerned issue is not a new one, but globalization and the end of the Cold War have shed light on it.

This study is founded on the results of two research areas:

– The re-emergence of religion and culture has influenced the study of international relations. A paradigm shift is taking place due to both the increasing importance of religion and culture (e.g. Mazrui 1999; Lapid and Kratochwil 1996; Haynes 1994: 122–145; Fox and Sandler 2004), and the renewed interest in normative approaches and values (e.g. Finnemore 1996; Brown 1992). Accordingly, the motives and justifications of building an Islamic paradigm, the characteristics of this paradigm and its contribution in the debates between paradigms have been elaborated (Mostafa 2002).

– The era of relations between cultures has revealed changes in international relations in the globalization époque (Mostafa 2004a; b). Globalization as a process, an ideology or policies offers evidence of the rise of cultural and religious aspects in international politics in general, and in politics related to the Muslim world in particular. Propositions about globalization presented by contemporary Muslim figures have been distinguished from those presented by other schools.

In the post-Cold War period, the relationship between civilizations[2] has appeared to be indicating a new kind or a new form of power conflicts and power balances. This relationship has become an issue of debate between comparative paradigms of international relations. The debate has also produced a number of questions on the degree of transformation of the study of International Relations, as to whether a new paradigm is actually emerging. This would be a paradigm based on a cultural/religious approach from which it derives the level of analysis, variables and hypotheses, something which would make it quite distinct from other paradigms well established in the study of International Relations.

Accordingly, extensive debates have emerged on the type of relations between cultures-civilizations on the one hand, and the relationship between these religious, cultural-civilizational aspects and the political aspects on the other hand. The exploring of these debates in Arab-Islamic discourses is the core of this study.

The relationship between cultures-civilizations has attracted many authors since the publication of Huntington's famous article. Following the September 11th events, the contributions on these relationships reached a climax, indicating the new weight acquired by the religion-culture-civilization dimension and by the normative dimension in the analysis of International Relations. As a result, the concepts dialogue and conflict of civilizations (or cultures or religions) became basic complementary concepts, and the growing concern with them led to the creation of what could be described as 'an area of research and debate'. Addressing this area of research has become an academic, theoretical and practical necessity, similar to the previous necessity to address concepts like the new world order or globalization. So, the concern with the new power structure in the world (unipolarity) and its new processes (globalization), is shifting gradually to become a concern with the context of these processes (dialectical-conflictual) in areas that seem rather new (culture-civilization).

My approach to this area of research and debate reflects my interactive experience and acquaintance with Arabic and Islamic trends in the field during the last decade.[3] I believe that this time span can be divided into three main stages, the first stage starting with Huntington's proposition, the second stage with the September 11th events, and the third stage with the crisis stimulated by the publication of the Danish caricature drawings. My conclusion is that the discourse on dialogue between civilizations has always been strongly linked to the discourse on conflict between civilizations, and that both discourses had emerged a long time before the September 11th events, although both discourses attracted more attention from that date.

My reason for studying and closely monitoring the different trends on this subject is my conviction that there is a need for a theoretical contribution – originating from within an Islamic paradigm. This would to add to other theoretical contributions approaching the study of International Relations from a cultural/religious perspective, contributions gradually forming a new subfield within the study of International Relations in particular and within political sciences in general. Making a contribution specifically from within an Islamic paradigm might also help to solve the problem of ambiguity, chaos, intersection, and cyclical movements that has characterized the study of this subject in Arabic and Islamic circles since the publication of Huntington's proposition.

The following three items present the accumulated results of my experience. The first item addresses the problem of whether the relationship between civilizations is originally a relationship of conflict or of dialogue. The second item addresses the preconditions for a dialogue, the possibilities for its continuation and the determinants of its effectiveness. The third item presents a personal theoretical and political stance, suggesting that the dialogue has lost its credibility due to increased hostility against Islam and Muslims (something distinct from Islam phobia), shown by indicators whose significance has become apparent all over the world since September 11th.

The relationship between civilizations[4]

Huntington's proposition and other western theoretical propositions concerned with the reality of 'the Islamic threat' together constitute a theoretical current offering a western cosmopolitan view. This could also be called a view of the world from within a western paradigm, a view of the role and position of the West in the world and consequently a view of the West's relationship with Islam and Muslims, and the impact of this relationship on the West's international role and position.

Huntington's concepts of civilization, culture, and identity have been thoroughly scrutinized and described as imprecise and confused. The model suggesting a world future dominated by conflict between 'civilizations, cultures, religions', knowing no compromise or rationality, only fanaticism against the other, has been rejected by those who advocate a global pluralism to explain world politics with special emphasis on dialogue and cooperation. Huntington's description of the Islamic borders as the bloody borders and the pivot of conflict – both at the macro-level (between civilizations) and at the micro-level (between states belonging to different civilizations) – has also been strongly criticized. Apologetic defendants of Islam have totally rejected the accusations that such propositions direct at Islam and Muslims, including the description of Islam as the future enemy of the West. That description has also been criticized by those who reject the philosophical and theoretical foundations of Huntington's proposition, and who could identify Huntington as another defendant of western interests, values and material hegemony, as another symbol of the western secular model whose impact on humanity they reject and fear.

These different points of criticism demonstrate only some of the main aspects of the debate on the 'clash of civilizations' proposition. The debate on Huntington's proposition took three different courses (Mostafa 2003a): The first course rejected the possibilities of a dialogue because of global realities such as the imbalance characterizing international power distribution. Some stressed that western policies towards the Arab and Muslim world are of a cultural, civilization-oriented nature and specifically pointed out that there is a conflict between civilizations initiated by the West against the Islamic World and Muslims. Therefore, the advocates of this course considered the dialogue as another tool for securing the dominance of western civilization and imposing western cultural hegemony.

The second course rejected either the epistemological basis, that the relationship between civilizations can be the main explaining factor in international relations, or the accusations directed at Islam and Muslims, instead stressing that Islam actually accepts 'the other', and rejecting the proposition because of believing in cultural plurality and considering the dialogue between cultures and civilizations as the real basis of international relations. Some who rejected the proposition on the grounds of cultural plurality adopted a globalist humanitarian view. Others adopted an Islamic view, stressing the importance of dialogue and the need for nations and peoples to get culturally acquainted because such acquaintance is a main element of the global Islamic mission, i.e. they rejected the proposition not from an apologetic or defensive position, but from a constructive one.

The third course suggested that the dialogue and the conflict between civilizations are nothing but variations in the relationship between civilizations. Some considered the present international condition as uninviting for true and sincere dialogues because of the extreme imbalance characterizing international power distribution, which implies that dialogue would only lead to the imposition of specific models of culture and civilization. Others regarded the dialogue as essential in leading the world out of its crisis. Yet, they stressed, a successful dialogue requires certain conditions in order to achieve real results of mutual understanding and healthy relationships.

The concern with a 'dialogue between civilizations' was thus a by-product of the concern – in Arabic and Islamic circles – with the clash of civilizations proposition. It is important to note that the delineating marks between the above mentioned three courses seem quite compatible with the marks delineating three main schools of thought – the liberal, the realist and the Islamic. Each of these schools has its own conception of the factor 'civilization' (or culture) and its limits as an explaining factor for political interactions, as well as its own conception of the nature of international interactions themselves, whether revolving around conflict or cooperation (Mostafa 2002).

The positions held by these three schools on the relationship between civilizations are extensions of the positions they hold on globalization, its impact and consequences for the international system (Mostafa 2004a). While liberals think that globalization leads to more cooperation and stability, nationalists, leftists, and Islamists – despite their differences – suggest that globalization leads to conflict and fragmentation.

Despite the fact that some within the three schools agree on the possibilities or the limitations of holding a dialogue, their stances differ, originating from different cognitive arguments and from different assessments of reality.

My interpretation of Huntington's proposition and the debate on it (Mostafa 1999c) led me to reject the attitude of welcoming a dialogue unconditionally – which was a quite common attitude until the end of the 1990s – because that seemed to be an apologetic attitude, used just for defending Islam in the face of Huntington's proposition. At the same time, I rejected the attitude suggesting that the relationship between civilizations is doomed to be a relationship of conflict. I felt that I had to get past these two attitudes and analyses, and offer a more constructive view (Mostafa 2002), whose main aspects could be summarized as follows (Mostafa 2004b):

First, the Islamic conception of 'conflict' does not treat it as an absolute law of history – unlike the various trends of the realist school, including the one represented by Huntington. In an Islamic view, 'conflict' is differently defined, and constitutes only one out of many features characterizing the human social existence. We see that jihad – in its broadest definition (Mostafa 2003b; 2006) – is not a war seeking the annihilation of the other, and that war is just one of the tools available for managing conflict. This acquaintance can also be achieved through the resort to pacific tools. Since both types of tools have their limitations and restrictions, none of them can be an absolute alternative or replacement of the other. Hence, to claim that the relationship between Muslims and non-Muslims – according to the Islamic view – is basically a relationship of peace or of war lacks a lot of precision. Instead one should ask: when does war take place and when does peace take place? This is how we should proceed to discuss the different Islamic schools and interpretations of Islamic teachings. The question is quite similar to one in the western paradigm: conflict as a driving force between whom and against what?

At the same time this Islamic view of conflict – be it military or non-military – does not aim at making one nation superior to the other, or one culture dominant over the other. Instead it aims at securing the Da'awa, i.e. making sure that Islamic teachings reach everyone.[5]

Second, the Islamic conception of the relationship between civilizations as a relationship of 'acquaintance' (e.g. Abdel Fattah forthcoming) derives its origins from the Quran and Sunnah, and indeed differs from a western conception and definition of a dialogue between cultures and civilizations. It also differs from the western conception as far as motives and goals are concerned. Using the concept 'dialogue' in Islamic circles and within the present context of globalization is of a defensive apologetic character, while the concept 'acquaintance' reflects a rather 'positive' conception of the relationship between the Islamic and other civilizations, regardless of their weakness or strength. The concept stresses that it is never enough to look at material factors, but that there should always be room for non-material factors, for ethics and morality.

Relevance of a dialogue after September 11th

Is the conflict between civilizations dominating the world? What is the origin of this conflict? How can it be confronted? Can a dialogue between civilizations manage the post-September 11th phase? These questions were profoundly and extensively debated after September 11th, and the Muslim world was openly accused, no longer considered as merely a potential threat (Mostafa 2003c; 2003d; 2004c).

In this phase too, the question was about the relative weight of cultural aspects compared to other aspects. Yet, this time the debate revolved specifically around the American policies towards Muslims and the Muslim world following the September 11th events. Despite the increasing recognition that there was an evident cultural tone characterizing the American official and unofficial discourses on conflict as well as on dialogue, there remained a trend totally rejecting cultural explanations, stressing that, since cultures do not give up their convictions easily, cultural aspects would only complicate the picture and make it extremely difficult to reach a solution. This trend stressed the importance of dialogue as the only way out of the crisis, but also the importance of establishing the proper preconditions of a dialogue.

Another trend recognized that the American policies in the aftermath of the September 11th events carried elements of cultural conflict, specifically directed against Muslims and Islam. This trend considered any discussion of a dialogue between civilizations as a sign of weakness and surrender, because at this stage of the relationship a dialogue would be subjected to western conditions, inspired by the western view of the world and moving towards a fixed western goal, i.e. 'a modified Islam'. The view was that the American administration was basically employing cultural aspects to serve political interests and goals.

A third trend viewed the dialogue as a tactic to manage this stage of the relationship between the West and the Muslim world, in which interests are in real conflict with each other.

To this classification of trends corresponds the classification that had characterized responses to Huntington's proposition, and that was based on a belief in the possibility of holding a dialogue between Muslims and the Islamic world on the one hand and the United States on the other.

Therefore, a dialogue on what? Or a conflict about what? And how? Actually a number of issues were addressed by various paradigms: above all came the issues of violence and human rights – human rights culturally unique or globally universal. However, studies addressing the relationship between civilizations seemed to be somewhat relegating the agenda of the dialogue, instead occupying themselves intensively with the dispute over the dialogue's credibility and relevance. Meanwhile the cultural-religious challenges and threats that face the Muslim world were badly rising. The repercussions of the September 11th events have deeply complicated the consequences of globalization (Mostafa 2004b; 2005a).

In the meantime, endless series of conferences, meetings and gatherings – at official and unofficial, national, regional and global levels – were being held. The question arose of to what extent there should be a general strategy that could give sense to the gatherings, instead of them being targeted or constituting unorganized responses to the increasing attacks on Arabs and Muslims, and to the critical situation characterized by serious threats to international peace and security.

It should be noted that in the aftermath of the September 11th events, there was an increased concern with the practical aspects of the dialogue. Both governments and theorists felt a strong pressure to address the dialogue, its needs and requirements as well as its relevance and utility.

Here again three main trends could be identified (Mostafa 2003a):

– The liberal trend, whose propositions can be summarized as follows:
Globalization strongly affects the dialogue, its content and trends, turning democracy, pluralism and respect for human rights into core issues.

A dialogue between two materially unequal civilizations is possible, even necessary. It is the way out for retarded civilizations, their chance to make real progress towards joining the civilized world. Such progress can basically be achieved through the imitation of a number of values, institutions and achievements characterizing the European civilization. Imitation will not negatively affect the cultural uniqueness of the Arabic and Islamic civilizations because values promoting human rights are universal, shared by civilizations throughout the globe. So, the dialogue should not be limited to issues of relations between the West and Islam, and Islamic values should contribute to solving global issues.

– The leftist trend, whose main elements can be summarized as follows:
The view of the world as involved in theoretical and cultural conflict is rejected. What we have is a condition of unequal power distribution that makes the capitalist system quite dominant at the material as well as the cultural level. In such a situation of imbalance, a cultural and intellectual dialogue loses its relevance. Unipolarity confers only a symbolic meaning to the dialogue. Accordingly, a new agenda

of dialogue is needed to address issues of anti-Americanization and anti-globalization.

– The third trend is represented by the approach of the Islamic official institutions and a wave of Islamic thinkers, accepting or rejecting the concept of dialogue. Their main focus is on the image of Islam and the refutation of accusations directed at it. This trend calls upon the real nature of Islam as understandable from the original teachings of Islamic jurisprudence, and from manners and values promoted by Islam.

While westerners were calling on Muslims to join their dialogue, the American policies towards the Muslim World – within the context of the war on terrorism – were intensively resorting to military and economic coercive tools, and the question remained unresolved: What were the supposed benefits for Muslims in joining the dialogue that everyone was inviting for? The question was no longer whether the relationship between the West and the Muslim world was one of conflict or of dialogue, as the American policies were definitely disclosing a relationship dominated by conflict. Instead, the question was now about the credibility of a dialogue, mainly sponsored and called for by western agencies and institutions, and taking place within a deteriorating global and regional context.

There were, on the one hand, developments of a conflict or clash led by the West and directed against the Muslim world (Afghanistan, Palestine, and Iraq), described as 'a global war against terrorism', and, on the other hand, a huge number of forums, meetings and conferences full of controversial discourses on the utility and relevance of dialogue and the real motives behind it. Comparing the two produced the following question: had the experience of the two years following September 11th not already provided enough evidence to resolve the question of whether the relationship between the Muslim and the western worlds was one of a conflict of civilizations or a conflict of interests, and the question of whether a dialogue was still possible and capable of effectively contributing to the management of this relationship in the twenty-first century? The debates on the relevance, utility, credibility, and goals of dialogues illustrated how complicated they are.

Ambiguity and confusion

In light of the conference organized by the Programme for Dialogue of Civilizations in October 2002 to record some of the experiences related to the dialogue at national, regional and global levels, a condition of ambiguity and confusion about the dialogue could be identified. That condition can best be described with reference to the following features (Mostafa and Said 2003):

– There was a strong feeling that the issue of the dialogue between civilizations was quite important, deriving its importance not only from contemporary considerations.

There was also a dominant feeling that the Arabic Islamic institutional treatment of the dialogue had been far below what was required. Some described it as superficial, others as lacking tools, organization and resource mobilization capabilities, and yet others as 'carnivalic' rather than academic, tempting people to use the title as a façade to sell his products regardless of their quality. Also, of course, some commented on this treatment's apologetic and defensive nature.

Therefore, the main concern of the Programme for Dialogue of Civilizations was to identify and explore the academic contribution on the issue of dialogue.

Unfortunately, the main conclusion was that what was there was a dialogue on the dialogue, not a dialogue between civilizations.

– There were many voices discussing the issue of dialogue, but a complete lack of coordination between them. There was not even a common view on what a dialogue is or on its real content.

– There was an evident inequality between us and the opposite party of the dialogue, manifested in differences in organizational capacity, resource mobilization capabilities, and the utilization of instruments and tools. This inequality hindered the possibilities for a dialogue to reach positive results.

– In the dialogue, we always adopted an apologetic and defensive position, revolving around issues imposed by the other and moulded into an accusation. While exerting every possible effort to refute it, we forgot to introduce ourselves in a positive way. Therefore, a dialogue between civilizations led quite frequently to strengthening barriers rather than lifting them. Moreover, most initiatives calling for a dialogue originated either from the West or from Christian national or regional institutions in the East. The initiatives were usually well armed, not only with speeches and oral discourses inviting to a dialogue between cultures, and to peace, tolerance, and pluralism – as was the case with Arabic and Islamic institutions addressing the dialogue – but also with tools and work plans for applying the dialogue at various levels and among various sectors (youth, media, education, training, etc.).

– While the international and European agencies realized that the cultural dimension has become an integral part of politics, our institutions still missed this perspective.

– As a result – and closely linked to that – many participants in the Islamic-western dialogue who were supposed to represent the Muslim party did not really adopt a cultural Islamic model, but were strongly influenced by the western cultural model. Therefore, we needed to pose a number of questions: Who is holding a discussion with whom? Are we holding a discussion with the West from within a western model or from within an Arabic-Islamic cultural model? Who represents the latter? What stance do the various trends – the liberal, the nationalist, the Islamic, and the leftist – have on a dialogue with the West? What are the issues that really need to be addressed in the dialogue?

– The dialogue must not be limited to academic debates enumerating the positive characteristics of different cultures and civilizations, or to conferences led by men of religion, each asserting how tolerant his religion is. We need a clear strategy, characterized by seriousness and continuity, identifying the issues that are of real concern to us and that truly represent our motives and serve our needs at the present stage of the dialogue. These should be issues that do not force us to defend ourselves, that derive from an awareness that cultural dimensions and political-economic dimensions are no longer separated, that arise out of an understanding that the West is employing the dialogue to serve political goals – dictated by the nature of our current relationship. This relationship is characterized by western global hegemony and deliberate attempts to ignore real issues that arise from the West's relationship with the South, i.e. issues of liberation and justice, as opposed to issues of violence, terrorism, pluralism, and tolerance.

A strategy for dialogue

Such a long term strategy, stressing the importance of dialogue as a means of co-existence and of respecting and cherishing diversity, must fulfil a number of basic requirements:

– We need to realize that the dialogue of civilizations is a political issue with a cultural basis – that mainly calls on religion. Therefore, we need to improve our ability to employ the cultural tool as a foreign policy tool (note, for example, the different weights assigned to a cultural strategy in the Egyptian and the Iranian foreign policies).

We also need to work on religious reform and renovation, in order to introduce our cultural system and disclose its real image. Since internal distortions of Islam are a main source of deliberate distortions and accusations against Islam in some western circles, there must be a dialogue and an improvement of the image of Islam among ourselves, before trying to improve that image towards the West.

– We need to admit that the dialogue of civilizations can never take place in isolation from the balance of power. If the international scene leaves us with a unipolar hegemony, enjoying all possible material advantage, the least we can do is to try to balance its power intellectually and normatively. We have very good potential for intellectual contributions, though quite sporadic and lacking in methodology. We also have a set of original values that can contribute to global cultural renewal, if correctly introduced and explained.

– We need to find a unifying thread that can pull together the dispersed efforts and isolated institutional attempts within individual state. We could, for example, establish special units in the Foreign Ministries concerned with the dialogue between civilizations. As a final step, such units could also be established at the regional and the Ummah (the Muslim nation) levels, for example through involvement of the Organization of the Islamic Conference.

– We need to realize that the dialogue is multi-levelled, and that all levels are important. There are dialogues of ordinary people, of common projects, of experience exchange, of cultures led by professionals, and dialogues between NGOs – seen as the main future sponsors of the dialogue due to the incompetence of official institutions. Some actually see a chance that interaction between civil society in the Muslim world and the global civil society might create a different kind of dialogue. Such a dialogue could neutralize the negative impact of western attempts to influence the rising cultural role of the United Nations and to redirect the course of the dialogue of civilizations to best serve western goals and to impose western values at the global level. Activating a dialogue between people could be the way to get around the negative impact of the imbalanced power distribution that heavily influences official dialogues between governments. Politicization of the dialogue has deprived it its merits, which makes it important to distinguish between the dialogue as an international issue or a tool of foreign policy, and as a continuous human activity as old as human existence.

– We should not confuse the issues of political dialogues with those of religious and cultural dialogues, or with the cultural dimensions of political issues. For example, women's rights, human rights, terrorism, citizenship, and democracy are political issues, and the dialogue on them cannot leave aside the cultural dimensions. While the religious point of view on issues such as justice, pluralism, violence, and values must be considered, the social and political role of religions should be identified as distinct from the religious foundations of such societal, political, and economic issues.

 – We must be able to improve our internal conditions. We cannot transmit a positive image of ourselves unless our reality is truly positive. Consequently, we must be ready to criticize ourselves. We have a lot of shortcomings, and if we intend to indulge in a serious dialogue with others, we must be receptive to criticism. We must be able to admit that there is a culture of dialogue that starts with oneself.

 – The establishment of a dialogue between civilizations must be preceded by a dialogue within the civilization, an internal Islamic-Islamic dialogue on the one hand, and a dialogue between various trends of thought on the other hand.

Relevance of the dialogue

In light of a series of lectures held between September 2002 and June 2003 (Mostafa and Zeid 2004), the topic dominating the discussions was the relevance of the dialogue and its conditions, while violent conflicts in Iraq and Palestine continued to escalate. Three main trends could be identified (ibid.: 5–11):

The first trend is represented by those who considered the whole issue of a dialogue of civilizations as of carnivalic nature, suddenly emerging as a reaction to Huntington's clash of civilizations proposition. They hence suggested that the issue should not be considered as a genuine subject to be seriously addressed. They based their scepticism about the relevance and usefulness of the dialogue on the impact of the uneven power distribution on the dialogue, claiming that the lack of balance between the parties would definitely lead to one party dictating the rules. They also pointed out that, since the West had always been setting the agenda, most issues submitted to dialogue were issues of freedom and individual rights, especially women's rights, pluralism, freedom of expression, the universality of human rights, and of traditional interpretations of Islamic jurisprudence. While all of such issues directly served the western attempts to mould the East into western shapes under the pretext of uprooting terrorism, tolerance really should mean respecting the other's right to be different.

The second trend is represented by those who believed in the importance of the dialogue and in its relevance. Their stance was based on treating globalization as an existing fact, a fact that called for co-existence rather than conflict. Everyone would have to accept that, and the sooner all parties started working together to find a common ground, the more time they would save. Yet, to achieve this, each party had to fulfil certain obligations. The West would have to redirect its foreign policy so as to avoid unilateral actions at the international level, and to admit it being partially responsible for the negative image associated with Islam in the West and the role played by western mass media in disseminating that image. The East would have to exert every possible effort to move beyond the role of the recipient. Both the West and the East would have to direct those who reject the dialogue towards accepting it. They would also have to start utilizing unconventional methods for activating the dialogue, for example limiting the role of official parties and instead opening more channels for the participation of individuals and societies.

The third trend represents the intermediate position between the sceptics and the defendants of the dialogue. This position was held by those who believed that the invitation to a dialogue between civilizations is something deeply rooted in the original Islamic teachings, strongly distinguishing Islam from, for example, Judaism where a total rejection of the concept of a dialogue between religions or civilizations could be identified. Even the western invitation to a dialogue was regarded as a political proposition aimed at political goals, and, hence, totally different from the Islamic genuine proposition, acknowledging religious and cultural plurality, promoting diversity, recognising 'others', and calling for acquaintance with dialogue as a tool. Such a politicization of the dialogue between civilizations – making it the root cause of conflict and war – was considered to have an extremely negative impact on civilizations and on the relationship between them. Consequently, the advocates of this third trend suggested that it was extremely important to pay attention to the growing tendency to link the political and the cultural, which they identified as characterizing the western – and particularly the American – strategy at the then present stage of the world system.

Conspiracy theory and self-criticism

Closely related to the debate on the relevance of the dialogue is the debate on two extremely important issues, conspiracy theory and self-criticism.

Some – basically sceptical about the relevance of the dialogue – suggested that we should always keep the conspiracy theory in mind, for it reminded us of what had been done to us in the past, is being done to us in the present, and awaits us in the future. The same kind of talk is recorded at the western side. Discourses of 'why do they hate us?' reflect, implicitly or explicitly, symptoms of conspiracy theory, proposed not by Islamists or Arab nationalists, but by westerners. This new western version of conspiracy theory is based on religious-cultural accusations that Muslims are threatening the West by violent, intolerant, and terrorist Islam.

Others totally rejected the conspiracy theory. Offering a different explanation, they suggested that Muslim retardation and dependency were products of the inability to follow the routes of reason, science, freedom, and justice, which had led to success and development in the West. They also claimed that the conspiracy theory had always been the surest route to rid oneself of any sense of guilt or responsibility. In addition, they suggested that claims about us being totally tolerant, and open to dialogue and pluralism were exaggerated and misleading. In reality the East too – when it had the upper hand – exercized imperialism, domination and hegemony, and exacerbated conflict. They thought that the issue of the dialogue of civilizations was given much more weight than it deserved, suggesting that history was nothing else than a series of cycles of conflict of interests. Though conflict in each historical episode was dominated by a different feature, be it cultural, economic, or military, one fact remained constant, i.e. that conflict had always been won by the more powerful, whoever that was and whatever the tools of conflict were. The advocates of this stance also suggested that the contemporary stage of human history was clearly characterized by a lead of cultural tools over other tools of conflict, highly synchronized with political-economic tools and goals.

In opposition to the conspiracy theory comes the self-criticism theory. It mainly addresses the issue of dialogue with reference to various Arabic discourses during the Renaissance with reference to the problem of interaction between various Arabic trends of thought – the Islamic, the leftist and the liberal – and the stance that each of them adopts towards the West. The theory critically assesses and evaluates the contribution and development of each of these trends, applying several criteria for the evaluation. A main criterion is the position that the trends adopt on modernization, and the extent to which they suggest that the failure of the Arabic region to make necessary and desired changes is attributable to its failure to adopt the modernization model.

The advocates of the self-criticism theory suggested that the most important preconditions for a successful dialogue of civilizations were the critical assessment of secularism and modernization on the one hand, and of Islamic history and Islamic thought on the other hand. Such multi-dimensional criticism was supposed to disclose areas of common values shared by all civilizations.

It is beyond dispute that the conspiracy theory is facing strong criticism, attacking its position on the dialogue of civilizations. The liberally oriented self-criticism theory is however also facing strong criticism, attacking its position on the goals, tools and mechanisms of the dialogue. The criticism of the self-criticism theory highlights a number of questions, such as: Self-criticism in what way? Self-criticism getting us closer to modernization (westernization) and further away from our own cultural model? Is the dialogue – as fostered by the liberal trend – just another channel for imitating the West? Do we need to criticize ourselves only on liberal bases, do we not also need to defend our Islamic roots that are being widely attacked?

Issues at the core of the dialogue

At the international conference 'The Dialogue of Civilizations: Tracks and Experiences', held in Cairo in September 2003, a number of epistemological, theoretical and political issues at the core of the ongoing dialogues were discussed. The most important issues were (Mostafa 2005b):

– The agenda of the dialogue between western and Islamic perspectives, the role of the West in determining this agenda, and the role of the political realities in the East and the West in determining the main problems emanating from the issues on the agenda.

For instance, the issue of 'religion and secularism' lead to questions on the difference in the concept of religion between the Islamic and secular perspectives: Does the renewed concern with religion – in theory and practice – in the West imply a crisis in secularism? Does the revival of religiosity, or at least spirituality, in the West have positive or negative impact on the dialogue? Does the 'religionization' of politics, or the politicization of religion, have positive or negative impact on the relationship between the different cultures? Do they include more or less opportunities for conflict and for peace?

– The role of traditional and modern Orientalism in the epistemological and intellectual foundation of the western discourses. The discourses on the clash of civilizations present distorted images of Islam and Islamic symbols. Other discourses discuss the hypothesis that Islam includes an epistemological foundation that is in conflict with modernism, i.e. with positivist rationalism. This hypothesis is based on the conviction that the concept of 'Allah' in the Islamic belief, according to certain viewpoints, is opposite to the concept of existence on earth, which means that the role of mind comes next to the revealed text. According to this point of view, this leads to hindering modernism.

Therefore, propositions arose on the opportunities for reviving the so-called traditional Islam, the future of fundamentalism and the possibilities of a third way towards a 'civil democratic Islam'. Other propositions arose on our ability to contribute to and take initiatives in the global dialogue of civilizations, as it is not only about defending Islam or ourselves, but also about contributing to its agenda.

– Aspects of the dialogue on life or 'co-living' between different cultures and religions. How do different areas of the world reflect various experiences on the nature of 'cultural pluralism' and its patterns? What is the difference between such experiences as of India and Singapore, western Europe in general and France in particular, or the Balkans and eastern Europe (Bosnia-Herzegovina in particular)? What is the difference between the models of 'cultural pluralism' and models of 'integration'? Can Muslims integrate while preserving their religious identity? What is meant by European Islam or secular Islam?

– Prospects for a dialogue for youth that make them a driving force behind self-reform based on self-criticism in comparison to the others. What are its motives, constraints, fields and outcomes? Forums of alternative globalization are among the most important spheres of interaction for youth.

These interrelated issues are at the core of debates on 'reform and change in the Muslim world'.

Is a dialogue still possible?

The question of whether a dialogue is still possible gained special significance in light of the crisis following the publication of the Danish caricatures. It had already been raised and addressed throughout a number of previous crises of two basic types.

The first type is crises resulting from the blunt use of force by western countries against the Muslim world, and crises excited by interventions resorting to soft power tools (the renovation of the religious discourse, civic education, modernizing youth and women, etc.). As the epistemological-theoretical attack and media attack on Muslims and Islam went on, the Danish caricatures seemed to be only the tip of an iceberg.

The second type is crises initiated by players exercising violence in the name of Islam, or crimes for which Muslims are directly accused. They are associated with incidents such as the explosions in Bali (2003), the explosions in Madrid (2004), the explosions in London (2005), the violence in Paris suburbs (2005), the explosions in Sharm Elsheikh (2005), the explosions in Jordan (2005), and the explosions in Morocco (2004), along with violence in Saudi Arabia, Turkey, and Tunisia. We face a widespread map of violence – within and outside the Islamic world – showing that things are getting more and more complicated since 2001, in opposition to the hopes of the American war on terrorism.

Between the two types of crises came civil efforts on both sides to stress the importance of dialogue and to call for justice before peace. At the same time, the official national and regional efforts (Arabic and Islamic) failed to achieve the coordination among themselves which is necessary in order to influence western societies and balance their ability to influence our societies.[6]

The reaction in Arabic and Islamic discourses to the Danish caricatures truly demonstrated the depth of the setback to the dialogue efforts. Two main features became quite identifiable. The first feature was the retreat of some Islamic symbols, which used to call for and strongly participate in dialogue, from their original position regarding the dialogue expressing their rejection of the politicization and humiliation involved in it.

The second feature was the unprecedented agreement between representatives of various trends – nationalist, liberal and Islamic – in condemning the European arrogance and the claimed freedom of expression according to the western liberal model.

The main features of the Arabic discourses (as identified from a close survey of Al-ahram and Al-hayat newspapers in February and March 2006) on the explanation of the Danish caricature crisis, its impact on the status of the dialogue, and the extent of politicization involved in it were the following (Mostafa 2006b):

The crisis triggered by the sarcastic cartoons is unprecedented due to the nature of the incident that provoked it, the reactions towards it and its repercussions, the multiplicity and overlapping of the issues of concern, and the multiplicity of players – formal, civil, and public. This created a need to contemplate and rethink what happened and what was said about the dialogue, because the crisis and its aftermath showed that, in an environment where interests and emotions – offensive and defensive – are intermingled, 'conflict' is prior to 'dialogue'. In the meantime, there is an obvious imbalance of power (in both a material and a non-material sense) between two cognitive systems and worldviews, i.e. between the Muslim world and the West. So, the crisis was not sudden or unusual, but a manifestation of the escalated animosity towards Islam and Muslims, signalled by many previous incidents. The crisis also illustrated the increasing politicization of the cultural/religious dimensions of the relationship between the West and the Muslim world.

The political context

Where do these incidents – the consecutive Danish and European actions and the Arab and Muslim reactions – that relate to a cultural-religious issue lie within the current political framework of the relationship between the West and the Muslim world, in the light of the American and European strategies towards the Muslim world and the so-called 'war on terrorism' and 'war for reform, democratization and human rights'?

One can argue that the deliberate publishing of the cartoons is another episode in the series of targeting the Muslim existence in Europe and the United States. But this time it took place in the Scandinavian arena that does not yet know the complexities of other areas in Europe. Thus, creating a new battlefield in Europe is consistent with the so called 'war on terrorism'. This means that the two wings of the Ummah – the Muslim countries and Muslims in the West – are two sides of one coin in the strategic planning of the American administration and its European allies in the war on terrorism. The indicators of collaboration or rapprochement between the European right and the neo-conservatives in the United States tend to augment this, which in turn augments the dangers of confrontation between the East and the West on religious and cultural bases that intensify and serve the war of interests. Hereby, the rapprochement between the European religious right and the American religious right proves to be dangerous.

The epistemological intellectual context

The epistemological intellectual context includes many side issues of crucial significance regarding the differences between two epistemological and cultural models, which essentially differ in the priority given to religion.

On one side, we find a perspective that completely excludes religion, and hence uses the freedom of expression as a pretext for insulting religions, and even insulting God. Though the laws in the European countries criminalize such abuses, it seems that these laws are not enforced to protect this side of human existence (religion) unless there are strict conditions. Such conditions do not yet exist, even in the case of the

Danish cartoons, while – contrary to this – there are procedures to protect other rights such as the rights of homosexuals.

On the other side is the perspective that refuses to accept the misuse of the freedom of expression to insult religions or offend certain ethnicities or nationalities, no matter how important this freedom is as a pillar for liberal democratic regimes. Some advocates of this perspective believe that there are limits to the freedom of expression, but advocate these limits only regarding Jews and anti-Semitism. When it comes to Islam and Muslims, these limits no longer exist. This explains how the practice of insulting Islam and Muslims escalates in various forms and on different levels, while the practice of criminalizing anti-Semitism continues unabatedly.

Therefore, the current crisis asserted the double-standard western policies, after having tested some of the most crucial features of the cognitive system and the worldview on which these policies are based. These features – conflict, racism, and materialism – led to the emergence of critical intellectual streams within the West, warning against the dangers of the built-in crisis of the western civilization.

Also, the shortcomings of the western civilization are criticized by cultural Islamic perspectives, some of which affirm that the current crisis of the western civilization cannot be solved from within this civilization, especially after the peak of arrogance and denial of other civilizations and cultures. Thus, the western civilization needs to pay attention to values introduced by other cultural models, like values of just and equivalent human development introduced by the Islamic model. Some of these values are related to the rights of freedom of expression.

Moreover, one can say that the current phase of interaction – or of crisis of the dialogue – between religions and cultures introduces important significance, referring to the nature and evolution of the Danish incident. Not only Islamist figures, but also liberal, nationalist, and leftist ones, warned of the efforts exerted by some in the West to impose a cultural value system that contradicts our cultural specificity, in order to impose the concept of freedom of expression as defined by western secularism, or to intentionally insult and degrade Muslims and Islam. In addition, there are indicators of deliberate imposition of the western concept of 'freedom of expression'. Some of the most obvious evidences of this deliberate behaviour are 'refusing to apologize', 'conditional apology', manipulating apology, emphasising the vitality of the 'freedom of expression', and diffusing justifications for the impossibility of an international legislation to criminalize insulting religions, and the impossibility of depriving whoever wants to criticize religions of his rights.

A political issue with cultural-religious dimensions

With the re-emergence of the conflicting issue of freedom of expression between the Muslims and Muslim paradigms, another issue emerged, i.e. the relationship between Islam, politics, and society, or, to be specific, the relationship between Islam and democracy. The issue emerged as a result of the victories of the Muslim Brotherhood in the Egyptian parliamentary elections and of Hamas in the Palestinian elections, and was enormously revived with the post-September 11th debate on the relationship between terrorism, resistance, and Jihad.

Thus, in the political sphere and in light of the actual power balance, debates are being imposed from above (sometimes from the American political hegemony or the excessive secular modernist epistemological hegemony, both of which are now facing serious challenges). Yes! These debates are imposed from above and emanate from the major debate established and launched by Huntington – also from above – on the conflict of civilizations.

However, the Islamic discourses need to be renewed in order to prompt the Ummah's potentials to protect against internal injustice, tyranny, and oppression, in the same way as defending the Prophet.

It is legitimate to wonder when religion will become a stimulator of social and political change in our societies, rather than put aside to achieve progress. We must ask who stole the 'essence' of Islam over many centuries of stagnation followed by centuries of westernization and secularism in the name of modernization. And we must ask how Islam can become a source of change.

Moreover, it is time to face 'the other', telling them loudly that 'you are responsible as well, and you must see how your racism and intended offence to Islam and Muslims tend to escalate'. In other words, it is time for an offensive strategy that obliges them to fix the bases and requirements of a just and equivalent dialogue. This should happen before we again get into responding to the flood of European formal and civil initiatives (collective and national), that do not seek to prevent repeating what has happened, but only to repair the relations with 'moderate Muslims'.

In sum, the issue, within the context of which this and previous crises lie, is not only an issue of Da'wah that necessitates introducing Islam and correcting the image of its origins and its Prophet to Europeans, by those who practice Da'wah as a job (Do'ah). Nor is it a political issue that has nothing to do with religions and cultures. Rather, it is a political issue with cultural-religious dimensions where the power balances and the interests of involved parties are tested.

A perusal of the events, discourses and interactions of the crisis has helped show that in order for future dialogues to be just and equivalent, international legislation is needed that criminalizes insulting or degrading Islam and Muslims as is the case of criminalizing anti-Semitism. Insulting and degrading Islam and Muslims, and condemning them according to false accusations, is no longer merely a matter of ignorance or freedom of expression. It is being used politically to provide an environment to prove that Muslims of the West are not willing to integrate, and that Muslims of the world jeopardize peace and stability, which allows for justifying all types of offensive and interventionist policies against Muslims, for either political or religious reasons. This subtracts from the need for and motives of a dialogue.

Coordination of efforts and roles is needed according to a strategy where dialogue between religions and cultures is not perceived as an alternative to conflict, but as a political issue and a tool for conflict management. Hence, the political context and the political aims of the dialogue must be known, keeping in mind that dialogue is essentially a strategic principle.

Conclusions

The previous accumulated analysis shows that the debates between the discourses on dialogue and those on conflict constitute a clear case of the cultural-civilizational arguing with the political. In addition, the current events all along the last decade (1996–2006) clarify to what extent the official western call for a dialogue has been politicized, while the cultural and religious aspects have been used intensively to justify political-military intervention and goals.

In other words, the suggested strategy will help test to what extent the politicization of the dialogue as a tool of foreign policy – while arms of aggression are destructing humanity – would deeply damage the dialogue as a strategy, worldview and principle in the eyes of Arabs and Muslims.

Notes

1. For similar arguments see, for example, Ezzat 2002.
2. In the chapter civilizations, cultures (and religions) are used interchangeably. I mean by cultural-civilizational aspects in studying International

Relations those related to the impact of differences between cultures and religions on the differences between world views. These aspects shape the following: the bases for world divisions, motives for international interactions and determinants for the state of the international system, tools of policies, issues, explanatory factors, and finally a component of power.

3. Although there are rich Arabic publications in the area, the study's references are those related to my own experience. Each of these references is based on collective and edited research.

4. The results have already been recorded at a number of Arabic and Islamic conferences and meetings 1998–2000, which were only some of many gatherings organized in Islamic and Arabic circles during the second half of the 1990s, especially after the Tehran summit in 1997, in which president Khatamy introduced his initiative calling for a dialogue between civilizations.

5. Da'awa (call) is the key concept of an Islamic paradigm of International Relations, like power is key in the realistic paradigm. For more details on various aspects of the comparison, see Mostafa 2002 and 1999b. See also Abdel Fattah 1996. For comparison between different Islamic legal thoughts on the bases of external Islamic relations, see Wanis (1996).

6. Compare for example the establishment of the Anna Lindh Foundation for the dialogue between Euro-Mediterranean cultures, stressing the cultural dimension of the Euro-Mediterranean partnership with the dispersed efforts of Islamic and Arabic institutions. For a critical assessment of the objectives, tools, and relations between the political and the cultural of the Euro-Mediterranean partnership, see Mostafa forthcoming. See also Assia BenSalah Alaoui (volume 2).

References

Abdel Fattah, S. E. (1996) 'The values as the frame of reference for studying international relations in Islam', in Mostafa, N. M. (ed) (1996) *The project of international relations in Islam*, volume 2 'The International Institute for Islamic Thought', Cairo (in Arabic).

Abdel Fattah, S. E. (forthcoming) 'Globalization and Universalism of Islam', in El Fadl, M. A. and N. M. Mostafa (eds) (forthcoming) *The proceedings of a project research on 'Theorizing about civilizational studies'*, Programme for Dialogue of Civilizations, Cairo University (in Arabic).

Brown, S. (1992) *International Relations in a changing global system: Toward a theory of the world polity*, Boulder: Westview Press.

El Fadl, M. A. and N. M. Mostafa (eds) (forthcoming) *The proceedings of a project research on 'Theorizing about civilizational studies'*, Programme for Dialogue of Civilizations, Cairo University (in Arabic).

Ezzat, H. R. (2002) *Co-Citizenship: Bringing religion back*, Paper presented to the International Consultations on Christian and Muslims in dialogue and beyond, Convened by World Church Council, Geneva, October 2002.

Finnemore, M. (1996) 'Norms, culture and world politics: insights from sociology's institutionalism', *International Organization* 50, 2: 325–345.

Fox, J. and Sandler, S. (2004) *Bringing religion into international relations*, New York: Palgrave Macmillan.

Haynes, J. (1994) *Religion in the third world politics*, Boulder: Lynne Rienner Publishers.

Lapid, Y. and Kratochwil, F. (eds) (1996) *The Return of Culture and Identity in International Relations Theory*, Boulder: Lynne Rienner Publishers.

Mazrui, A. (1999) *Cultural Forces and World Politics*, London: James Currey.

Mostafa, N. M. (ed) (1996) *The project of international relations in Islam*, volume 1 'The International Institute for Islamic Thought', Cairo (in Arabic).

Mostafa, N. M. (ed) (1999a) The Project of International Relations in Islam, volume 1 (in Arabic).

Mostafa, N. M. (1999b) 'The introduction to the project of international relations in Islam: The objectives, the methodology', in Mostafa, N. M. (ed) (1999a) The Project of International Relations in Islam, volume 1 (in Arabic).

Mostafa, N.M. (1999c) The Foreign political challenges for Muslim world (in) Association of Muslim universities, A project on the challenges that faces Muslim world in the next century, Part (3), Cairo.

Mostafa, N. M. (2002) 'The process of founding an Islamic paradigm for studying international relations: The problematics of research and teaching', in Mostafa, N. M. and Abdel Fattah, S. E. (eds) (2002) *The Islamic methodology for social sciences: The model of political science*, Cairo: The Centre of Civilization for Political Studies, The International Institute for Islamic thought (in Arabic).

Mostafa, N. M. (2003a) 'Problematics of approaching the concept of dialogue of civilizations in Arab discourses', in *The annual report on My Ummah (Muslim community) in the world (2002– 2003)*, The Centre of Civilization for Political Studies, Cairo, 2003 (in Arabic).

Mostafa, N. M. (2003b) 'How to comprehend Jihad', Islamonline, 25 March 2003: http://www.islamonline.net/english/Contemporary/2003/03/Article02.shtml.

Mostafa, N. M. (2003c) 'The American policy toward Islam and Muslims: Between cultural and strategic aspects', Programme for Dialogue of Civilizations, Cairo University (in Arabic).

Mostafa, N. M. (2003d) 'The first war of the 21st century, The position of the Muslim Ummah: The rise of cultural-civilizational challenges and the conditions for the continuity for dialogue of civilizations', in the Proceedings of the conference on 'How do we continue the dialogues of civilizations?' (January 2002), Damascus: The Center for Iranian Arab relations (in Arabic).

Mostafa, N. M. and Zeid, O. A. (eds) (2003) *Experiences of dialogue of civilizations: National, regional, global*, Programme for Dialogue of Civilizations, Cairo university (in Arabic).

Mostafa, N. M. (2004a) 'The Globalization challenges and Normative-cultural-civilizational aspects (an Islamic perspective)', in group of authors (2004) *The future of Islam*, Damascus: Dar El Fikr-el Arabi (in Arabic).

Mostafa, N. M. (2004b) 'The foreign political challenges to the Muslin world, the rise of the cultural aspects', in Mostafa, N. M. and Abdel Fattah, S. E. (eds) (2004) *The Ummah in a century*, volume 6 'The relevance of challenges, responses and initiative toward the future', Cairo: The Centre of Civilization for Political Studies (in Arabic).

Mostafa, N. M. (2004c) 'The first war of the 21st century', *International politics*, Cairo, January 2004 (in Arabic).

Mostafa, N. M. (2005a) 'The cultural aspects of the political-economic globalization', *Arab dialogue*, number 4, March 2005, Beirut (in Arabic).

Mostafa, N. M. (ed) (2005b) *Experiences and courses in dialogue of civilizations: Variant perspectives in a changing world*, Programme for Dialogue of Civilizations, Cairo University (in Arabic).

Mostafa, N. M. (2006a) 'The missing Logic in the discourse of peace and Violence in Islam', in Said, A-A., Abu-Nemr, M. and Sharify-Funk, M. (eds) (2006) *Contemporary Islam: Dynamic, not Static*, Oxford: Routledge.

Mostafa, N. M. (2006b) *The Danish cartoons and its consequences, Crisis in the course of dialogue of culture and religions: Reading in the significance of the relationship between Political and Cultural aspects, and in the conditions for just and equivalent Dialogue* (in Arabic): http://www.hewaronline.net/denmark/2lrosom2ldenemarkya.htm

Mostafa, N. M. (forthcoming) 'The cultural aspect of the Euro-Mediterranean partnership', in *The proceedings of international conference on 'Europe and the Euro-Mediterranean dialogue of cultures'*, organized in April 2005 by the Programme for Dialogue of Civilizations, Cairo University.

Mostafa, N. M. and Zeid, O. A. (eds) (2004) *Arab and Western discourses on dialogue of civilizations*, Programme for Dialogue of Civilizations, Cairo University (in Arabic).

Wanis, A. A. (1996) 'Legal Foundation and main principles for the external relations of Muslim state', volume 1, chapter 3 in Mostafa, N. M. (ed) (1996) *The project of International Relations in Islam* (in Arabic).

6

Fostering Intercultural Dialogue in the Euro-Mediterranean Area

Assia BenSalah Alaoui

Never has intercultural dialogue been more necessary. Never have the initiatives to promote it been so numerous. But never has the divide, especially between the 'West' and the 'Islamic World' been so deep and the cultural gap so wide. We can wonder: 'What went wrong with the dialogue between cultures'?[1] Why did 'The dialogue between cultures and civilizations [fail] the first critical test during the recent cultural crisis?'[2]

If the 'satirical cartoons', depicting the Prophet Muhammad[3] played only a catalyst role in the cultural crisis, as most seem to assume, then myriad questions have still to be answered.

'Accumulated frustrations in the Muslim world [having] their roots in the many unresolved conflicts affecting Muslims', as recently recalled by the Finnish Minister of Foreign Affairs, Erkki Tuomiojo, have still to be addressed. And so should many other inducing factors of structural violence, within the North/South divide.

There is a crying need for new strategies to foster dialogue between peoples and cultures. Intercultural dialogue is the only way to build the bridges of tomorrow for a shared future in our common space! It is a must to defeat the 'clash of civilizations' which was announced by Samuel Huntington and so well reinforced by Bin Laden after September 11th 2001, albeit in the minds of only a few. More profoundly, the dialogue is more necessary than ever to fight 'ignorance', which looms over all.

The question is then how to establish an efficient process for fostering dialogue. What corrections are needed to ongoing efforts? Are there success stories to build on and expand? Or is a novel approach and new strategies needed? How can a culture of dialogue be built? What roles are there for what stakeholders? Vast questions, to which this paper will attempt to provide some elements of answer.

The need for intercultural dialogue

How we look at diversity and at 'the other' is indeed at the core of how we behave. Is diversity an element of wealth, or a threat? Such questions are related to the nature and temper of each of us, to our historical, national and family backgrounds, to our environments and experiences, to our education. And in those respects, there are huge differences between, for example, well-read and well-travelled people and others.

The need for intercultural dialogue is equal only to the magnitude of the task which its achievement demands, and to the challenges of the present situations. Challenges are also inherent to culture itself.

Creating the future

If one believes with Paul Valéry that the essential function of man is to create the future, one will have no difficulty in grasping the very function of intercultural dialogue. Creating the future requires, first of all, a dialogue with ourselves and within nations. In this era, where frontiers between nations are blurred, and where identities are changing, we need to address our respective pasts, to revive the memory so central to the core identity of each of us, to help us understand and accept ourselves, in order to better accept the other; to heal the wounds of past conflicts and tensions as well as more vivid present ones. Creating the future is to pave the way, not for a cold peace, but for genuine reconciliation, a much more difficult exercize.

Creating the future is also confronting the present with its huge and complex challenges, including reducing inequality and exclusion within nations and between them. It is adapting through painful adjustments, fostering civil societies and securing the participation of all in a better shared socio-economic and political development. Creating the future is, finally, investing in children, creativity, and education. A life-long process is required to build the culture of dialogue, educate for peace, cultivate openness, and accompany the emergence of the new identities in the making, forged through cross-cultural practice and cross-fertilization.

Tremendous changes are occurring across the world, and many questions remain unanswered. There is a need for dialogue within the wider

Europe, which gets richer with new cultural heritages, languages and religions, where Islam is perceived as a challenge, and where the 'new Europeans', from immigration, are in need of better integration and harmony.

Dialogue is also necessary within the fragmented 'South', struggling with ill-development, and facing demographic, economic, political, migration and other sorts of transition. Before the long term benefits of democratic peace and potential prosperity through 'liberalization', the transition implies painful and costly adjustment, while instability is also inherent to modernization and political change.

Dialogue is necessary between the North and the South, including of course, the superpower, who is the dominant player in the Mediterranean. The question is how to find common ground between a North, obviously concerned about its security, and a South perceived as a threat to the prosperity and security of the North.

There is an urgent need to deconstruct mutual biased images. Complex images have been built over time by shared geography and history, but are lately subject to oversimplification, close to caricatures.

The dialogue is necessary also to humanise globalization, which affects all, but whose benefits go only to a few! Along with 'regionalization', globalization generates, on the one hand, integration of the 'knows' and the 'haves', between nations and among them and, on the other hand, exclusion of the 'know-nots' and 'have-nots'. One should be more aware of the devastating effects of the illiteracy and poverty across the southern shore, with sad records for women, who are the poorest of the poorer and the most illiterate of the ignorant!

Reappraisal of culture

Cultures are no longer invisible inner parts of us. They are increasingly exposed to erosion and transformation and need to be taken care of. However, for too long, culture has been marginalized. What room is there for culture, in an era when the ideal of nations is expressed in market shares and competitive gains, and when the globalization of risks and the privatization of violence have made security the top priority everywhere, while individual and collective security are extremely difficult to achieve? What room is there for cultural diversity in the era of the politically and culturally correct? What room is there for inter-cultural dialogue when culture and 'the sacred' are instrumentalized to contest the established order?

Cultures are sensitive domains, where ideologies can 'manipulate' despair and exclusion, which are not lacking nowadays! Among the mega-trends, 'standardization' of ways of life and behaviours can be observed mainly through consumption patterns, the media and the youth culture. Meanwhile, deep aspirations to differentiation are expressed across the planet. The return of culture and 'the sacred' to contest the established order, whether national or international, occurs among violence and fragmentation.

However, there is an urgent need for more expertise in the field of culture, just as for economics and politics. While time is a central component of culture, the information society imposes the acceleration of history. Culture seems confined to the past and patrimony, while it should be alive, nurturing all other sectors! Paradoxically, the context commands such a change but also makes it much more difficult.

The global and Mediterranean challenges

Beyond the global gloomy context, a number of events and evolutions seem to have made the Mediterranean more of a barrier than a bridge.

Rising cultural distance, cultural ignorance, and mutual misperceptions of Islam and the West are major challenges, which all learning devices and media should deal with. The Iranian revolution, the collapse of the USSR, the first Gulf war, the Balkan conflicts, the emergence of domestic instability, the rise of extremisms, of negative mutual perceptions and even xenophobia, the deepening of the prosperity gap... All these phenomena had already made the tow rims of the Mediterranean drift apart, leaving them sometimes with only common perils! Then came September 11th, the Afghanistan war, the global war against terrorism, striking on both rims of the Mediterranean, the radicalization of the Israeli-Palestinian conflict, and the quagmire in Iraq. There are great risks that the amalgam between Islam and terrorism further deepens the divide between the West and Islam, with the Mediterranean becoming the line of all fractures!

A new paradigm of development has to be elaborated – development as freedom, as A. Sen qualifies it. The vital link between development and security is more relevant than ever, particularly since the turning point of September 11th, as the reading of international relations through 'terrorism' has drastically altered the picture. With security as the top priority, attention and resources are diverted from development and human rights. However, providing genuine stakes to the concerned populations in their own societies, through socio-economic development and political participation, is the only valid base for sustainable security!

The global war against terror, as conducted, seems counterproductive, having become a war against 'Islam'! Ethnic profiling and discrimination against Arabs and Muslims across the United States and in some European countries further deepen the cultural divide.

The war against Iraq offered a vast field for conflicts and turmoil, from resistance to insurgency and all forms of criminality and terrorism. Moreover it introduced Al-Qaeda into a country where it was absent, giving that movement renewed strength. The presence of American soldiers in Iraq also offers 'icononic' targets – otherwise unreachable – along with the tremendous power of American and international medias. The extremists can, at no cost, considerably expand their recruiting base among young Arabs and Muslims, who are unemployed, resource weak, and angry.

What credibility is there then for the initiatives devised to promote democracy, equality, the rule of law and respect for human rights in the region? While international cooperation is more necessary than ever, its very legitimacy is questioned. What room is there for dialogue?

Initiatives for intercultural dialogue

In the vast field of intercultural dialogue, there was a promising trend of initiatives, seminars, conferences, declarations, recommendations, events, and so forth, especially after September 11th. Yet, the results are mixed and getting into concrete issues proves to be extremely challenging.

Reviewing what is being carried out on various levels is far beyond this framework. Rather, I would like to only mention a few noteworthy developments on the universal level, on the multilateral one, and some flagship achievements by some institutions and countries, before focussing on the Euro-Mediterranean area.

Enhanced cooperation at various levels

On the multilateral level, cooperation in this field is carried out mainly by the specialized institutions in education and culture: UNESCO for the universal level, ALECSO for the Arab world, ISESCO for the Islamic world (OIC), and more recently, the Anna Lindh Euro-Mediterranean Foundation for Dialogue between Cultures, to name only those relevant for our region.

The 'Convention on Cultural Diversity' is probably the best news in years. Expected for a long time, it was finally adopted by UNESCO on 20 October 2005, after lengthy and heated debates. Responsibility of implementing such a breakthrough text rests with all the respective parties.

However, for Europe, this Convention should not mean only the possibility to preserve the cultural specificity of European countries, and to protect, encourage and subsidize European artistic productions against the American landslide. Europe should also make sure to promote and implement cultural diversity. Special attention must be paid to the new Europeans, trapped between cultures and ill-integrated in their host countries, and especially to the alienation of younger generations. Europe is under watch. It should set the example with coherent and consistent policies, for its normative power is huge.

For Azouz Begag, the French minister, diversity should become more visible and commonplace, far beyond the special treatment reserved to stars, like the football player Zidane.[4] Education and innovative approaches should make diversity a natural part of European societies, including representation on TV screens.

Extremely diverse, the Arab world as well, has to pay particular attention to its minorities, which are sometimes the 'majority', like the Berbers in certain countries. Ethnicity and identity are not necessarily political factors per se, but can be rapidly mobilized and politicized. To live together in harmony, the diverse ethnic, religious and minority groups must be better integrated, and their participation in public positions duly enforced.

The UN is endeavouring to improve intercultural dialogue. At the initiative of the Iranian President Khatami, a special session on this theme, was held in the UN headquarters in New York in September 2000. More recently the 'Alliance of Civilizations' High Level Group, with a specific feature on Islam, was established by the Secretary-General Kofi Annan in response to the Turkish-Spanish proposal (see volume 2, by Candido Mendes).

However, 'the new divide over religion [which] is getting deeper and will not vanish even after the waves over the cartoons get lower' (Schofthaler 2006). A reason behind this gloomy prospect lies in the confrontation over the UN General Assembly Resolution 60/150 'Combating defamation of religions'.[5] This resolution was voted for on 16 December 2005, by 101 against 53 countries. The positive votes were those of all Arab, Muslim and non-'western' countries, while the no votes were those of EU and other 'western' countries. The resolution was submitted by the OIC alone to the Human Rights Commission in Geneva in April 2004, after the failure of the EU and OIC to go further than 'good will and common values' in the joint forum in Istanbul

(12–13 February 2002).[6] The resolution was accepted by two thirds against one third of the countries – the 'West against the rest of the world', as some western media put it. Actually, the West stood fast and refused the proposal of the OIC to include a special mentioning of 'discrimination of Muslims' in the resolution.

Notwithstanding this confrontation, dialogue seems to be progressing between Arab and Islamic institutions and other institutions in charge, as the 'Rabat Commitment' testifies.

This commitment, adopted on 16 June 2005, is a unique partnership initiative, testifying the importance of common ground among so diverse regions and institutions. Under the high patronage of His Majesty King Mohamed VI, six co-sponsor organizations – UNESCO, OIC, ISESCO, ALECSO, the Danish Centre for Culture and Development, and the Anna Lindh Euro-Mediterranean Foundation for Dialogue between Cultures – and the Council of Europe as an observer held the 'Conference on Fostering Dialogue among Cultures and Civilizations through Concrete and Sustained Initiatives' (Rabat, Morocco, 14–16 June 2005). The conclusions and recommendations of the conference represent a major and exhaustive platform to foster dialogue. It included visions, achievements, and recommendations within education, culture, and communication, from grass root issues to research. The hope rests with the capacity of the signatory institutions to translate the many proposals into real actions and behaviours of their constituencies!

ALECSO and ISESCO seem to be moving in the right direction. At the Abu Dhabi Expert Meeting, 4–7 January 2006, they jointly started the elaboration of 'principles of a balanced dialogue' which 'should be based on rationalism, scientific methods, and self-criticism'.

Some individual Arab initiatives and practices are also worth mentioning. The Bibliotheca Alexandrina, inaugerated five years ago, aims to become, among other domains of excellence, the 'Meeting point for dialogue and understanding between people', not only within the Arab world, but also between the Arabs and the rest of the world (www. bibalex.org). Under the direction of its dynamic director Ismail Serageldine, the Bibliotheca has taken a serious option on this trend as shown by the dazzling number of events, symposiums, conferences, and exhibitions that it organizes. The conference on 'Issues of Reform in the Arab World: Vision and Implementation', held with civil society institutions in the Arab world (12–14 March 2004) adopted the 'Alexandria Statement', which calls for 'the necessary and urgent' political, economic, social, and cultural reform.[7] The Bibliotheca also houses the Anna Lindh Euro-Mediterranean Foundation in partnership with the Swedish Institute in Alexandria, which is extremely active in the rapprochement between Europe and the Arab world and the West and the Islamic world at large.

Prince Hassan Bin Tallal of Jordan, endlessly advocates intercultural and interfaith dialogue on various fronts. His 'Arab Thought Forum' has built a solid credibility, he is very active in many other similar organizations, and his well-known eloquence and commitment to peace and dialogue are very present in western and Arab media.

Morocco has made dialogue a way of life. Its secular identity, but rich ethnic diversity has allowed this 12 centuries-old nation to develop a solid art of living together, with Islam and the Arabic language as the glue and with monarchy in a central role of mediation and federation. Morocco was the pioneer of, and is increasingly active in, the domains of intercultural and interfaith dialogue, not only on its own land but also abroad. King Mohamed V protected the Jewish Moroccan citizens against the Vichy regime during the Second World War. For decades, His Majesty Hassan II advocated a dialogue with Israel to spare loss of Arab land and lives, and mediated in the Middle East conflict, including in the success of Camp David.

His Majesty King Mohamed VI co-chairs with His Majesty King Juan Carlos of Spain the very dynamic 'Tres Culturas' Foundation. The last event held on 20 March 2006 brought together 400 Imams and Rabbins at a very tense moment of the Middle East conflict.

The 'Festival of sacred music of Fès', among the numerous festivals and intercultural events organized both by nationals and foreigners in Morocco, has become a flagship event in intercultural exchange, known across the world. For 15 years, music groups from all over the world, and particularly Muslim, Jewish and Christian ones, have been gathering for ten days, even at moments of great tension. Besides the official shows, the music expands in the whole city and in 'off-festival places', mixing youth from the entire world in a unique convivial atmosphere. 'The spirit of Fès Foundation' has also launched, the Fès informal seminars where, in pure African tradition under the 'centennial tree' of the Batha Museum, all the hot subjects are discussed, particularly 'divisive' ones which seem to make the West and the Islamic world drift apart. Remarkably, these events are attracting more outstanding American intellectuals and NGOs every year.

A lot is being carried out in the European countries as well, especially in Scandinavia as testified by this book. However, the rise of far-right parties, the restrictive policies on immigration, the failure of integration policies, terrorist acts, and some violent outbursts such as the turmoil in French suburbs in November 2005, destroy the benefits of the endeavours. Such trends also give a flavour of the huge and difficult task which must still be carried out on all levels, especially in our common area.

The Euro-Mediterranean area

The most structured dialogue between peoples and cultures seem to have been initiated in the Euro-Mediterranean area. From the 'High Level Advisory Group', set by Romano Prodi in 2002, to the creation of the Anna Lindh Foundation and the Euro-Mediterranean Parliamentary Assembly, to the launching, in June 2006, of the 'Ibn Khaldoun' network of universities, the dialogue is being translated into concrete actions.

The 'High Level Advisory Group on Dialogue Between Culture and Peoples in the Euro-Mediterranean Area'

In October 2002, Romano Prodi created this group to rethink intercultural dialogue, in the context of a wider Europe and of the Euro-Mediterranean Partnership. The initiative stemmed from all the concerns identified above, and bearing in mind – in the terms of the UNESCO Constitution – that 'since wars begin in the minds of men, it is in the minds of men that the defences of peace must be constructed'.

With this strong conviction and enthusiasm, I accepted Romano Prodi's invitation, to co-chair this group with Jean Daniel. It functioned in harmony for about one year, perhaps thanks to the diversity of nationalities, religions, genders, expertise and experiences – and despite the hugeness of the egos of the intellectuals. There was an intercultural dialogue in process, and a report and concrete proposals were produced, published on the EU website in all Euro-Mediterranean languages.

'The High Level Advisory Group' established that the dialogue between peoples and cultures needs to be based on founding principles (European Commission 2004). It has to be materialized in concrete projects and actions, and carried out within an institutional framework. General principles are well known: respect of the other, freedom of conscience and worship, equality in diversity, solidarity, and knowledge prevailing over impressions. Operational principles comprise equity, cooperation, cross-fertilization and co-ownership. The proposals concern all stakeholders: states, local bodies, civil society, and NGOs. Focussing on the human dimension, the identified proposals evolve around three main domains: education, mobility and exchange, and the media.

– Education, especially education to diversity, appears to be the cornerstone of cross-cultural dialogue.

Pedagogy of diversity has to be promoted and implemented, as has lifelong education, raising the awareness of cultural diversity, and allowing us to better digest our respective pasts to prepare us better for our common future!

Education of the youngest is crucial, as is education of women, who have a central role to play, but who are suffering from poverty and illiteracy. The trickle-down effect of the education of women can never be overemphasized!

The group has also recommended comparative teaching of religions. Knowledge about religion is important to be a good citizen, even for atheists!

Furthermore, shared knowledge is promoted. The Centres for Mediterranean studies should improve and expand knowledge about our common sea. A 'Braudel-Ibn Khaldoun network' of university professors should be created and connected to the Jean Monet one.

Short-, medium- and longer-term actions should prepare everybody for exposure to 'the other' and for taking responsibility. This lifelong process is completed by the second cluster of proposals.

– Mobility and exchange of experience in all fields are extremely fruitful avenues to promote the daily practice of intercultural dialogue.

The group has proposed a number of actions such as the creation and development of networks of civic meeting places to foster dialogue between social groups and generations, and voluntary service for the youth on both rims and across the Mediterranean. So exchanges are more necessary than ever to promote mutual knowledge and fight stereotypes. They must be carried out on a much larger scale, particularly among the youth.

– Last, but not least, media has a central responsibility in the pedagogy of diversity. They are indeed vital vectors of mutual knowledge and intercultural dialogue.

Proposals in this field evolve around training, elaborating specific programmes and developing new media vehicles. Media students, journalists, and teachers must be trained to face cultural diversity. Their awareness about their responsibility needs to be drastically raised, far from the devastating stereotypes and misconceptions often conveyed. They should make knowledge prevail over impressions. Studies which defeat commonly admitted mutual biased images should be widely publicized.

To foster mutual knowledge in the common area, specific programmes, co-produced ones, and satellite channels connecting people should be developed. The creation in Qatar of 'Al Jazeera Children's Channel' in September 2005 provides an interesting South-North initiative and joint venture in that respect.[8] It could, if properly managed, help foster the so badly needed integration of the Arab world.

The group has also recommended the creation of an independent media observatory, linked to the Euro-Mediterranean Foundation.

Promoting the emergence of 'the Euro-Mediterranean of peoples and societies', next to that of states, is the rationale behind the Prodi report, which has largely inspired a number of institutions and particularly the Anna Lindh Euro-Mediterranean Foundation for the Dialogue between Cultures.[9]

This rationale is behind the establishment of all the Euro-Mediterranean Partnership institutions.

The Euro-Mediterranean Partnership institutions

– The Euro-Mediterranean Parliamentary Assembly, established in Naples in December 2003, 'will enable parliamentarians from both sides of the Mediterranean to exchange ideas on how a democratic system should function in a modern state, on how to fight terrorism and organized crime while respecting human rights and the rule of law, including an independent Judiciary. The Assembly will also provide a forum for Parliamentarians from countries like Morocco or Jordan to present their experiences of pursuing democratic reform within a system fully respectful of Islam'.[10] On 27 March 2006, the assembly adopted a detailed resolution, urging all political representatives of the Euro-Mediterranean Partnership 'to abstain from any action or attitude which might offend religions and/or provoke any hostile acts in respective public opinions'. The assembly has subscribed to the proposal of eight Arab countries to call 'on the Anna Lindh Euro-Mediterranean Foundation to take action conducive to the establishment of [...] an ad hoc committee, including wise persons and experts from both shores of the Mediterranean, to strengthen mutual knowledge among peoples and intercultural dialogue and mediation'.

– The Anna Lindh Euro-Mediterranean Foundation for the Dialogue between Cultures was initiated by the Valencia Action Plan, and finally created by the Euro-Mediterranean Ministerial Conference in Dublin on 6 May 2004.[11] Based in the Bibliotheca Alexandrina and the Swedish Institute in Alexandria, the Foundation will act as the network of national networks.[12] The Foundation is supposed to receive input from the civil society in the Mediterranean countries. Its mission is to allow the differences to dialogue and to promote education to diversity.

After a rather slow beginning, the initial projects identified by the Foundation seemed encouraging: 'our common future', 'avenues for multiperspectivity', 'creative diversity', 'sciences without frontiers', and 'information society'. Since then, the last programme, 'women and gender equality', recalls the mission statement, identifies the strategy, the modalities of action, and details the components of the six flagship projects, the other projects relying on synergy actions and added value.

On 16 February 2006 the Foundation presented a 'Draft strategy and action plan for re-launching the dialogue between cultures in the Euro-Mediterranean region'. The strategy draws lessons from the failure of the dialogue. It proposes to capitalize on best practices, as the High Level Group had recommended, ensure the follow-up of texts and explore new avenues. The key argument underlines that the dialogue failed because its traditional modalities focussed for the last decades on what cultures and religions have in common, instead of on differences and diversity, based on the common value of non-discrimination. The Foundation was invited, on 22 February 2006, to present this strategy to the meeting of the EuroMed Committee, during which the EU Commission presented a 'Decalogue' of instruments regrouping ten Euro-Mediterranean regional programmes, projects and networks.

However we can deplore that a few guidelines and proposals formulated by the High Level Advisory Group have not been followed by the Euro-Mediterranean officials. We had insisted on the autonomy of the foundation in all respects: conceptual, financial, and administrative. The states are rather reluctant to lose such control, and the bureaucratic EU procedures and methods which were imposed for its 'light' administrative structure, had already considerably delayed its launching and real work.

Neither have they been generous in the allocation of funds, which are extremely modest considering the importance and scope of its mission.[13] The efficiency of the Foundation and the very spirit of this innovative initiative may be endangered by the drawbacks of the broader Euro-Mediterranean Partnership.

The Anna Lindh Foundation represents our common permanent institution, our common home in a way, where each of us, no matter his rim of origin, can feel at home. It carries people's hope, demonstrating, I hope, that institutionalization and innovation are not an antinomy.

– The Ibn Khaldoun Univerties' Network has been proposed by the Prodi Report to improve connectivity and interaction among the knowledge-based institutions across the Euro-Mediterranean area. Such a network should promote multilateralism among the ongoing cooperation between universities of the two shores, improve the dialogue, knowledge and expertise exchange, in line with the philosophy of the European neighbourhood policy 'share all, but the institutions'.

New strategies and novel approaches

To re-launch the intercultural dialogue on viable bases and enhance its impact and cost-effectiveness, new strategies and novel approaches are necessary, some of which are discussed below:

Implementation, follow-up, and building on best practices

Common sense invites us to capitalize on previous experiences. Though innovative approaches and new strategies seem necessary to face the mighty challenges, one cannot reinvent the wheel indefinitely. The progress and innovations do build on humanity's huge memory.

First of all the most noteworthy recommendations, enshrined in diverse and numerous texts, which are the fruits of long endeavours, like the 'Convention on Cultural Diversity' or the 'Rabat Commitment', mentioned above, have to be implemented. 'One cannot change the society by decree', as wrote the French sociologist Michel Crozier. To be effective, laws and recommendations have to generate states' practices and individual behaviours, which pave the way for societal change. Follow-up is also critical. Too often, lack of financial and/or human resources, among other things, prevents initiatives and projects from being finalized and producing full impact.

For the sake of capitalizing on previous experiences and avoiding duplication and waste, and for permanent innovation and dialogue, The High Level Advisory Group proposed the establishment of a task force within the Euro-Mediterranean Foundation. This unity would identify best practices, listening to suggestions from all over the Euro-Mediterranean and beyond. I still believe that such a task force may be valuable to save time and expand the process. Although not totally in line with this proposal, the Anna Lindh Foundation seems to be moving in that direction. It has proposed to establish an 'observatory' of good practices, and other institutions follow this trend. The Rabat Commitment recommends that 'international and regional organizations should identify, document and analyse 'best practice' approaches...'

Identification of stakeholders' roles

Given the changing functions of the various stakeholders in dialogue and education, their respective roles must be clearly identified, for increased complementarities and synergies. In the era of the retrenchment of states, and of intertwined public and private spheres, it is the relations between civil societies, NGOs, intellectual and cultural institutions, business firms, private sectors, and so forth, which will make up the very substance of the Euro-Mediterranean partnership. The Mediterranean is a place of close contact, where looks, flavours, smells, and words exchanged play a central role.

Beyond the changing roles of the *states* and their 'disengagement', they still play an important role in shaping the framework of our daily life. They have to elaborate environments which secure freedom and facilitate initiatives and creativity. The states still play a central role in education and in border control, even in the very integrated EU. These two domains are critical, as we will see, for intercultural dialogue.

On the one hand, it is imperative that the southern countries, individually and collectively, do their homework, clean up their own backyards, and carry out the appropriate reforms to provide a better life and participation for all their citizens. In particular, they have to carry out wide reforms and, especially in education systems, promote a culture of openness and tolerance. For the very dignity of the people – we know that dignity represents a cardinal virtue in the region – the Arab governments have to address the expectations of a growing, and overwhelmingly young population. They have to change the realities on the ground for the better, in their respective countries. Some have indeed launched ambitious reforms. Morocco, for instance, has considerably consolidated the democratization process, the rule of law and respect for human rights. Additionally, vast economic and social reforms, refocussing on human development, are paving the way for increased international investment.

On the other hand, the European Union and its member countries must pay special attention to their southern frontier. With its colonial past, its geographic proximity and overwhelming asymmetries, Europe has to reassure,, and not threaten, its Mediterranean neighbours. It has to restore confidence in the Euro-Mediterranean partnership through an effective rethinking of the whole process. Barcelona plus ten seems to have been a lost opportunity for such an exercize! There is certainly a need for a more even-handed strategy in the Arab-Israeli conflict and a more coherent approach, making sure that the practice is conforming to the prevailing speech!

The local bodies and decentralized cooperation between the two rims also have a crucial role to play. They can secure better knowledge of the backgrounds and environments, facilitating implementation, follow-up and creativity. Despite obvious disparities and asymmetries of players, means, and procedures, 'proximity-cooperation' offers a great potential for enhancing dialogue. Moreover, exchange of experiences and best practices foster mutual knowledge, understanding and tolerance. Some regions, particularly in southern Europe, are seriously engaged in such activities. An association like 'L'Arc Latin' is endeavouring to build bridges over the Mediterranean Sea and share learning with their southern Mediterranean counterparts.

The respective regions and autonomies like PACA in France, or Andalucia, Cataluna, and Madrid Communidad in Spain, deploy many efforts to initiate and improve cooperation with the southern regions. There is certainly room for innovation to support the endeavours of the emerging locally-elected bodies in the South for the promotion of development, democracy and openness. Associating the South at early stages, as the Communidad of Madrid did in February 2005 for the elaboration of its cooperation development plan, is certainly a very encouraging example.

Civil societies and NGOs, which are emerging and blossoming in the Arab countries, should play an important role in the dialogue between the two rims of the Mediterranean. They cannot be a substitute for political parties as some are tempted to think, but they have a significant role to play in the reforms and the democratization processes. They are still embryonic in certain countries, and sometimes between 'repression' and 'recuperation' and there are still suspicions about their lack of transparency, real intents, and financing. However, they can play an important role in the learning process, to promote an open society, raise consciousness, facilitate and disseminate knowledge, and carry out tasks complementary to schools.

Women in particular have a unique role in promoting intercultural dialogue. They do play a central role in development at large, often under the shadow of discrimination. Moreover, they are at the centre of polemics about the future of the region. The evolving situations are challenging men, women, governments, and societies at large to re-evaluate the status and roles of women across the region. I would like to support the view that beyond the gloomy indicators of the Gender empowerment measure (GEM) – lagging behind in a region itself lagging behind! – the improvement of women's status and empowerment can be a key to enhancing, speeding-up, and expanding reforms. The recent amendment of the family code in Morocco illustrates such a turning point, launching a cultural revolution. The new code, which came into force in January 2004, grants equal responsibility in managing family matters to women, whose rights have been upgraded to meet such an aim and responsibility. Such a move has wide ranging impact: harmonization of legislation, acceleration of the judiciary reform, creation of special family courts, and training of judges in implementing the new law. Campaigns of 'legal literacy' and massive literacy – to allow men to better understand and admit, and women to better exercize their new rights – have been launched, partly in mosques. The use of mosques can help restore the real message of Islam, which prefers 'the ink of the erudite to the blood of the martyr'!

The Moroccan approach is the fruit of an encounter of two wills, two legitimacies: the considerable grassroots work carried out by human rights and women's organizations for over a decade, and the royal will to enhance the respect for human rights and consolidate democracy. This is an even greater determination in that respect by His Majesty Mohamed VI, after the terrorist attacks on 16 May 2003.

Special attention has to be paid to the youth and their increasing expectations. Next to job creation, education, including education to diversity, is the biggest challenge for the Arab region.

Education tools and approaches

Reforming education systems to improve education to diversity and peace is urgent on both rims of the Mediterranean.

Traditional learning tools should be modernized and updated. Despite new technologies, textbooks are still a major – often the only – instrument for educating students in the Arab world. They enjoy a strong normative and legitimating power, and have to be used as instruments of peace-building. Unfortunately however, they are often outdated and expensive.

They need to become free from stereotypes, and move from 'negative tolerance to inclusiveness' (Hopken 2004: 142). Joint textbook revision among former enemies to comply with new contexts, for instance, must be part of a more comprehensive strategy. It requires not only favourable political environments, but also time and strong commitment, as testified by the history textbook which was recently jointly published by the French and the Germans.

New tools and technologies have a great potential for knowledge dissemination. However, the youth at large must learn to confront the 'non culturally-correct' programmes and devices in order to develop their own capacity of analysis, criticism, and defence. Here, the youngest and the most vulnerable must be protected and prepared. The internet, for instance, can channel stereotypes, hatred, and extreme violence.

Curricula should be revised to meet the challenge of diversity. Student teachers and in-service teachers should be exposed to a paradigm of critical multicultural education, transcending the liberal four Ds: 'dance, diet, dress, dialect'. Self-criticism about one's own contradictions should pave the way for positive hybridization and multiculturalism, along with the teaching of languages, especially of the Euro-Mediterranean area. Languages are a key component of intercultural education, ensuring respect for human rights. Here, the three UNESCO principles should be implemented. First, support of mother tongue instruction is basic. The Arabic language, for instance, should be reinforced not only at home but also in Europe and expanded to pupils who are not of Arabic descent, to give them opportunities to know Arabic culture better. Minority languages, as part of national wealth, have to be taught. Languages are not only a medium of communication, but provide opportunities to learn and reflect on other ways of life, literatures, and customs. So bilingual and/or multilingual education, at all levels, as a means of promoting social and gender equality, is a key element of diversity. Reading materials and adequate learning resources must be supplied.

Alleviate obstacles for mobility and exchanges

Socio-cultural exchanges are taking place on the bilateral level, between EU member states and their southern partners. This trend is developing between cities, regions, economic operators, cultural institutions, and civil societies, and so forth. However, these promising trends meet tremendous obstacles that prevent the expansion of exchanges and the maximization of the impact of the initiatives, and at times nourish frustrations and resentment. We touch here on the major contradiction of the Euro-Mediterranean Partnership, whose ambition is to promote democracy and civil society, but who does it mainly through intergovernmental means. The states in a globalizing world are still hampering free circulation of people, despite the Euro-Mediterranean Partnership promise to 'share [with them] everything except the institutions'. Free circulation is hampered by increasingly restrictive migration policies.

After September 11th 2001, there is a serious and increasing trend towards very restrictive immigration policies in contradiction with a globalizing world. Migration has dominated the news for a few years, with its dramatic images and heated debates. I would like to make just a few observations about this very complex phenomenon.

Involving over 170 millions people a year, migration will not stop. Rather, it is expanding, particularly in the Euro-Mediterranean region, where it is favoured by the demo-economic unbalance, making Europe a real magnet that no Schengenland, no specialized agency can isolate!

Migration is a happy phenomenon, rich in potential cross-fertilization. However, it is a source of growing tension: North/South, South/South, and even North/North. Moreover, Arabs and Muslims in general, are often seen in Europe through the biased lenses of immigration. Migration implies multidimensional stakes: cultural, political, security related, and economic, bearing in mind that the transfer of remittances are higher than the FDI and development aid combined. There are huge challenges ahead of recipient countries, sending and transit countries, and of the migrant themselves.

The management of this problem within the Euro-Mediterranean Partnership is far from satisfactory. Migration has dominated the third basket, hampered its impact and moved to the first basket, i.e. the political and security one, without receiving the rational strategic treatment that it deserves. Migration should be better managed by all stakeholders together: in the interest of an ageing Europe that needs new blood to pay its pensions and maintain its living standards, of developing sending and transit countries who face tremendous transition problems, and of the migrants themselves and their rights and dignity!

The promise of the European Neighbourhood Policy to share with the Mediterranean partners 'everything except the institutions' may become a simple slogan contradicted by actual behaviour. Joint North-South research programmes, through a comprehensive approach around the three terms – demography, migration-integration, and brain-drain – should be developed!

The prospects for selective migration legislation in France lately, for instance, are frightening. Beyond lost opportunities for many, there is a great risk that this unlawful competition will drain our countries of our best trained human resources. Ironically, the South will end up paying for the education and training of the North! Moreover, in the present knowledge society, the knowledge gap will further deepen the prosperity gap and perpetuate the vicious circle of poverty. Significant steps have to be taken to curb this trend, as the 2003 UNDP Arab Human Development Report recommends.

Enhancing partnerships and connectivity

Building partnerships, networking and connectivity have become keys to living in the globalizing world, and to improving impacts and efficiency. Such modalities also pave the way for genuine open-minded behaviour and favour intercultural dialogue at all levels.

The few examples below give an idea of the potential of partnership in fostering dialogue.

Ahmed Medhoune, a Belgian citizen of Moroccan origin, professor in the free university of Brussels (ULB), in partnership with the Ministry of Secondary and special Education, the Official Authorities of the Francophone Community of Brussels, and with the collaboration of the Executive Representatives of the Muslims of Belgium, published a small book, in French entitled: 'L'Islam, vous connaissez?'(Islam: do you know it?). The clear objective is to bring forward a better understanding of Islam, which is at the centre of polemics, not to say hostility (Bouhoute et al. 2003). The targets are the teachers, the students, and the larger audience and public. The book offers many advantages. First of all, it enjoys a double legitimacy of the representatives of Islam and the authorities of the host country. Second, the book is short and simple, and sheds light on the essential pillars of Islam. It offers a base of discussion, through the information it provides. It seeks to deconstruct misconceptions about the second religion in Belgium. Misconceptions of Islam are persistent and widespread among the European public opinion.

The second initiative, also conducted in Brussels by the same young man, received the UNESCO reward of 'the best education action in the world' in 2004. Ahmed Medhoune imagined a programme of tutorship, carried out by Belgian students for younger immigrant students, in order to fight school failure.[14] Beyond the obvious benefits for the targeted pupils and their community, this operation sends various messages. It shows the sense of responsibility of young immigrants, who are perceived by host countries as problems, but who can also offer solutions. The very process recreates the social link, solidarity channels and, above all, better understanding among citizens. This example which restores hope could be expanded and adapted elsewhere. It should be largely funded to give incentives and income to students.

An experience from Egypt shows the importance of innovation and partnerships, which could be provided by international cooperation in education for peace. A pedagogic tool was developed in Alexandria, to provide an initiation to archaeology and Egyptian history, but as a sort of game: the 'trunk' ('la malle'). Under the auspices of a French research institute, many stakeholders are engaged in partnership to implement this programme: the local authorities of the PACA region in France, the Ministry of Education of Egypt, the city of Alexandria, and the Bibliotheca Alexandrina acting as a catalyst and offering its premises to the young participants. This tool offers the opportunity for pupils from public and private schools, from Moslem and Coptic backgrounds, to move from learning through books to learning through doing. As in a game, they undo the trunk completely and discover archaeology. The programme is part of the European 'Youth and sports'. Numbers of beneficiaries are still modest, but the potential is great.[15] Beyond the difficulty to coordinate so many partners, this is a perfect example of partnership, capitalizing on specific strengths and expertise, and developing synergies to promote diversity and education for peace in the Euro-Mediterranean area.

The need for comprehensive strategies

Just as the survival of the planet demands a change of our devastating lifestyles and the adoption of environmentally-friendly behaviour, for the survival of humanity we need to kick the confrontation habit and build a culture of dialogue, generating dialogue-friendly actions and attitudes.

Comprehensive strategies and the involvement of whole societies are required, through a whole spectrum of short-term and long-term measures! Building the culture of dialogue, fighting stereotypes, changing mind-sets and behaviour, promoting mutual knowledge and tolerance, are life-long processes and shared responsibilities. Learning is at the core of such a holistic approach. Education to diversity and learning to live together require re-focussing policies on the human dimension.

Stereotypes and misperceptions must be challenged within wider contexts, across a variety of sources: the curricula, textbooks, popular media, the internet and influences of arts, associations, and civil society, which need to be assertive and proactive.

Language is a key component to foster diversity. New avenues are being explored. A decision has been taken to apply the approach used to promote gender issues in the institutions to intercultural dialogue, starting with the language. Too much work has been carried out on universal values. Cultural and religious differences have to be addressed. The challenge is to build a common language for the differences and terminology which excludes discrimination.

Vocabulary matters. As Douglas E. Strusand writes: 'leaders, journalists, authors, and speakers must use the most accurate terms to describe ideas'. By using the words 'Jihad and Djihadist', which are positive terms for Muslims 'we [the US] designate ourselves as the enemies of Islam' (National Defense University 2006). However, we can deplore that the author uses the expression 'Islamic Terrorism' in the title of this very paper precisely about language! Over 1.3 billion Muslims feel offended by such a qualifier linked to Islam at large when only a few extremists are using biased interpretations of Islam to justify their horrible acts. Muslims feel discriminated against as well. For decades, terrorism has been inflaming Ireland, but has never been qualified as 'Catholic' terrorism!

There is a crucial need to move away from the strategy of confrontation with Islam, which is prevailing in the West, despite the rhetoric of denial. How can one fight what they call the 'Jihad' and practice 'Crusades', a word actually used by President Bush? Moreover, notwithstanding the freedom of expression, the satirical cartoons depicting the Prophet Muhammad, illustrate at best ignorance and at worst provocation! Societies should show more sense of responsibility and not put oil on fire, deepening the cultural divide and resentment in this particularly tense context.

Stereotypes and biased images are often hard to change! It is important, for instance, to correct the 'amnesia', duly maintained in Europe about the role played by the Arabs in the Renaissance, and about Islam's contribution to universal civilization!

I am aware that there is an initiative fatigue in the Mediterranean. Moreover, proliferation in this field is certainly counterproductive. However, I have long been advocating a larger institution on the Mediterranean level.

A permanent institution for the Mediterranean

Only a permanent institution for the Mediterranean, with the dominant Mediterranean player – the US – along with the European countries and all other Mediterranean countries, enjoying equal status, thus becoming real and responsible players, and not only mere figureheads of their own history, could help restore genuine dialogue and confidence in the area.

Such a permanent institution should be located on the Mediterranean shores, far from Brussels, which houses already the NATO headquarters and the EU institutions. Such visibility is important for the sphere of symbols, but also to make up for the democratic deficit, which is the first characteristic of the relational 'order' in the Mediterranean.

Within this institution, cooperation among all the stakeholders would have to prevail over devastating competitive strategies and unilateralism, so detrimental to both development and peace. It could offer the framework, where we could all together deconstruct terror, avoiding the sinister synergy of terrorism and exclusion, and building development and peace.

We are all aware that cross-cultural dialogue will not wipe out conflicts and tensions. It is true that culture and identity often lie at the heart of the world's most intricate conflicts. They are the domains where sidelined and wounded identities express themselves violently. But they are also the only realm which provides the ammunition to solve conflicts peacefully and prevent them!

Intercultural dialogue is neither a panacea, nor an end in itself. Rather it is the modus operandi to make cooperation prevail over confrontation and conviviality over conflicts, these contradictions being inherent to life itself. We need to make sure that we can use our different cultures as bridges that bring us closer together, not barriers that drive us apart. Dialogue is the only vehicle to achieve this aim.

Notes

1. Traugot Schoefthaler, Executive Director of the Anna Lindh Foundation in a speech to the Forum 'Europe in Dialogue and Interaction between Cultures' at the Finnish-Swedish Cultural Centre/Hanaforum, Helsinki, Finland, 5 April 2006.
2. President Husni Mubarak's declaration during the Khartoum Summit of the League of Arab States, 27 March 2006.
3. In September 2005, the Danish newspaper Jyllands-Posten published satirical cartoons depicting the Prophet Muhammad, which a few months later provoked extremely violent protests across the Islamic World.
4. Interview with the French minister in Le Monde, 11–12 September 2005.
5. Presented by western countries and supposed to be 'more balanced', a resolution on 'Elimination of all forms of intolerance and discrimination based on religion and belief' was adopted by consensus the same day (UN AG 60/166).
6. The EU-OIC (Organization of the Islamic Conference) joint forum on the political dimensions of 'civilizations and harmony'.
7. The conference was organized by the Bibliotheca in collaboration with Arab Academy for Science and Technology, Arab Business Council, Arab Women's Organization, Economic Arab Forum and Arab Organization of Human Rights. For further information, consult the Bibliotheca website, and especially theme 9 of the project proposals.

8. This was a joint venture between a Qatar Fund and the French group of A. Lagardère. See Le Figaro, 10–11 September 2005.
9. 'The foundation is the first concrete action of the neighbourhood policy – as Mr Prodi said – based on the principles of co-responsibility, co-ownership and on dialogue among equals, it should be the agent of cross cultural dialogue, between our civil societies and within them.'
10. Speech by Chris Patten at the Oxford Centre for Islamic Studies, 24 May 2004.
11. The foundation was named after Anna Lindh, former Minister of Foreign Affairs of Sweden, assassinated on 11 September 2003, both to pay tribute to her exceptional personal qualities and as a dedication to 'the other' and to the dialogue.
12. The Foundation is set on a non-governmental basis, with a light and independent administrative structure – a director, Traugott Shofhaler, named for three years, and no more than eight staff members.
13. The Commission has promised 5 million euros and the member states should grant an equivalent amount. However, almost one year after its creation, the funds had not been disbursed.
14. In 15 years, about 1,000 undergraduates have helped 8,000 pupils at the secondary level to achieve 80 per cent success in their exams.
15. From October 2004 to June 2005, 1,700 pupils participated in the programme.

References

Bouhoute, H., Manço, U. and Medhoune, A. (2003) *L'Islam, vous connaissez?*, Communauté Wallonie Bruxelles.

European Commission (2004) Dialogue between Peoples and Culture in the Euro-Mediterranean Area, European Communities, Luxembourg, 2004.

Hopken, W. (2004) 'Learning to live together: fighting stereotypes', in UNESCO (2004) *New Ignorances, New Literacies, Learning to live together in a globalizing world*, Paris: UNESCO.

National Defense University (2006) Choosing Words Carefully: Language to help fight Islamic Terrorism, Center for Strategic Communication, LTCD, Tunell IV, Working Draft.

Schofthaler, T. (2006) *What went wrong with dialogue?*, Doc. n° 67/06, p.4, Anna Lindh Foundation, Alexandria, 25 April 2006.

UNESCO (2004) *New Ignorances, New Literacies, Learning to live together in a globalizing world*, Paris: UNESCO.

7
Globalization, Hegemony and Difference

Candido Mendes

Any concern nowadays with the world after September 11th has to deal not only with the 'civilization of fear', out of the general alert to terrorism, but also with the inducement of globalization into the emergent logics of hegemony. The crisis of the Prophet's cartoons and the condemnation of the evangelism of Bush as the embodiment of the West are just initial examples of a world torn into reciprocal fundamentalisms. We moved far away from the 'culture of peace' and from a possible international détente, as envisaged in the 1990s, after the thaw of the Cold War. Are we just following the threat of the much widespread idea of a 'clash of civilizations', probably already anticipated as a 'war of religions'?

Or is there room for a completely different scenario: an 'Alliance of Civilizations' as I will argue.

First let me outline the global ideological landscape in the globalized condition.

Any attempt to look for a new global 'vis-à-vis' has to start with the discussion of the Huntingtonian idea of a 'clash of civilizations' by the analysis of that concept and the correlative one of a 'culture'. It requires an epistemological approach, to avoid, in any search for a world dialogue, the disruption of irretrievable semantic gaps (Bessis 2002).

Civilization refers to the broad impact of technology and rationalization upon nature and the social collectivity – giving birth to the objective transformation of man's context to the benefit of his needs and wellbeing. Culture concerns the emergence of a sense within a collectivity, responding to its inner perception of its identity, as 'being in the world' (Heidegger 2006) and becoming a subject of freedom and difference.

The present clash may have come out of a sudden global feeling or perception of the Islamic world, of being hurt by a trespassing of the process of civilization into the cultural one, with the reification (Lukács 1967) of the subjective realm, and the deprivation of the collective self.

What is at stake in the present reflection is the rendering of such an approach, and its effects, among the remaining cultures of the world, and the difficulties raised – after September 11th – for a comeback to the culture of peace, as a simple return to the ethics of overcoming conflicts, without the appraisal of the visions of the world involved to the extreme of confrontation at the verge of becoming hegemonic (Nair 2003).

An holistic approach to culture and civilization

The first half of the last century showed how, in the encompassing idea of the process of history, the very key concept of culture moves from the Weberian, to the Lukacsian-Marxist revision and to the Frankfurt School, in order to assure the holistic stance required to face the risks of an expropriation of a collective subjectivity.

The idea of civilization, under such perspective, involves a dialectic counterpoint to the one of culture, at the edge where universals move in the interplay between idiomacy and identity.

On the general acknowledgement of the present 'state of the world', the overcoming of the September 11th syndrome implies not only the assumption of the West as the *lieu* – the place – of civilization, but also of its reified way to be perceived in its development, both in terms of technological achievements and power controls, and of its representation, turned into a simulacrum. The threshold of the new era shows this defined universal extension of the West, along with the imposition of its reified inner self, to the context it permeates, seen previously as the necessary sequence – in the Hegelian sense of the word – of the 'realm of reason'.

The fall of the Twin Towers happened at the moment of the final virtualization, as stressed by Baudrillard and Valiente Noailles (2005), of this long-standing attempt to seize a world subjectivity. Cultures are thus faced with this literal abduction, and not any more with a loose domination by an imperial power. Such a catastrophic 'limit-situation' disrupts the former development of the process of 'meaning-building' within history, seen as the long-run consciousness-raising in terms of a social self. Difference, its end-product, draws from a memory work through the interplay of a unique individual and collective identity. No 'other' is the distinctive matrix in the networking of this process, built on protagonisms and remembrances that mould its social players, through the achievement of a 'vision of the world' and the 'style of life' it embeds.

The present impending virtualization, indeed, supposes a different stand to the classical clashes of the old dominance of the West as 'the' civilization. The 'outer' cultures are no more exposed to a face-to-face, in an interplay that could subsist – still – at the threshold of the technological involvement and its full embracement. Nowadays, along with such a 'built-in' seizure, the West reverberates already in its simulacra, in framing any collective identity in the same looking-glass.

The unique, the uniform, the various

Globalization is thus identified, in the cognitive dimension, with the imperative of search and imposition of 'the unique, in the face of uniformity, above and beyond that of uniformity in the face of variety' (Sztompka and Alexander 1990), in contrast to the tolerance with the particular, as we have been accustomed to in the former spontaneous keeping of a subjectivity under classic dominations. Because of this conditioning of consciousness by uniformity, globalization erodes the impact of representation on the objective set of historical causation. How to react to this tendency in the name of freedom and self-determination of the human adventure? This amounts to seeing the existence of pluralism as a constitutive feature of cultural policy to the extent that it is open to the direct intervention of social reflection on history. Here lies the urgency of the imperative of difference in the context of globalization. This imperative can be considered to be a heuristic requirement, even before we have decided whether the present process of multicausation has an open or a closed nature. In this complex situation, we do not know yet whether the new system seems closed by the repeated accumulation of its multiple variables, or whether it shapes them in successive repercussions. In this case, there would be interactions and counter-responses implying representations and performances extraneous to the new external order. This would mean a dissonant subjectivity, for the good of difference, in the context of an open globalization (Lamchichi 2001a, 2001b).

In any case, in the inner world the ongoing process leaves no doubt as to the countervailing and founding action of the imperative of differentiation in the face of the unsettling effect that the modernizing 'disembedding' (Giddens 1991), as an early consequence of globalization, has already had on the subjective architecture of these collectivities. The reducing impact of the new order tends to affect the consciousness with previously formed identities, whether deriving from the consciousness-raising in regard to successful development, abortive change, or to the structures and routines of ages-old tradition. But it is on the basis of such niches that resist the new currents that difference is still built at the heart of the cultural policies of our time. The territory where these policies are active is all the more threatened by the fact that the induction of a collective specificity now relies on the existence of exceptional pockets of resistance to a uniformization of contemporary subjectivity, which takes place simultaneously with the disrupting effect of modernization and the systemic multi-dependence of globalization. In the struggle against the raising of innerness, remnants have all the value of reality, and the figurations of true development and its projection, however mimetic, have the worth of good currency for a reflection that is still differentiated and able, in any case, to resist the last stage of a 'repressive sameness' (Calhoun 1994).

The national, the 'glocal', and the canonic interplay of identity and difference

The full architecture of nation-building processes of collective identity, its catharsis and its charismas, are completely put at stake by globalization, and the full new set it proposes for the interplay of history (Goldsmith and Mander 2001; Barret and Cavanagh 2001).

Two questions are immediately raised. To what extent does the national scenario become indeed contradictory in this emerging context? Does it intrinsically collide with the interplay of the new forces and agencies unleashed by the vision of the market as a *mare ignotum*, in its currents and shapings of the new moulding of that said cultural dimension of man; of the building of significance?

And in such a challenge, is the nation-framed identity an effective mediation in the process of building a new and larger social subjectivity (Habermas 2000)? Does it collapse, immediately, in this kind of landslide forced by globalization in this interior world in the making. Is that, exactly, what is shown by the instant sticking to fundamentalism, in the peripheries, as sheer resistance becomes the only way to survive, in this fully unknown new universe of social conditionings?

The national *corpus* simply vanishes, or works as a brake in the emerging set of the sole market, only pliable to the dimension of the *glocal*? Or even worse, is the incoming frame washing out the placenta itself and the nurturing of the 'interior world'? How does its representation become the prey of the simulacra, brought in by the mediatic universe, together with globalization? Does it become just its 'second nature' or a fatal interface with the hegemonic emerging set? Anyway, what is at stake now, in the full dimension of the plight of social identity, is the very breakdown of the canonic interplay, assured by modernity, of identity and difference, as the proper tension of culture, as still in the event of a 'being-in-the-world' (Shohat and Stam 1994).

It is not just the case of facing, for once, the disruption of the social *continua* as the established support to the framing of collective memory, representation, and the profiling of the historic persona. The question is to see to what extent this previous memory can resist to such a qualitative change for what is still, today, a need to configurate, in order to express a historical protagonism, so to say, of modes of existence and styles of life framed out of a confrontation, in a pluralistic horizon of achievement. No 'other' is the known context in which difference *per se* is the ultimate requisite for this full exercize of self-determination, and the 'proper' of man.

The simulacra and the singular concrete

What is at stake, then, is the loss of deeply rooted canon to provide for the basic features of representation, and its linkage with recognition, identity, and difference. What faces an emerging phenomenology of worldliness or 'mundaneness' nowadays is not only the problem of seizing that rupture, started by the new rules of the *glocal*, implying the trouncing of the national stance where the category of people is produced, as the paramount feature of social subjectivity. What is at quest is the very consistency of such subjectivity vis-à-vis the cancellation of the social concrete via the simulacra, and the multiplicity of inner intakes that blows up all framing, as the *loci* of the person. Or of the very idea of time exposure, in the new artifacts or placebos offered to real time, in the form of its virtuality, its edition, its deconstruction of memory (Baudrillard 1999).

Perhaps, it is the very notion of identity that is foreclosed by the rape of globalization. Communication, indeed, can go forward as a strict minimalist operation of recognition, if not turned to a zero ground, via the new codes for that almost void form of linkage or relationships. A modular environment produces a setting, without an interaction. 'Circumstance' is then engulfed without any real possible graft of difference. Endless repetition – the *ersatz* of an interplay – is the opposite of time, as a rendering of a mode, that exactly provides the declination of existence, the uniqueness of man out of the liturgical array vis-à-vis nature. More and more gone are those 'decants' of difference, preserved in the set remembrances of the nations (Dieckhoff 2000).

At the verge of a loss may also be the very rules of the imprint on the issues of memory itself, all based in that emergence of the egregious; lost the background for the gestures and the meaning of an all-binding coalescence and identity. Jeopardized, then, is the final set of a collective persona based on the division of difference, playing out of its social unconscious as the container of the subjective.

One can then immediately imagine, at the sight of globalization, how this former idea of culture, nurtured by the beat of the outstanding of its memory, disappears before the immense, empty, new scenario, and the lack of any niche to identify, recognize, and cling to our creative reminiscence. That millenary framing, however, still nurtures a certain logic of expectations, or a notion of the stage to frame the protagonist and the significance of our present time, and hence, also of the roots of the world at large , and its vagrant, immense constellations of meaning.

Gone is the differentiation of collectivities we were used to, thus blocking all penetration by the context that marks a distinction about to emerge. Fundamentalism is not a response to this inner, irreversible disruption. In fact, those cultures that go under that shelter are forced to the absolute immobility of its content of representation, impervious even to any revival, brought by the former continued change of its social frame, or the trade-offs of its memory.

No fertilization – thus, no grafts – takes place in that utter resistance, only able to repeat itself indefinitely. Cultures forced into this Zealotic stand are exposed less to the demolition of their structures than to the full remoulding of their contents, by what is the average of the 'imaginary correct' accepted by globalization – or incompatible with it.

Indeed, exposed to so many shades and sequences of an internal representation of reality, cultures face today this 'de-territorialization' of any rooting of a nation, as a historical *corpus* and the stalwart of difference. It does not imply only a mere change of grounds for the keeping of the same perspective, of an 'in-and-out,' as dictated by the walls of the subjective and objective, that decanted the 'world' and its view, built by the West.

We face nowadays a new multiple social self, exposed to the emergence of complexity, its apparata and its feedback, even to the point of an algebraic-sum-like trap. Its immediate impact builds a universe of straight, eerie deambulation of what was, before, subdued to the panopticon of a life, commanding the flux of its *vécu*, and the plotting of its growing unique memory. Even more, as the 'other' is subtracted by the *simulacrum*-like inner representation, we have to face, in its vacuum, the mere 'reproduction of the same' in such an operation yields to a more and more opaque subjectivity, forced to exchange genuine alterity for a rudimentary simulation of one's self (Mesure and Renault 1999).

A new syntax for the imaginary

What is really to be examined nowadays is to what extent, inside the walls of virtuality and hegemony, the very eradication of the world of culture is taking place, under the western civilization process.

For sure, this mediatization of the world comes together with the full empire of the market, of capital circulation and of the games of its choice, involving the building of an 'interior time', capable of fitting a sole world. What matters is to see how the very notion of identity survives these new times of subjective exposure, of a syntax of expectations of a completely different kind. Or of how a full new moulding of the former idea of a sequence meets the over-complex, and the virtual builds a new instance for the former discourse. It is in fact the very change of 'interior time' that disrupts all classic rules of the *raconto*, or of the recollection, in the right seizure of its tension.

The side effect of collective subjectivity hence brings a new, unusual screen for the old Platonic cavern. What can still stand to this interior landslide, and how can we still think of the old identity process, based on the rule of thumb, of seeing from within and being seen, as the quest for meaning emerges, in this new *iter* of man, facing tamed differences and the nonchalant, new oblivion of memory?

Reciprocity of perspectives and
logics of hegemony

The very discussion immediately after September 11th, as stated, for instance, by the dialogue of Habermas and Baudrillard (Baudrillard and

Valiente Noailles 2005), pointed out to what extent the objective effects of the globalization process led to the logics of hegemony over that of the classical imperial domination. The new virtualization of the so-called civilizatory process involves a new pragmatic acknowledgment, regardless of the very philosophical discussion itself, concerning the mediatic globalization system, up to the point of a possible pre-emption of the world imaginary.

Thus, all approaches to the emerging horizon, searching for any 'reciprocity of perspectives' post- September 11th, turn back to the old classical interplay between civilization and culture. At the sheer encompassing of modernity, it could still be perceived in terms of resistance, integration or eventual synthesis. In a world to be engulfed by hegemony, gone are the good old days of dominance, in the clear-cut of the profile to be assumed by the peripheries, as either an accomplice or a foe.

One refers here to the two Toynbeean classical archetypes for a collective response to an imperial embrace, taken from the examples of the Judaic confrontation with the Roman *aegis*. The Herodian answer was the compromise with the winner, at the risk of the very losing of its identity, and the Zealotic, the one to resist to any assimilation, through a culture turned into a stern and aggressive traditionalism.

The old paradigmatic views before September 11th disappear, through either the assimilationist response, or a full resistance, even as a condemned last stand. Terrorism awakes, in a blind anticipation of a reductionist universal world. It is useless, in this context, to call for mobilization or disarmament of the tight targeted assembling, of which are made the old crusades, the *jihads*, their polarities and further decompressions.

Out of the Khomeyni endeavour, Mohammad Khatami warned about the grounds of pseudo-holistic conflicts that are at stake for a possible dialogue of civilizations, before the deconstruction of its ideology, in terms of a critical appraisal of a world turned hegemonic, according to the Oval Office.

The Khomeyni successful 'last resistance' unleashed a sense of 'uneasiness' in the social unconscious in our times with regard to the receptiveness towards the West and its benefits, in a feeling of a subjective displacement or *malaise* – if not, already, of a rejection vis-à-vis the overall outcome of modernization.

The expropriation of collective subjectivity: delayed and instant revulsion

The apocalyptic impact of September 11th turned from a diluted sense of a day-by-day loss into a smashing consciousness-raising process in terms of that overall assimilation, and hampered, at the same time, the perception of progress, seen as a real sharing in time, much more than an imposition *anima dominandi*.

On the other side, the shock suffered by the West, with the fall of the Towers brought a new ambiguity to the rising self-perception of a world-power turned – finally – into an *über alles* profile, after the crumbling of the Berlin Wall in 1989. It blended a sense of overpowering, with a general defensive attitude, never found in the classical imperial domination. The horror of the sacrificial destruction of the WTC had, also, an unknown potential threat, of a killing of the collective soul of the outer cultures, threatened by the hegemonic approach, brought to modernization.

We moved, hence, after September 11th into a 'culture of fear' without mediated steps, far different from the world alertness of a nuclear war, and plunged into unpredictable anonymity. The burdens of terrorism, as topical and punctual as they are, escape any counterbalance of menace, assured previously by the over-control of the Cold War.

Beyond canonical exclusion

Derrida and Habermas (2004) see this new stand of ultimate violence as the very break of communication itself, when it is not just a sense of 'reciprocity' that disappears, despite the degree of antagonism, but that of the very 'otherness'. A confrontation of survivals erupts, cancelling the 'canon' of its established sequence, or protocol of acknowledgement, either by the western pre-emption, or by protest turned into erratic extermination.

One, hence, may speak today of a social unconscious of repulsion on both sides, made agonistic by the fall of the Twin Towers. One, coming from a sudden triggering of a protracted, diffused, and mixed feeling of historical expropriation; the other from this attempt against rationality and civilization, an ultimate horror, perceived by the West as much more than just a case of strict social pathology (Ferro 2002).

Towards a terrorism of no return

The utter complexity of a new fundamentalist vision does not just re-enact the atmosphere of the 100 years war of religious tensions at the brink of Renaissance. Indeed, we entered – as so well stated in Mallorca[1] by Mohammad Khatami – into the vicious circle; into the network of violence where civil warfare drives a fragmented and infinite uprising, even more rooted or different as triggered by faith or ethnic claims. It expresses an outburst of identity taken out of its nest by the impending hegemony, pushed to a sacrificial testimony of a collective soul.

Terrorism escapes the length of amenable responses, as pre-emption made irreversible the climax of confrontation, away from the simple *crescendos* of protest, lost for good after September 11th. The simultaneous emergence of crusades or *jihads*, in such a regressive ground, escapes the gestures of a decanted 'rearguard', typical of any imperial culture. Threatened by pre-emption, the remaining players in the world scenario confront 'threatening limit situations', different from the old days of massive, target-defined extermination. In this world of successive discontinuities, we can speak of the ontological disruption of the event (Baudrillard 1999). We are far away now from the days of the Cold War and of conflict resolution practices, always compatible in their outstanding visibility and contention.

The overcoming of the post-September 11th syndrome cannot count on a simple return to social ethics with all the feelings of otherness, of discourse, of a disarmed will, or radical generosity. The repertoire of reconciliation simply disappears, as long as any effective interactive movement is replaced by the naked urge of survival in a subjective abyss. Not to mention the ideal of retrogressive integrations, and then *pardons*, neither a scaling-down, between extreme and moderate standing against the world impeding blows.

Social unconscious and subjective destitution

The new 'limit situation' does not explode by an increasing level of domination, but from a sudden seizure of a protracted subjective destitution, in a path turned into a short circuit from the Khomeini Revolution to the Twin Towers fall.

Habermas and Baudrillard (Baudrillard and Valiente Noailles 2005) pointed out the horrendous – and 'portentous' (Stockhausen) – spectacle of the Manhattan sacrifice vindicating in that social unconscious of the outer West, a time length expropriation of its identity. Regardless of its revulsion, it brought in the rupture of the former assimilations or Heroditan compromises in the co-existence of cultures today, as world players. Such an awakening, in its own dynamics, cannot be associated to a – still – over-organized confrontation, or a strict disciplined strategy, or of a unique never-ceasing fight against the West as the protagonist of an inescapable world civilization.

The September 11th catastrophe took over the current social imaginary, blocking a new critical and mediating processing of those extreme tensions. It requires a whole methodology of deconstruction and awareness to face and understand modernity as a transcendental, common to all cultures in their advance to an inner rationality and their chance to remain as such vis-à-vis the West, seen also as a culture and not as a pretender of an engulfing universality.

Domination and hegemony

An expropriation of the collective self through the simulacra and the banning of any heteronomy of representation is in sheer contrast to the traditional take-over of the colonial era and of the classical empires, and builds a new scenario to which old fundamentalism had never been exposed.

Until the twentieth century, one could still speak of a residual capacity of resistance to the West, as a compromise, in time and concessions, according to a final Herodian profile, in an assimilationist-like dynamism of history. Vis-à-vis the new era of an impending virtualization of the world, fundamentalism is condemned to vanish, regardless of its compromise to die or be removed within the lapse of one generation. No last standing, in fact, prevails over the dialectics of reification, at the ladder of its simulacra, and its generated artefacts against any claim of authenticity even committed to a terminal testimony.

There is no historical perspective yet to assess how much such abduction took over the social unconscious of the turn-of-the-century pushed by September 11th. It may have turned from an overall diffused resistance against the classical imperial dominances into a gesture of survival as a basic affirmation of a social self (Delacampagne 2003).

When the little girls of Gaza, in their dynamite coats, kiss their parents and explode in the bus, to what extent are they responding to an organized command, the more efficient or radical it may still be, for a programmed action? The ignition of an unknown and expanding encompassed a doomed last push for difference vis-à-vis a landslide burying of a collective soul.

One has to face the world reception of a formal democratic access of a government, in demand for the erasing of Israel, as feared with the Hamas victory at the Palestine Authority. Or, at the same time, at the very heart of the platform of human rights, the emerging tension between the right to religion, offended in the Islamic faith by the portraying of the Prophet in the western press, and the intrinsic right of expression, assimilated to the core of the modern conquests of freedom. For once, the acknowledgment of an 'irretrievable abyss' is assumed by the very inner soul of Europe in a near fundamentalist stand of no apologies or tactical surrounding to a strategy of keeping a world dialogue.

The relevance of such a quest reflects a first and fundamental priority, in terms of the limits of 'contextuality' in the present frames of mind, among countries, for the understanding of the universal of values.

It is then crucial to provide for an exchange on the views of post-modernity by scholars from both Islam and the West to face the stereotypes, blurring the real confrontation on collective identities (Benzine 2004). What is needed is a critique of the values and concepts that would enable an effective approach on secularity and the ideologies of the 'clash of civilizations', giving birth to new fundamentalisms, starting by the one of reason itself (Buck-Morss 2003).

A further proposal, and already oriented towards an action programme, concerns the common platform of human rights, as able to establish a 'culture of peace', under an effective world platform. Such an initiative will face the boundaries of the exception of national security opposed nowadays to privacy, or physical integrity, or the right of expression.

One has thus to discuss the contextual injustice that may come out of the very context of these rights concerning, for instance, the effective grievances of torture, on its physical and moral impact, of the right to religion vis-à-vis the freedom of expression, as expressed by the cartoon crisis. Such requests coincide with a full restructuring of the UN

Commission of Human Rights together with its Islamic counterpart. The final intent of this purpose is of course to reduce the disparagement still remaining in these issues, for a common progress towards a world 'rule of law'.

The present historical insertion of terrorism – in its new congenital extremist stand – leads to a new, subtle consequence, in the setting of the horizons and policies for an 'Alliance of Civilizations'. They go beyond the underscoring of the emerging limit situations built by the cumulative, inertia-bounded interplays of complexity, in the postmodern society, still built under the belief of its aggregate impact, always *in bonam partem*.

To advance the Alliance of Civilizations, the UN Secretary-General established a High-Level Group of eminent personalities to produce a report containing an analysis of the rise in cross-cultural polarization and extremism and a set of practical recommendations to counter this phenomenon.[2] The report strongly stressed that the conflict between the West and the Muslim world is a political and not a religious problem. The role of religion is, in spite of the claims of modernization theories, growing in many areas, but very few religiously motivated groups take part in acts of violence. Religion can in fact play a critical role in promoting appreciation of other cultures. As discussed by Jan Nederveen Pieterse in volume 1, the report on the Alliance of Civilizations points out that Islamic civilization was a major source of civilization during medieval times, and that Jews and Christians were free to practice their religion in Muslim empires. But as also stressed by Raj Isar in this volume, as communities face discrimination, humiliation and marginalization based on ethnic or religious identity markers, they tend to assert their identity more aggressively. In this respect the Millennium Development Goals play a strategic role. As Peter Wallensteen stresses in the last chapter of this volume, the UN system as a whole must undergo fundamental reforms. The report was based on a multi-polar perspective, advocating adherence to international law and an effective multilateral system. It stressed resolution of the Israeli-Palestinian conflict as the key issue, together with violence in Afghanistan and Iraq. It also underlined the need for political pluralism in the Muslim countries (cf. volume 1 by Saad Eddin Ibrahim). It presented recommendations in four thematic areas: education, youth, migration, and media. Education about one's own history is important but has to be combined by knowledge of global issues (Global Studies). Migration is part of the current global order, representing problems as well as benefits. Problems must be addressed proactively and cooperatively. Press freedom is essential for democracy but must be combined with responsibility and objectivity. Thus improved knowledge and understanding, particularly among youth, can be seen as the main message of the report and this will also be the core of future, continuous work.

The debate is only starting, in a historic process that disrupts the classical mental architecture, to discuss alternatives and utopias in unobstructed dialectics and scenarios.

Notes

1. Reference to the inaugural meeting of the High-Level Group for the Alliance of Civilizations (ONU) that took place in Mallorca/Spain in November 2005.
2. The High-Level Group met five times from November 2005 to November 2006, and as a conclusion produced a report which takes a multi-polar approach within which it prioritizes relations between Muslim and western societies. The Report of the High-Level Group was presented to UN Secretary-General Kofi Annan and to Prime Ministers José Luis Rodríguez Zapatero and Recep Tayyip Erdoğan on 13 November 2006 at the final meeting of the High-Level Group in Istanbul, Turkey. See www.unaoc.org.

References

Baudrillard, J. (1999) *L'Exchange Impossible*, especially pp. 131–141 'Société dissociée, société parallèle' and 'Evènement réel, évènement fatal: singularité de l'évènement', Paris: Galilée.

Baudrillard, J. and Valiente Noailles, E. (2005) *Les éxilés du dialogue*, Paris: Galilée.

Benzine, R. (2004) *Les nouveaux penseurs de l'islam*, Paris: Albin Michel.

Barret, R. and Cavanagh, J. (2001) 'L'uniformisation de la culture planétaire', pp. 279–289 in Goldsmith, E. and Mander, J. (2001) *Les procès de la mondialisation*, Paris: Fayard.

Bessis, S. (2002) *L'Occident et les autres – Histoire d'une suprématie*, Paris: La Découverte & Syros.

Buck-Morss, S. (2003) *Thinking Past Terror – Islamism and Critical Theory on the Left*, London and New York: Verso.

Calhoun, C. (2004) 'It's Time To Be Post National?', in Mendes, C. (2004) *Hégémonie et civilisation de la peur*, Rio de Janeiro: Educam-Académie de la Latinité.

Delacampagne, C. (2003) *Islam et Occident, les raisons d'un conflit*, Paris: PUF.

Derida, J. and Habermas, J. (2004) *Le concept du 11 Septembre. Dialogues à New York (Octobre-Décembre 2001) avec Giovanna Borradori*, Paris: Galilée.

Dieckhoff, A. (2000) *La nation dans tous ses états*, Paris: Flammarion.

Ferro, M. (2002) *Le Choc de l'Islam (XVIIIe–XXIe Siècle)*, Paris: Odile Jacob.

Giddens, A. (1991) *Modernity and Self Identity – Self and Society in the Late Modern Age*, Palo Alto: Stanford University Press.

Goldsmith, E. and Mander, J. (2001) *Les procès de la mondialisation*, Paris: Fayard.

Habermas, J. (2000) *Après l'état nation*, Paris: Fayard.

Heidegger, M. (2006) *La devastation et l'attente. Entretiens sur le chemin de Campagne*, Paris, Gallimard.

Lamchichi, A. (2001a) *Islam et Occident: la confrontation?*, Paris: L'Harmattan.

Lamchichi, A. (2001b) *Pour comprendre l'Islamisme politique*, Paris: L'Harmattan.

Lukács, G. (1967) *History & Class Consciousness*, London: The Merlin Press.

Mendes, C. (2004) *Hégémonie et civilisation de la peur*, Rio de Janeiro: Educam-Académie de la Latinité.

Mesure, S. and Renault, A. (1999) *Alter ego. Les paradoxes de l'identité démocratique*, Paris: Aubier.

Nair, S. (2003) *L'Empire face à la diversité*, Paris: Hachette.

Shohat, E. and Stam, R. (1994) *Unthinking Eurocentrism: Multiculturalism and the Media*, New York: Routledge.

Stockhausen, K. (2001) Deutsche Presse Agentur, 18 September, 2001, www.andante.com/maginez/article.cfm?id=14256.

Sztompka, P. and Alexander, J. (eds) (1990) *Rethinking Progress: Movements, Forces and Ideas at the End of the 20th Century*, London: Unwin Hyman.

8
The Moral Voice Can be Heard in Different Ways. Global Ethics and Cultural Diversity

Göran Bexell

Fundamentals in ethics

Love is one of the most intimate and private phenomena in the world. Almost every individual has her or his love story or stories, expressed in thousands of poems, novels, and movies. But it is curious that we today on a certain spot of the globe understand – or believe to understand – such expressions of love from other people, other cultures, other times. When Sappho writes about love or when Jesus teaches about love, our experience is that we understand something, even if there is a risk of misunderstanding. When girls and boys from China, Zimbabwe, and Sweden talk about love, they understand each other.

The explanation is that we have our own experiences – in a social context – as a source of knowledge, often the knowledge of emotions and experiences. Love is, on the one hand, the most intimate and private experience, on the other hand, a common human experience, founded in psychophysical and emotional reactions and human needs, and expressed in many different private and culturally specific ways. Almost every person around the world and across history and cultures has experienced something that can be called love, not only in combination with sex but also in a broad meaning, including love for friends, children, music, and ideas and so on. It is not only empathy, it is more passionate and personal.

The question in this chapter is whether we have good reasons or not to believe in the possibility of globally shared values as a ground for, or at least a contribution to, building an international society and global governance, and, if so, how such an ethics is constructed. As a first observation I will argue that morality is, in many ways, equivalent with love in the example above. If we start our thinking from the unique we can reach something common human, and from the common human we can reach the individual and the unique. This is not true for every phenomenon, but for some fundamentals in morality.

I will elaborate on some aspects of these two starting points. The first is the very private sphere, the micro-perspective, concerning the individual and her or his experiences in smaller interpersonal and social formations. The second is cultural and religious traditions, the macro-perspective, and some contemporary principles and theories on shared values on an international or global scene. Between them, on a scale from the narrow to the wide setting, we find different kinds of communities: families, work places, networks, neighbours, regional, and in a wider sense cultural, traditions, religions, and global networks.

Love is an ethical phenomenon just like hate, trust, hope, and mercy. They have biochemical and psychophysical roots, but cannot be reduced to chemical reactions. They are conditioned by and expressed in social conventions and they give us moral knowledge. They are important for the individual as a person.

One interesting observation concerning ethical phenomena is that they, so to speak, bring their own interpretation before we decide to interpret them as morally good or bad. The Danish ethicist K. E. Lögstrup (died 1981) has elaborated a view on this. In a spontaneous way we prefer love and trust to hate and mistrust. According to Lögstrup, we do not make a moral choice first and value love and trust as something good. But we have to take responsibility and decide or interpret what love means in every specific situation. I have to decide in many questions concerning love, not least when it comes to social and political questions. Some kind of transformation of love and trust to a socially possible level is necessary (Lögstrup 1997).

If a child receives love, trust, and care, she or he will grow as a person, become ready to give love to others and through empathy be ready to respect other people's integrity. But if you do not get these necessary things as a child – and later during your life – you will be hurt in one way or another. It often starts with the relationship with your parents and continues with other social relationships, with the family, neighbours, the village or city. There are numerous examples in history and literature, in criminality, and among terrorists and dictators, that there has been a fundamental lack of love and trust, and of real empathy, in their lives. Empathy is one of the conditions for a good morality.

The need for love and trust, and the spontaneous giving of love and trust, belong to the basis of morality. The commandments of love and social care have their roots in both human needs and social conditions. In that way, the commandments correspond to what human beings need in order to live and prosper. In all cultures, nations, and religions, in liberalism and socialism, in the East and the West, in Islam and Christianity, these fundamentals in morality are the same, albeit expressed in different socially and culturally conditioned forms. This is one of the most hopeful and important arguments for the possibility of shared values on a fundamental and common human basis. The future of the world and humankind depends on how we succeed in managing these fundamentals, for example, the role of parents, families, social rituals, education, and public defence of moral values such as trust and truth, not only in rhetoric but in concrete actions and international agreements.

Almost every human community has formulated positive values that express these fundamentals and promote social support, for example, caring for children and the sick. There are negative restrictions concerning murder, violence, lying, rape, and so on, but the aim is the same: to make it possible to live together in social communities. Such values and norms can be considered self-evident, but are still important for the ethical analysis. They aim at making social coexistence and survival possible, but do not explicitly formulate any visions of the good life and the good society.

This view is opposed to the theory that moral values are nothing but a consequence of the social and economic development. Such development is important for people's attitudes and values, but it is not the only foundation of morality. Moral values are deeply connected with human needs and aspirations, and with basic social demands. Moral convictions can stimulate criticism against the social and economic development. Not even basic moral values are, however, static. They can slowly change over time, more or less. The applications of basic values are changing faster than the basic values themselves.

I have mentioned this basis because of its fundamental importance for ethics. When arguing for and against shared common values, also on a macro- and global level, applied values and specific ethical problems are often at the fore, such as disagreement concerning the death penalty, partnership for homosexuals, and cloning. But the fact that there is disagreement on the death penalty is not a very good argument against the fundamental value of protecting human life.

Although these values are basic and common human, they are threatened by opposing values, and by hate, mistrust, and destructive actions. All people are tempted to act against basic human values, especially in certain situations. In war, extreme poverty, and enduring social injustice, all of us can act against these norms and values, but also out of sheer self-interest. In order to protect life, and to make it possible to have trust and give love, long historic and cultural traditions have formed moral commandments. They are often short and negative, such as 'don't lie', or positive such as 'love your neighbour as yourself'. They all have, as stated above, the positive aim to protect fragile human life and social community.

From this point of view it is not astonishing that all great world religions share some basic values, norms, and virtues. The moralities of the religions have these phenomenological, social, and historical roots, but are embedded in different religious contexts and vary in cultural expressions. For example, there is deep moral agreement on anti-egoistic norms. Positively expressed, this is the norm wherein the individual's own interests are restrained by a broader social consideration of other individuals and larger communities. The Golden Rule is one example. With some variations this rule is widely accepted in many world religions. Examples are found in Islam's 'sharia', in Judaism's 'Torah', and in Hinduism's 'dharma'. Examples of negative commandments common to Islam, Judaism, Christianity, Hinduism, and Buddhism are: do not murder; do not steal; do not lie! Examples of positive norms are: show responsibility and love for all living beings; show self-control and self-respect; take care of orphans and the poor; honour your parents (cf.Bexell 2002).

On the basis of such a morality, the social community can survive and prosper. In social and other relations we cannot act according to the demand of the great love commandment in a direct and spontaneous way. We have to transform love and trust to general and abstract moral principles that express the basis, for example, principles of justice, equality, and dignity of the human individual.

Trust as an ethical, social, and political phenomenon is one of the core elements in a society. When trust declines, the social institutions like the police, schools, and care also decline. Interpersonal trust is one of the conditions for a stable society and thus for a democratic state. It is well-known that interpersonal trust among the US public has declined during the last decades. If interpersonal and social trust disappear, social institutions are in a very difficult position.

Trust in governments and political elites is also decreasing in most industrial countries, e.g. in the United States and Sweden. Russell J. Dalton argues that the greatest declines are among the better-educated. The changes are not so much dependent on failures of governments or scandals as on the social process of modernization, with less trust and more doubts in the institutions of democracy (Dalton 2005). There is a close relationship between the levels of interpersonal and social trust within a society. Decreasing trust and empathy are serious threats against an open and democratic society.

The conclusion regarding the main question of this chapter, good arguments for globally shared values, is that these perspectives and observations are good arguments for an ethics that is not restricted by borders of nations, religions, ethnic communities, or ideologies. The basis of ethics is quite a stable foundation, outside of governments' and even dictators' control. If this is true, this basis is a good starting-point for dialogues.

If we have the ambition to promote global governance, the task is to build sustainable societies that defend and promote the basis of ethics, for example, social movements like sports, music, good education, and care of the sick and poor, parents and families, dialogues between social groups, justice, constructive social rituals, and international exchanges. On a more abstract and macro-level, national and international players have to defend the same values, promote dialogues, and combine the micro- and the macro-perspectives.

Global ethics: initiatives and debates

In his contribution to this book, Peter Wallensteen discusses the rise of a vibrant international civil society, partly building on human rights and cross-border solidarity. Part of this is the production of ethical consensus documents, panels, conferences, and initiatives on globally shared values from leaders within politics, culture, universities, and the United Nations. These new forms of global governance are important as expressions of opinions, preparing for political action. I will give four examples of global ethics initiatives, and discuss what values they promote. I will argue that there is convergence between the personal sphere, the micro-level, and the global and macro-level of morality.

Some of the most important initiatives on global ethics belong to late history, for example, Gro Harlem Brundtland's report 'Our common future' (1987) with its global perspectives on development and ethical dimensions of sustainable development. The report was a sign of the growing global awareness and the need for value-based political action at an international level. Social justice, the elimination of poverty, and justice between generations were some of the central values of the report.

The Commission on Global Governance, endorsed by the UN Secretary-General and headed by the former Swedish Prime Minister Ingvar Carlsson, produced a report of high quality, entitled 'Our Global Neighbourhood' (Commission on Global Governance 1987). The ambition was to find a firm ethical foundation for a new global governance underpinned by democracy and the rule of law and consisting of 'a set of core values that can unite people of all cultural, political, religious, or philosophical backgrounds [...] We believe that all humanity could uphold the core values of respect for life, liberty, justice and equity, mutual respect, caring, and integrity' (ibid.).

These values correspond to what I call the basis of ethics. As these core values are adopted, the Commission believes, a 'global ethic' will emerge. The possibility of such an ethics depends on the willingness and ability to promote what I label the common good, i.e. 'the ability of people and governments to transcend narrow self-interests and agree that the interests of humanity as a whole will be best served by acceptance of a set of common rights and responsibilities' (ibid.).

Among the rights promoted in a global ethics is a secure life, an opportunity to earn a fair living, and equal access to the global commons. Security means not only peace but freedom from threats of 'hunger, disease, and repression, as well as protection from sudden and harmful disruptions in the patterns of daily life. The Commission believes that the security of people must be regarded as a goal as important as the security of states.' (ibid.). Everybody's right to a 'fair living' challenges the developed countries, where 20 per cent of the world's population live and where 80 per cent of the world's natural resources are used. A commitment to equity is the only secure foundation for a more humane world order and the principle of intergenerational equity underlies the strategy of sustainable development.

Within UNESCO there are different projects on global ethics. The report 'Our Creative Diversity' (UNESCO 1995), compiled by the World Commission for Culture and Development, is one example. This report, just like the others, confirms that there are recurrent moral values in nearly all cultural traditions, exemplified by the variations of the Golden Rule. Not only traditions, but also a new global civic culture, are sources of global ethics, mainly building on human rights, democratic legitimacy, and public accountability.

Another focus predominates in Hans Küng's 'Projekt Weltethos', based in Tübingen. The focus is on the ethics of the world's religions. Küng believes that there will not be any global ethics without a consensus among religions. The most well-known and important document on this is the Declaration from the Chicago meeting in 1993. This document reflects the very typical focus when world religions try to reach consensus on ethical questions. There are many moral disagreements between religions about, for example, the role of women, homosexuality, medical ethics, the death penalty, and so on, but there is a wide value consensus on fundamentals and non-self-evident values in basic ethics, for example, trust, love, care, and human dignity. The following quotation is representative:

> In the face of all inhumanity our religions and ethical convictions demand that every human being must be treated humanely! That means that every human being – without distinction of sex, age, race, skin colour, language, religion, political view, or national or social origin – possesses an inalienable and untouchable dignity. And everyone, individuals as well as the state, is therefore obliged to honour this dignity and guarantee its effective protection. Humans must always be the subjects of rights, must be ends, never mere means, never objects of commercialization and industrialization in economics, politics, and media, in research institutes and industrial undertakings. (Second Parliament of the World's Religions 1993)

Küng's project reminds us of the importance of the great religions of the world in fostering morality. It is important that dialogues between religions continue as well as between religious ethics and secular ethics. Although the moral basis can be the same, the religions have different social movements and rituals, confirming and promoting the values. One of the problems in secular societies is how to give morality a solid base in socially common rituals.

These four examples of initiatives promoting global ethics have a strong converging structure and content. First, the moral values, norms, and virtues are the same as or converging with what in the first part of this chapter was called the basis of ethics. Let us call them a set of core values, for example, caring, integrity, and respect for life, freedom, and justice. Second, there is nothing or very little in the public debates on morality, for example, disagreements on homosexuality or bioethical questions.

These examples illustrate the starting point, not from the personal sphere but from the abstract and general human level. The common and universal strengthen the personal and unique, and the personal strengthen the common and universal. Without the foundation in human needs and aspirations, and basic social demands, these projects were unrealistic.

What about theoretical analysis and academic projects on global ethics? Today quite a few universities give courses on global ethics. Academics, especially from ethics, philosophy, theology, and sociology, have contributed with analysis, debate, and literature. Different positions are debated and defended. There are communitarian positions, such as the one provided by Charles Taylor, arguing that morality is always strongly connected with its social basis in different communities, and that communities with different values sometimes overlap, although their ultimate goals can differ (cf. Etzioni 2001: 245). An extreme view is that the moral landscape consists of isolated moral islands without moral connections. One of the problems for such hard communitarians is the risk of relativism, founded on the claim that all morality depends on special cultural conditions. An interesting position is upheld by Amitai Etzioni, who combines a communitarian view with a distinct argumentation for a core of globally shared values (ibid.).

A position based on an individual and liberal perspective is often defended by western intellectuals, emphasizing the rights of the individual. Sissela Bok has, for example, elucidated some cross-cultural values: mutual care, injunctions against violence and deceit, and elementary justice. Such minimal basic values are 'indispensable to human coexistence, though far from sufficient' (Bok 1995: 13ff). According to Peter Singer, the injustices of globalization demand new ethical guidelines for international behaviour, which challenge the sovereignty of states (Singer 2002).

There are defenders of modern post-modernism. A strong post-modernism cannot be combined with the efforts to find a new global ethics, but the criticism against the abstract, general, non-historic, and non-contextual approaches can be rebuffed in the manner exemplified in the beginning of this article.

Global ethics is often connected with globalization. The opinion of the critics is that economic and political interests driving globalization are the real force behind the new interest for global ethics, not least from the only superpower, the United States. The criticism is, of course, a serious one. In a theory of global ethics it is necessary to give globally shared values another basis than such interests. That is one of the assumptions in the first part of this article. The explanation of moral origin and changes is, as shown, complex. Globalization and economic development, of course, have great impact on the development of morality, but there are other explanations as well.

One criticism of global ethics is that all kinds of globalism and universalism are one-dimensional. In other articles, however, I have launched a combination of a new form of universal or global ethics with cultural diversity, grounded on empirical evidences, dialogues and common human needs and ambitions, and political decisions, on this ground (Bexell 2002).

There is a need for clarifying analysis of the whole range of questions. Today, there exist many unclear assumptions on how morality functions and how deep and widespread ethical consensus and disagreements really are. Many intellectuals are sceptical of every tendency to argue for shared values and global ethics. Empirically founded research is therefore necessary, which will be discussed in the following section.

Moral conflicts

After the Second World War, the Cold War dominated the western world which was kept together not least, though not only, by its interpretation of freedom within its capitalistic system versus communism. After the fall of the Berlin wall, we saw, on the one hand, more national ethnocentric social movements and conflicts, and, on the other hand, a strong globalization. The latter aspect made some people believe that we lived in the best of times and that history had come to an end. September 11th was a reminder of another reality. There have been many interpretations of September 11th from cultural, religious, and political value perspectives. One question is, of course, which real value conflicts are demonstrated in the symbolic date (Bexell 2004). Is there a real moral clash of civilizations?

Despite the above sketched basis for a global civic ethics, it is a fact that moral conflicts exist and that cultural and religious conflicts have moral dimensions. But which value conflicts are dominating in today's world, and how deep are those conflicts: are they real conflicts on basic ethics with potential social and political conflict dimensions, or are they moral disagreements within a moral basis of moral consensus on fundamental values? Do they promote a real democracy with moral vitality, or do they foster military, political, and religious conflicts? Are moral disagreements a hindrance for globally shared values, global governance, and international society?

The first task is to find out which value conflicts dominate the world today. The answers depend on the ways of asking, on what is observed, and on how the analysis is structured. If you, for example, ask for people's attitudes towards the environment or health, you will focus on disagreements, and perhaps find a great diversity around the globe. The choice of analytical perspective is, of course, important for the result. I will give a few but central examples.

Being conventional is too easy, i.e. to believe that moral differences always follow traditional borders such as the West versus the East, and Islam versus Christianity. I will discuss some of these questions, bringing up some results from the most important research project concerning globally shared values and value changes over time, the World Values Study (WVS), led by Professor Ronald Inglehart in Michigan. The project presents empirical research on ethics and analysis based on empirical evidence on value changes and value opinions in many countries. Today there are many research groups dealing with this project around the world. Empirical ethics gives answers on how people act, think, and make moral choices, quite independent of theories of universalism versus particularism in ethics (Inglehart and Welzel 2005).

There have been speculations on a conflict between Islam and Christianity, though it is impossible to put the two religions against one another as uniform entities supposedly in conflict. If they are compared with, for example, atheistic materialism, they probably have more in common than in what distinguishes them. Neither Muslims nor Christians can be treated as homogeneous groups. There are fanatical Protestants in Northern Ireland, there are Christian opponents of abortion who will murder for their cause, and there is the most profound piety in Islamic Sufism.

There are, however, in both religions, elements that can inspire conflicts and even war, and elements that can be, and indeed are, exploited to create conflict. Individual representatives and groups are actual or potential hotbeds of conflict, or are exploited by sharp propagandists, especially when potential conflicts shaping disagreements are exploited by religious fundamentalists. Seen not least from that point of view, the morality and practice of the religions should be examined more critically on the basis of globally shared values. Taking into consideration the fear of generating conflicts between religious groups, the ethical theory and practice of religions should be more discussed in public debate. International society has a great and difficult task to criticize fundamentalists, violence, oppression or resistance against human rights and democracy in the name of religion.

There are fundamentalist movements in combination with political-ideological movements that oppose values agreed upon by the international society, using violence and terrorism. Such movements represent a fundamental clash, not only with western humanism and the moral groundwork of the United Nations, but also with the above sketched basis of a shared human ethics.

If the perspective is widened to a conflict between cultures, influenced by Islamic or Christian movements respectively, one comes closer to a more complicated and perhaps realistic conflict. The symbolic effect of September 11th contains elements of cultural confrontation in a wide sense. The attack can be seen as aimed against western values and lifestyles. But there has not been any total confrontation or moral clash of civilizations. In the interpretations of September 11th, the criticism of Huntington's thesis has nonetheless been so fierce that what is sometimes justified in his views has been lost, for example, that people belong to what he calls civilizations and that these civilizations can foster moral identities. From a moral point of view, there are moral disagreements that in some respects follow culture more than politics.

As we know, Huntington argued that there is a clash between western Christianity and Islam in combination with Orthodox Christianity. In their article, 'The True Clash of Civilizations', Ronald Inglehart and Pippa Norris argue that Huntington is right in his thesis that culture does matter but 'mistaken in assuming that the core clash between the West and Islam is over political values' (Inglehart and Norris 2003: 68). According to results within the WVS, democracy has an overwhelmingly positive image throughout the world, also in Muslim- dominated countries except for Pakistan. But there is a moral clash concerning family, gender equality, and sexual liberalization. And this clash mirrors different stages of economic development, lack of democracy in practise, and of so-called self-expression values such as personal freedom and individual rights. The conclusion by Inglehart and Norris is the following:

> Although nearly the entire world pays lip service to democracy, there is still no global consensus on the self-expression values – such as social tolerance, gender equality, freedom of speech, and interpersonal trust – that are crucial to democracy. Today, these divergent

values constitute the real clash between Islamic societies and the West. (ibid: 73)

Culture and cultural values have great impact on societies but, as Inglehart and Norris write, 'culture does not have to be destiny'. Cultural values are changing, but rather slowly.

Another finding in the WVS is that cultural or moral conflicts or disagreements between secular and religious societies and values is not a gap between the West and Islam, but between secular states and values in the West, and more religious societies in Islamic, African, and Latin American countries. In many countries, it is almost impossible to be a political leader without holding faith in God.

What does this mean? From a moral point of view, a person who believes in God can be either a moral conservative or a moral liberal, a defender of human rights or an enemy of rights. The attitude can change from the conviction that God is on our side (President Bush) to the hope that we are on God's side (President Lincoln).

Another main result of the WVS project points to another but similar conflict, namely that traditional values contrast with secular/rational values. In some regions, values protecting children, parents, family, and nationalism are highly ranked. Another main result is that so-called survival values contrast with self-expressions values. Survival values are connected with industrial society with emphasis on economic and physical security. Self-expression values are connected with post-industrial society. Children of this society take economic welfare for granted and have subjective well-being, tolerance, and diversity as highly ranked values.

The tendency is, according to the WVS, quite clear for the future. With a growing economy, social welfare, and democracy, including more of so-called modernization and secularization, the consequence will be more self-expression values and more rights of the individual.

Sometimes a value conflict between western individualism and eastern communitarianism (or Asian values) is put to the front. So-called Asian values are sometimes used as arguments against, for example, individual human rights. However, there is not necessarily any contradiction. Harmony, the strong position of the family, and a well-balanced choice between the common good and individual rights are sometimes considered to be Asian values, but it is dangerous to generalize. Of course, such values must be respected by western liberals in intercultural dialogue and vice versa. It is not the origin of a value which determines its moral validity. If we want to promote global dialogue, the task is to find combinations of western individualism and eastern community values, combinations of individual rights, and protection of the common good and social duties. There is no contradiction between the promotion of human rights and the common good.

A classical and always present conflict is the one between the common good and individuals' or groups' self-interests (Bexell 2004, 2003: 117–143). The idea of the common good conflicts with the notion of favouring certain players, for example, economically or politically strong states or groups, selected ethnic groups, or one of the two sexes. The idea of the common good also requires certain common basic values.

The fact that the poorer part of the world is, or can be, opposed to the richer creates a potential moral conflict between participants and non-participants of globalization and modernization and their social and economic effects. Perhaps the real cultural confrontation is the more conflict-charged, but this is uncertain. This dimension concerns the basic conditions of life and is, as usual, not only an isolated conflict of values, but integrated with economical and political conflicts.

The value conflict between the common good and the particular is highly relevant in a global perspective. Expressed in a simplified way, the globalization process will be governed either by the common good or by particular interests, such as individual states, major economic interests or ethnic groups. The disagreements do not follow borders of religion, culture or political power.

One result of this short analysis is that there is not one single potential conflict, but many different conflicts or disagreements. Some of them follow borders of culture and/or religions, but others are crossing such borders, for example the disagreement between moral conservatives and liberals, and between promoters of self-expression values and survival values respectively. An individual can be a member of different value communities.

Another result is that greatest and most isolated value conflicts do not concern what I call basic ethics, but applications of the basis. There are, however, many political and economic conflicts with deeply integrated moral dimensions, such as conflicts between rich and poor countries and between influential and non-influential social groups.

Core values, cultural diversity, and dialogue

I agree with Amitai Etzioni. The great question is if it possible for the cultures of the world to find common fundamental moral and cultural values that express both commonalities and cultural vital diversities

(Etzioni 2001: 232ff). As far as I understand, these common values have to emanate from what I call basic values, for example trust and love and, on a more general level, justice and human dignity. The ultimate reasons and embodiment of these values can differ, but we can still agree upon them. On the basis of agreements of some core values, there must be space for moral disagreements and cultural diversity. In a vital democracy there is always a debate on which values are core values and on their applications.

As a result of globalization, common human and social problems need common solutions, for example, concerning the environment and the fight against terrorism and other criminal acts. As shown, there are many NGO and other initiatives on globally shared values, and these are evidences of strong criticism against cultural and moral relativism on a global level. These initiatives promote some core values for survival and self-expression.

All cultures have some problems in common, concerning, for example, survival, distribution of goods, and the possibilities of cultural development. Social life demands some kind of reciprocity, restriction of violence, justice, and basic truth telling. All cultures have some basic norms and values aiming to protect the survival of the society and the individual, and to take care of children, parents, families, and the social community.

Is this background enough as a base for also sharing common visions of a good life, a good society, and human prosperity? Today it is important to remember that a person and a community can belong to many families or circles of moral agreements or disagreements. We do not need to share the same vision of a good life, but we can share core values and an understanding of what is morally wrong in a fundamental way, what is without doubt outside the boundaries. This necessary foundation also needs a complement from international society, for example, international legislation, binding agreements on human rights, and realistic sanctions.

The main question in this chapter is whether we have good reasons or not to believe in the possibility of globally shared values as a contribution to building an international society. The answer is that we have many good reasons. A moral basis on human grounds provides the possibility for a new global ethics, and the development of an international society. The task is to combine globally shared values with moral vitality and cultural diversity. It is a difficult task, however, not to use the common to promote your own culture (elevated universalism), and not to use cultural diversity as an argument against accepted shared values (Bexell 2002).

In order to avoid misunderstandings, I will emphasize that I have not argued that all people or the majority of women and men are morally good, or that the moral development of the world is always going straight forward.

There is a converging moral voice coming from, on the one hand, the basis of ethics, and, on the other hand, the international and global level, as described above. The voice is focussed on some core values and can be heard in different ways, in a variety of cultural expressions. Military and economic powers are strong, but in the long run the moral voice is stronger, and without it a human global community cannot be built.

Observations on dialogues

I have discussed some moral conflicts, and will end with some observations on dialogues on these conflicts.

One conclusion concerning dialogues between representatives from different cultures, religions, and various interests is that dialogues on morality are possible and should be promoted. There are common human conditions, needs and aspirations, and some shared common values, and there are many initiatives on the global level pointing in the same direction. This is an enormous need for dialogue, and good conditions for it. Obviously, there is diversity and moral disagreement, but this is not a hindrance to dialogue, but a possibility.

International society has to defend fragile human values, by international laws on, for example, human rights. International society needs different kinds of sanctions and special military forces in case of crises. Dialogue is not an alternative but a necessary complement and precondition.

First, there are ongoing dialogues between representatives of Islam and Christianity, and a special analysis on such dialogues. One task is, of course, to identify common values, another to identify disagreements, and a third to analyse presumptions and conditions for dialogue, for example, whose values a dialogue in itself represents. One failure of such a dialogue is the construction of a common border against the secular world. The task is rather – from the point of view of international society – on the one hand, to build a common front against conflict elements within the own religions which are exploited by political interests, on the other hand, to make the common human moral fundamentals clear in societies with conflicting values.

One finding is that the moral clashes to discuss are not political controversies, but cultural and specific moral questions. The main moral clash, namely, the gap between traditional and modern values, on, for example, sexual liberation, family, free speech, and gender, needs dialogues. We have, on the one hand, traditional and often religiously motivated values along with survival values, and, on the other hand, self-expression values which are often secularly motivated. The task is, for example, to analyse what fundamental values different players want to promote, perhaps values such as human prospering and happiness, and to define the ethical problem.

Another interesting issue for dialogue is the diverse opinions on the role of the individual versus the family, the society or the religious community. The western world has, no doubt, much to learn from other cultures concerning the role of the individual without giving up the idea of human rights. On the basis of some shared values, there are many disagreements that need dialogues, for example on the death penalty, suicide, murder by honour, genital mutilation, the role of women and men, and partnerships for homosexuals.

A third task for dialogues is to identify, promote and express shared values and, at the same time, cultural and individual diversity, and moral vitality. This ambition is, as far I understand, the only way to build a global society, security, and cultural richness.

A fourth task is to foster dialogue, in schools, in public debate, and within universities.

The great task of the United Nations

Based on the facts, analysis, and conclusions in this article, I will address the Secretary-General of the United Nations to start promoting worldwide dialogues on moral questions, focussing on moral agreements and disagreements. A dialogue is not a place for political manifestations, but for giving and taking, for having one's own identity along with openness for other people's values, for searching for good arguments and – sometimes – searching for converging and shared values as a basis for a stable global community.

References

Bexell, G. (2002) 'Universalism in Ethics and Cultural Diversity', in Bexell, G. and Andersson, D-E. (eds) (2002) *Universal Ethics. Perspectives and Proposals from Scandinavian Scholars*, The Hague: Martinus Nijhoff Publishers.

Bexell, G. and Andersson, D-E. (eds) (2002) *Universal Ethics. Perspectives and Proposals from Scandinavian Scholars*, The Hague: Martinus Nijhoff Publishers.

Bexell, G. (2003) 'Det gemensamma bästa och det partikulära: kulturkonfrontationer och värdekonflikter', in Lundmark, F. (ed) (2003) *Kultur, säkerhet och hållbar samhällsutveckling efter 11 september*, Stockholm: Gidlunds förlag.

Bexell, G. (2004) 'Universal Values and Cultural Diversity: Driving forces for Good Government', in Mellbourn, A. (ed) (2004) *Developing a Culture of Conflict Prevention*, Stockholm: Gidlunds förlag.

Bok, S. (1995) *Common Values*, Columbia: University of Missouri Press.

Brundtland, G. H. (ed) (1987) *Our common future: The World Commission on Environment and Development*, Oxford: Oxford University Press.

Commission on Global Governance (1995) *Our Global Neighbourhood*, New York: Oxford University Press.

Dalton, R.J. (2005) 'The Social Transformation of Trust in Government', *The International Review of Sociology*, 15(1): 133–154.

Etzioni, A. (2001) *The Monochrome Society*, Princeton: Princeton University Press.

Lundmark, F. (ed) (2003) *Kultur, säkerhet och hållbar samhällsutveckling efter 11 september*, Stockholm: Gidlunds förlag.

Inglehart, R. and Norris, P. (2003) 'The True Clash of Civilizations', *Foreign Policy*, March/April 2003.

Inglehart, R. and Welzel, C. (2005) *Modernization, Cultural Change, and Democracy. The Human Development Sequence*, Cambridge: Cambridge University Press.

Lögstrup, K.E (1997) *The Ethical Demand*, English edition, Notre Dame: University of Notre Dame Press.

Mellbourn, A. (ed) (2004) *Developing a Culture of Conflict Prevention*, Stockholm: Gidlunds förlag.

Second Parliament of the World's Religions (1993) *Toward a Global Ethic: An Initial Declaration*, Declaration from the Chicago meeting.

Singer, P. (2002) *One World: The Ethics of Globalization*, New Haven: Yale University Press.

UNESCO (1995) *Our Creative Diversity*, Paris: UNESCO.

9

The Role of Solidarity in Institutions of Governance*

Gita Sen

Introduction

This paper addresses a question that becomes particularly important when a society is going through major social and economic changes such as those that were triggered by the Indian economic reforms of the 1990s. As existing institutions break down or become irrelevant, and as new ones struggle to come into existence, the possible basis for creating sustainable institutions becomes a central issue. Whatever one may think of the reforms, and however one assesses their impact on economic growth, poverty, inequality and economic performance overall, few would question that much has changed in the structure of economic interactions at many levels.

These changes pose challenges for policymakers and programme implementers as much as for citizens. In the pre-1990s 'shortages' economy, queues and rationing mechanisms of various kinds determined the interactions among citizens, between citizens and sellers of goods and service providers, and among providers themselves, whether private or public. While shortages continue to shape the options available to the poor in urban and rural areas, the problem for those at the middle and upper ends of the economic spectrum has become one of learning to cope with the problems of plenty. To give one example: with the rapid increase in vehicular traffic, traffic behaviour in cities such as Bangalore and Delhi has taken on the characteristics of a 'prisoners'

* An earlier version of this paper was presented at the Conference on Governance, Jawaharlal Nehru University, New Delhi, 9–10 February 2006. I am grateful to the participants for their questions and comments. I am also indebted to Chiranjib Sen, Aditi Iyer, Asha George, and Veloshnee Govender for many hours discussing these issues.

dilemma'. There are high pay-offs for successful non-cooperative rule-breaking, significant losses for those who follow the rules while others do not, and the resulting chaos of collective non-cooperation. What is most striking is the extent to which new informal behavioural rules, based on non-cooperation, appear to have evolved. In today's mean streets, those who follow traditional traffic rules based on cooperative principles, including courtesy to smaller vehicles and pedestrians, draw puzzled looks and set off aggressive behaviour.

Increased policing is one obvious answer, but a relatively ineffective one that may, in fact, serve to further break down social cooperation. In Bangalore, traffic police have been called upon to manage more and more intersections (including those with new traffic signals), but this appears to have the perverse effect of worsening behaviour in the unmanned areas. Nor has it eliminated rule-breaking at the manned intersections. It is fairly common to see rule-breakers whizzing by with impunity, with the traffic policeman shouting or shaking his fist at them!

Clearly, norms of cooperation have broken down and need to be rec-reated. Traditional economics' answer to problems of coordination and cooperation is to create private incentives or disincentives (including through policing), 'as if' markets, or private property rights. Social norms in this view are perceived to be the rules of thumb that evolve on the basis of these underpinning institutional characteristics. But what if incentives, policing, and property rights are difficult to create or sustain? There may be many circumstances, including the traffic example given above, where this may be so. What then? Can social norms, created in conjunction with, or independent of, private incentives and disincentives, provide a partial answer?

This paper is particularly concerned with one class of problems where norms of 'solidarity' (explained below) are, we believe, crucial, but difficult to create or sustain through traditional economic incentives and disincentives alone. In the Indian context of social and economic inequality, the provision of decent quality social services (schools, health centres, housing) to poor people continues to be an unresolved problem. It has been compounded by inadequate financing and weak budgetary allocations. The policy debate often pits those who argue for the need for more funds against those who argue that existing funds are very poorly utilized. On the ground, the availability and quality of public services remain woefully inadequate, especially those on which poor people depend. Creating viable and sustainable institutions is a key challenge.

Institutions and norms

I use the term 'institution' to refer to a normative frame that structures interactions among people (and other economic agents), and is held together by shared values that govern norms of behaviour, and a common and accepted language of communication and discourse. The emphasis on shared values and the language of discourse distinguishes this from Bowles who has a similar definition: '*Institutions* (as I use the term) *are the laws, informal rules, and conventions that give a durable structure to social interactions among the members of a population*' (Bowles 2005: 47f). The stronger its shared values and language of discourse become, the stronger the institution and the more enduring will be the organizational frame that is based on it.

Institutions can graduate from those that are *basic* (where the normative basis and its corresponding organizational frame are held together by incentives and disincentives) to those that are more *advanced* (where the glue is provided by shared values that may or may not be based on incentives or disincentives). Advanced institutions do not function primarily through policing or private incentives. In advanced institutions, people wait in queues, obey traffic rules, and treat health centre clients with courtesy even when there is no immediate pay-off or punishment. Might these behaviours be simply learned responses to underlying private incentives and disincentives, simply the rules of thumb that represent that structure? Or can norms have a rationale and life of their own? Can cooperative behaviours be learned even if they are not underpinned by private incentives or disincentives?

Standard economic theory has long assumed that the behaviour of economic agents, including individuals, is driven by private cost-benefit calculus. Despite considerable disagreement by psychologists, anthropologists, and other social scientists, it is only recently that economic experiments, made possible by rapid advances in game theory, have challenged these standard assumptions. For instance, as reported in Fehr and Fischbacher (2001), the rate of cooperation in 'prisoners' dilemma' experiments is as high as 40–60 per cent, contrary to the dominant strategy expectation of mutual non-cooperation. Bowles reports the results of other experiments with the Ultimate Game[1] to show that other-centredness (i.e. reciprocal behaviour) is quite common. When played by university students, responders often reject substantial offers if they feel that the proposer is being unfair, even though by doing so they know that they will end up with nothing. These results have been vindicated in similar experiments with small societies in

15 different parts of the world. Experimental results show that no society behaved as predicted by self-interest axioms, and there was also considerable variation in the size of the proposers' offers, depending on whether the society had a regular practice of collective sharing (Bowles 2004: 115f).

Such experimental results point to a significant presence of what Bowles calls 'social preferences', i.e. *other-regarding* or *process-regarding* motivations for behaviour. That is, time and again, people evaluate a state not only on the basis of its implications for themselves, but also based on what it might mean for others. They also evaluate a state based on the process by which it comes about. In the Ultimate Game experiments mentioned above, the evaluation is linked to whether or not the process is judged to be fair, an ethical judgement that often leads to behaviour that has a substantial cost for the player in question. Hirschman's (1981) argument that people's willingness to be patient when stuck in a traffic jam in a tunnel depends on how fast they are moving relative to the cars in the other lane, is another example of other-directed perceptions. As Bowles puts it: *'The key aspect of other-regarding preferences is that one's evaluation of a state depends on how it is experienced by others'* (2004: 109).

How do non-'selfish'[2] behaviours of this type come about? How do they become social norms, and how do such norms get built into organizations? In particular, how can social norms of solidarity with poor people's needs get ingrained in a society?

Solidarity as a social norm

I define solidarity as *an other-directed trait that views the needs and interests of others as inherently similar to one's own.* By definition, solidarity is an interpersonal value that cannot be defined independently of the other person. The idea of being 'inherently similar' does not necessarily mean they are identical, but that they are viewed as intrinsically having the same worthiness. Similarity may be measured on a number of different metrics, including common citizenship or common humanity. The fault-lines for solidarity are often precisely the commonly experienced bases of social difference – nationality, ethnicity, race, caste, gender, and economic class. The more unequal a society and the more fragmented along such lines, the less likely it is to recognize solidarity as a value or to build it into institutions or behaviour.[3]

A simple thought experiment can help to measure the extent to which a group values solidarity. The experiment asks for individual responses to the following question: Starting from an initial position of equality, if some people in a group can be made better-off without making others worse off, which position is better? While the self-directed will choose the Pareto-superior position, those concerned with solidarity are more likely to pick the initial position. In an informal Indian classroom setting[4] a number of people did prefer the initial position and people's responses did not vary much based on how the better-off became so. This may well be because of a generalized Indian belief that intrinsic worth or effort has little to do with economic performance or social superiority. More interesting were the reasons given by those who picked the initial position; a number of them said that they did not like the second position, not because they felt it was intrinsically unfair, but because they were afraid that it was the beginning of a slippery slope towards greater and greater inequality, as well as lack of concern of the better-off for those worse-off.

Experiments such as those above point to the fragility of the assumption of independent preferences that is at the heart of the standard theorems of welfare economics. Another important insight that can be culled from the new experimental economics is the malleability of human 'preferences' and behaviour. We have already cited evidence showing that people's behaviours are not purely 'selfish', but can be both other-directed and process-dependent. They also depend on the norms of the society within which one lives, and are hence variable over time as society itself changes.

Solidarity as a value grows out of concern for fairness and is the basis of many social justice movements in different societies. In the solidarity-rich societies of western Europe, particularly the Nordic countries, the development of social solidarity was a product of nineteenth century social democratic movements which attached intrinsic worth to social equality, and hence built this norm into many social and economic institutions and organizations. By contrast, the sharp racial inequality characterizing US society was only partially changed by the civil rights movement of the 1960s, and found renewed justification in Ronald Reagan's vituperative attacks on so-called 'welfare queens'.

Nearer home, the most dramatic example of how social justice movements can replace inequality with solidarity-based norms and behaviour is the transformation of caste relations in Kerala in the twentieth century. From a caste system described by Swami Vivekananda as among the most rigid in the country and built on norms of both untouchability and 'unseeability', the society changed in a relatively short period through a combination of social reform and communist movements. In today's Kerala, caste-based social norms and differentiation have all but disappeared, and solidarity as a basis for collective action is much more widely accepted.

An important aspect of solidarity is that it refers particularly to the view from the perspective of the better-off. While Sen's 'freedom to do and be' (Sen 1999) clarifies the rights of the have-nots, the idea of solidarity actualizes the other side of the human rights coin – the responsibilities of the haves.

But even if we recognize the value of solidarity as a social norm underpinning public action to meet the basic needs for food, health-care, education, housing etc. of the worse-off in society, is it necessary? Can public provision for these needs be justified without calling on solidarity?

The need for solidarity[5]

Traditional economics' treatment of the need for public action is based on the presence of externalities, public goods whose consumption is non-rivalrous and non-excludable, transactions costs, or incomplete information. However, much of what we would include under basic needs do not meet these criteria. While externalities certainly exist (particularly in such areas as public health and sanitation), much of basic needs – food, curative health services, education – are rivalrous and excludable and have few associated externalities.

Indeed, if we take curative health services as our example, there is usually a thriving private market for such services on which a considerable portion of health expenditure is spent. Private production and consumption are not only possible, but common. The problem is that over-reliance on private markets for the provision of curative health services divides people into haves and have-nots on the basis of affordability. This is the experience of both a rich country such as the United States, (with over 40 million people without health insurance), and India, where the bulk of health expenditures are out of pocket but the poor are increasingly forced to opt out of treatment because of rising costs (Sen et al. 2002). Unaffordability, rather than incomplete information about its public benefits (the idea behind merit goods), is the reason for consumption below the 'efficient' level. Catastrophic health expenditures have emerged as a major cause of households falling into poverty (Krishna 2005).

The justification for the public provision of basic needs is simply that the poor cannot afford them at the prices determined in the private sector, and without them life entails significant hardships and deprivation. Furthermore, private provision divides people on the basis of affordability, enforces rationing within the household on the basis of gender and age, and causes households to fall into poverty. This justification for the public provision of the basic needs of the poor is not on the basis of any of the standard public goods/externalities/incomplete information/transactions costs reasons; it is on the simple basis of solidarity – the basic needs of the poor are as worthy of fulfilment as those of the better-off. In some sense, one might call them 'solidarity' goods – a shorthand for the recognition of what these goods stand for, the recognition by the haves of the intrinsic worth of the basic needs of the have-nots. This argument about the need for public provision does not rule out the possibility that the social value of solidarity on which it is based can be a rule of thumb representation for underlying private incentives (something most economists would be comfortable with since one could then work on the private incentives and not worry about solidarity!).[6] It does not need to be based on strict altruism in the evolutionary biologist's sense.[7]

Provision of 'solidarity' goods

The argument that provision of the basic needs of poor people cannot be left to the mercies of private markets does not tell us exactly how such provision should occur. The following questions are addressed in this section. First, is solidarity only a matter of financing or is it needed at other levels also? Second, what combination of private incentives, policing, and social values such as solidarity could be the most effective glue to hold together the institutions for provision of the basic needs of the poor? Third, can the social value of solidarity be built into a society if it has not evolved on its own through historical processes?

Solidarity in provision

Examining the actual experience of efforts to meet the basic needs of poor people through public provision makes it clear that the social value of solidarity needs to operate at more than one level. As we have seen, the better-off certainly need to be willing to pay to ensure that the basic needs of the poor are met. This is, however, only the first step. The next and equally important level at which solidarity must be present is in the actual production or provision of the goods and services. No amount of funding will ensure a decent learning environment for a *dalit* child in a government run school dominated by the upper castes, if the teacher does not step in to change the default environment.

When a poor woman is in need of emergency obstetric care and the doctor in the primary health centre tells her to come back later, solidarity norms are being violated. Solidarity needs to work both at arm's length in relation to funding adequacy, and in the day-to-day functioning of public 'markets'. Improved management and supervision, better working conditions, and upgraded facilities need to be complemented by specific training for solidaristic behaviour (discussed further later) linked with greater accountability by providers to communities.

Private incentives, policing, and solidarity

It follows that, while private goods can be left to private incentives requiring neither policing (except to ensure competition) nor social values, this is not true either for standard public goods or for 'solidarity' goods. For public goods, private markets tend to fail as we know. In some instances it may be possible to create 'as if' markets (e.g. markets for emissions trading), but otherwise a combination of policing and social values creation are needed. For solidarity goods on the other hand, a combination of private production and social values based public production may be possible and necessary.[8] Depending on the effectiveness of provision by the public sector, policing of the private sector may also be needed.

Combinations of private and public production are quite common for basic needs, but their intent and mechanisms vary widely. Taking the example of curative health services again, private and public sectors may co-exist as in India, operating as largely parallel tracks which loop in to intersect at particular points. Poor people in backward rural areas go back and forth for services between the public health workers (such as the auxiliary nurse-midwife), the private rural medical practitioners, the public doctor at the primary or higher level health centre, and the private hospital. In the process, they lose time, spend large sums of money out of pocket, and may end up cured if they are lucky, but all too often uncured or even dead.[9]

A major problem is that not only do public providers need solidarity 'training', but private providers need policing and regulation if the poor are not to be taken advantage of. The experience of health systems in countries such as Canada, Sweden, and the United Kingdom is that the public health system acts as an 'automatic' regulator of the private sector. The competition provided by a well-functioning public system for needs such as health and education can serve to discipline the private sector and provide cost- and quality-assurance.

Solidarity in an environment of inequality

But what if historical processes have not enshrined solidarity as a social norm, and social and economic inequality run deep? Can solidarity be created if it does not already exist? This is a major dilemma in India today after several decades of under-financed and poorly functioning public services intended to meet the basic needs of the poor. The experiences of the health and education sectors provide different lessons which need to be brought together.

The health sector is, as we have seen, a poorly regulated plural system which by all accounts is quite low on solidarity values. Attempts by the government to improve the quality and reach of services have included multiple institutional experiments and a lot of confusion! By the 1990s, the government appeared increasingly to be giving up on public provision in the face of a process of creeping but ill-regulated privatization. Starting with contracting out or handing over primary health centres to NGOs, this has spread to increased use of private contract doctors, charging of user fees, drastic reduction of the scope of drug price controls, and subsidies for large corporate hospitals. Private contract doctors are also at the heart of the new National Rural Health Mission that is intended to improve health care in the most backward districts. Some attempts are also being made to increase local accountability by allowing the *panchayati raj* (local self-governance) institutions in some states to control the salaries of lower level health workers.

In none of these attempts has the core problem of social distance, disregard, and lack of solidarity of providers with their clients been acknowledged, let alone addressed.

The education sector provides a contrast. The National Literacy Mission following the landmark Education Policy of 1986 was the single most important process that brought the basic need of the poor for education to the centre of national awareness. It has been followed by other programmes with a focus on improving quality and reach such as the District Primary Education Programme, and the innovative Education Guaranteed Scheme of Madhya Pradesh. This is not the place to go into the details or the pros and cons. Nor is public education in the country as imbued with solidarity as one might wish. Nevertheless, it is not accidental that the haves in the country recognize literacy and the educational deficit of the poor much better than their equally desperate need for affordable health care.

What this shows is that a recognition of the need for solidarity as a social value can be a first step to policies and programmes that can have quite far-reaching effects. While history may be the most effective creator of new social norms, it is also unpredictable. But the imaginative policymaker does not have to be a good astrologer! Neither does she or he have to simply sit and wait!

Notes

1. The Ultimate Game in its simplest version is a two-person game in which one person, the proposer, is given a 'pie' and can decide how much of it to offer to the other person, the responder. If the responder accepts the offer, the pie is shared as proposed; if the responder rejects the offer, no-one gets anything.
2. It is not intended to be perjorative here; 'selfish' is simply a short-hand for self-directed behaviour based on costs and benefits to oneself.
3. Recent evidence from biological experiments identifies social inequality as a cause of higher stress levels and ill-health among both humans and other primates. This evidence is based on measuring the levels of the stress hormone cortisol in the bloodstream, and other non-psychometric measures (see Wilkinson 2005).
4. The class, being a group of mid-career civil servants, contained a number of people who had direct responsibility for managing anti-poverty programmes and were well aware of the problems posed on the ground by social inequality. In that sense it may not have been a very representative group.
5. In standard economics, treatment of consumer preferences and demand theory, both preferences and the rules for utility maximization, are invariant with respect to the level of the consumer's budget constraint. The rich and the poor may have different preference maps, but they adopt the same utility maximization behaviour. While such behaviour may be a reasonable approximation for those above the poverty line, it flies in the face of much ground-level observation of how poor households make consumption decisions and choices.
6. For instance, the health budget could be increased by offering individual income tax-payers the choice of earmarking a portion of their income tax for health in exchange for paying taxes at the slightly lower marginal rate.
7. 'A behaviour is *altruistic* if it confers a benefit on another while inflicting a cost on oneself (this standard biological definition is restricted to benefits and costs and does not concern intentions)' (Bowles 2005: 110).
8. Public production is needed because it is very difficult to imbue private production with social values such as solidarity that may run counter to profit maximization.
9. These remarks draw upon observations made from the Gender and Health Equity project that we have been implementing in Koppal, a poor and backward district of northern Karnataka over the last five years.

References

Bowles, S. (2005) *Microeconomics: Behaviour, Institutions, and Evolution*, New Delhi: Oxford University Press.

Fehr, E. and Fischbacher, U. (2001) 'Why social preferences matter', Stockholm, Nobel Symposium on Behavioural and Experimental Economics (quoted in Bowles 2005: 109).

Hirschman, A. O. (1981) *Essays in Trespassing. Economics to Politics and Beyond*, Cambridge: Cambridge University Press.

Hirschman, A. O. (1981) 'The changing tolerance for income inequality in the course of economic development', in Hirschman, A. O. (1981) *Essays in Trespassing. Economics to Politics and Beyond*, Cambridge: Cambridge University Press.

Krishna, A. (2005) 'Poverty knowledge and poverty action in India' (draft).

Sen, A. K. (1999) *Development as Freedom*, New York: Alfred Knopf.

Sen, G., Iyer, A. and George, A. (2002) 'Structural Reforms and Health Equity: A Comparison of NSS Surveys of 1986–87 and 1995–96', *Economic and Political Weekly*, XXXVII: 14.

Wilkinson, R. G. (2005) *The Impact of Inequality: How to Make Sick Societies Healthier*, London: Routledge.

10
Meeting Global Challenges.
The Role of Public Goods

Gun-Britt Andersson

The current system of global governance is not adequate for dealing appropriately with the most pressing common concerns. Too often, the debate on Global Public Goods blurs with that on development. The international community needs to find better ways of dealing with interests shared by all nations. The Paris Declaration on Aid Effectiveness provides an example, which, however, only relates to national development matters. Cooperation on global issues in national interests should have its own agenda. The French and Swedish governments have, following up on the Financing for Development Conference in Monterrey, Mexico in 2002, sponsored an International Task Force on Global Public Goods.[1] The Task Force has endeavoured to deepen the understanding on why in international cooperation it tends to be difficult to agree on measures to attain clearly desirable results such as halting global warming and the spread of communicable diseases. It provides structural and pragmatic proposals on how international cooperation in the national interest can be improved. The report of the Task Force with the title 'Meeting Global Challenges' was released in September 2006. The following gives a perspective on Global Public Goods from one of the members of the Task Force.

Background

Most peoples' economic, political, and social lives and livelihoods are grounded in local and national contexts and conditions. At the same time globalization is accompanied by ever more issues and concerns that cannot be handled by local or national action alone. The spread of diseases, climate change, the international financial architecture, and fighting terrorism are only a few examples of challenges that cannot be effectively handled at the level of the sovereign state alone. In every person's and every nation's interest, international cooperation is needed.

To respond to the growing need for international cooperation, an elaborate web of international organizations has been created since the Second World War, including the United Nations and the European Union. Over these past decades, enormous progress has been made towards greater freedom – freedom from fear, hunger, and want. The conventions on Universal Human Rights have been negotiated and are gaining respect in spite of frequent abuses. Democracy has spread. Human development indicators show that a majority of people in the world live longer and lead better lives materially than ever before (www.gapminder.org).

The vision that poverty can be eradicated is no longer purely utopian. World leaders have believed in it enough to proclaim the Millennium Development Goals (MDGs), including those of reducing by half the number of people living in poverty, and providing basic education and health for everyone by 2015. In important ways, there has also been progress on peace, security, and human dignity. Decolonization has been more or less completed. Europe has moved on from its history of violent conflict to the historic EU project. The Cold War is over.

These fundamental changes have liberated much energy and local aspirations. Men and women around the world are demanding better lives, self-determination, and a fair share of prosperity. Their ambitions can fuel sustainable development, but when frustrated, can also fuel aggression, protective fear, and regression.

The issues are complicated and the answers will have to be manifold. International cooperation, however, must definitely improve further. Along with worthy achievements, the international community has witnessed failures and shortcomings. All summed up, international bodies have been better at identifying problems, passing well-intended resolutions, and setting targets than at delivering results. While there is a fair degree of common understanding of the responsibilities of nations for their own development, including of best practices as to economic and many other policies, international cooperation and governance have neither managed to foster a conducive environment for national development efforts nor effectively address genuinely global concerns. There is under-provision of Global Public Goods such as peace and security, sustainable management of global commons, control of communicable diseases, enabling rules of the game in the economic sphere, and access to knowledge. All these have been identified by the International Task Force as Priority Global Public Goods.

Responsibility and legitimacy

As clearly stated by the Millennium Review Summit in the autumn of 2005, the global governance system needs to be improved. Too many governments consider it neither efficient nor effective and, as powerful nations and strong stakeholders are resorting to unilateral action because of perceived weaknesses, the system is further weakened. Another, equally dangerous, choice is to remain inactive and wait for others to sort out problems. Neither approach is acceptable.

In some cases, the international system has been up to task. Consider, for example, achievements in spite of set-backs of peace-keeping operations in Sierra Leone, the Balkans, and East Timor. In the environmental field, the implementation of the Montreal Protocol is helping to close the gap in our atmosphere's ozone layer. The World Health Organization (WHO) acted with authority to suppress a SARS outbreak and, as a result, was given enhanced powers to monitor and control diseases. The international community also proved competent in its response to the Indian Ocean tsunami. Unprecedented levels of assistance for relief and reconstruction was provided and a tsunami warning system is now being established in the Indian Ocean region. The International Oceanographic Commission of UNESCO is serving as a convener and catalyst in this endeavour.

These examples strikingly illustrate that governments need to cooperate, that individual action is insufficient. Peace and security, control of epidemics, and prevention and relief in cases of massive natural disaster, depend on international cooperation, regional and global.

However, it is obvious that international organizations have difficulties in setting priorities within their often broad mandates. There has been a proliferation of initiatives and projects. For every topical issue, donor conferences are convened and multilateral organizations rush to make their particular contributions. Intentions are good, but important motives for conveners are also to be seen to act and for organizations to get recognition and access to fresh or redirected funds. More attention is too often given to visibility than to careful prioritization and to achieving and accounting for results.

The international system has its own dynamic for better and worse. The main responsibility, however, for weaknesses and failures falls on the 'owners' – the member states.

The experiences of the European Union, and in particular its current crises, also provide lessons in this regard for wider international cooperation.

In a series of intergovernmental negotiations, the European Union has been given some supranational powers. They are mostly confined to areas where removal of obstacles for interaction across borders has opened up for more business, people, and civil society contacts. One category of issues concerns such things as food safety, environmental standards, and animal health, where the benefits of cross-border cooperation are obvious. This open space and internal market constitute a public good that everybody can enjoy at the expense of nobody. However, when the openness and measures beg for not so well understood adjustments of livelihoods and attitudes, and enhanced competition is, or is perceived as, a threat to job security, political problems arise. The legitimacy of decisions in far away Brussels is questioned. The images of a distant all encompassing bureaucratic centre of power can become a scapegoat for grievances over all sorts of domestic and global problems. This has been evident in the debate and referenda over the proposed EU constitution.

The advanced European experience of integration demonstrates that it is important to be clear about what to cooperate on and why. In modern democratic information societies, the wisdom and legitimacy of political decisions are always put to the test. At the national level, governments derive legitimacy from history, constitutions, and elections. Even as some degree of democratic governance and control are introduced at the regional level, national politicians and governments remain the first line of accountability. In the EU context, experience has reinforced the principle of subsidiarity. There is no point in referring problems and issues that can be settled at home to a higher level.

At the same time this also means that national governments must assume responsibility for international affairs. Only they can do it. In cases where issues cannot be handled by national action alone, political leaders must clarify to citizens and voters that international cooperation is in their national interest. As international cooperation is by nature voluntary, this is not an easy task. It entails explaining why resources should be committed and rules changed, how and why other nations and players could be expected, or made, to contribute to a common cause, and what the benefits of action and the costs of inaction would be. It also entails being clear about expectations and guidance of the various international organizations.

The nature of public goods

A typical feature of public goods is that once provided they are there for everybody's consumption irrespective of who has paid for, or assumed responsibility for, the provision. This creates a tendency to wait for others to act and also means that it can be genuinely difficult to determine what needs to be done by whom. Benefits can also be unevenly shared. Climate change might e.g. have positive effects in the short run in some regions, while others will experience more immediate negative consequences. Strong economic powers have a heavier stake in financial stability than smaller nations, but all are affected. The incentives for contributing towards global ends differ and nations frequently wait for others to take the initiative, or hide behind the excuse that it is futile to e.g. restrict over-fishing because others will take advantage.

There are different types of global public goods from the point of view of how they can be provided. In the case of mitigating climate change, achieving positive results will depend on the participation by everybody in lowering emissions of greenhouse gases (summation public goods). As to control of communicable disease, discovery of an effective vaccine constitutes a best shot public good – once discovered, it is in principle available for everybody's use. Knowledge also has that property, unless it is made private by property right rules. In an opposite situation, control of an epidemic will fail if one country or region is unable to take efficient preventive measures. Whether or not measures will succeed depends on the weakest link. Walls against flooding are another example in this context. Common for all are that, even if everybody is aware of the problems and would benefit from solutions, there are inbuilt tendencies to wait for others to act; to entertain a hope that free-riding will be possible. To overcome obstacles, commitment and initiatives by influential players and workable proposals on how to solve a problem and deliver a global public good are needed.

The Task Force on Global Public Goods has argued that these inherent difficulties for the provision of global public goods can be overcome only through enlightened responsible leadership and better performance of international organizations. As to leadership, there are examples where the G8 of heads of states has had such a catalytic role. The G20, which is comprised of Ministers of Finance from 20 countries, was similarly established to deal with financial stability issues. Building on these experiences, the International Task Force on Global Public Goods has proposed the formation of a G25, constituted of top leaders from the most influential players globally, with representation of all regions and also of the poorest developing countries, in Africa through the African Union. G25 would have a catalytic leadership role.

The dual roles of international organizations

Besides dealing with cross-border or global issues, international organizations are fora, where governments support one another in national development endeavours. The old 'rich' countries have, since the time of post-war reconstruction, benefited from exchange of experience, peer learning, and policy advice in and from the OECD. Membership has gradually expanded. The UN system and the international financial institutions are in similar and other ways providing support to developing countries, in particular the poorest among them. They are part of the so called donor community, contributing towards achieving the Millenium Development Goals (MDGs). For reasons of solidarity and enlightened self-interest, poverty eradication, and education for all are of shared global interest, but they are private or national goods or utilities rather than global public goods.

National governments can in these cases do the most by themselves to promote growth and development through sound policy choices. Mainly domestic resources are required for expanding education facilities, improving health systems, and meeting similar needs. Outside support can have the useful role of contributing to the design of better policies, to the scaling up of activities, and to enhancing institutions and capacities. However, attempts to do more will often not be sustainable or work. Responsibility and accountability for these matters must not be allowed to blur between national and international levels – as that could, in fact, discourage domestic efforts. These issues have been analysed and discussed systematically in recent years. The Paris Declaration on Aid Effectiveness of 2005 represents widely accepted conclusions.

The architecture and modalities for cooperation on cross-border, regional, and global issues which require common action – and, more often than not, joint funding – need similar analyses and conclusions as those on aid effectiveness.

The issues concerned are of crucial importance for sound global development, but are not per se belonging to the poverty/development agenda. Provision of global public goods, such as aviation safety, the mitigation of global warming, or containment of the avian flu depend on constructive multi-party interaction in much the same way as development interventions do. Nonetheless, there has been an unfortunate mixing – and sometimes even merging – of the agendas for development and initiatives to better address other global concerns in international politics. Reasons are that the same international organizations are involved and that national budgets for development cooperation are, more or less, the only available public sources of financing for international civilian matters.

Different from development assistance

In coalition with development agencies from donor countries, developing countries have naturally defended the use of such funds according to priorities as seen from their perspective. Some global or regional public goods are among these priorities, including, for instance, measures to combat communicable diseases, like HIV/AIDS and malaria. The same can be said of promoting security through conflict-prevention and post-conflict reconstruction. In the field of energy and environment, on the other hand, international debate and negotiations have been marked by a notion that sustainable management of global commons are matters of interest to rich nations primarily – something they should pay for beyond their disbursements of 0.7 per cent of their GDP for development.

However, it is obvious that, for instance, the sustainable use and protection of natural resources are of vital interest to all nations, often in the short run, but even more so in a longer run perspective. Sweden, like a few other countries, party to the Kyoto agreement, should and will continue to impose high taxes on fossil fuels and take other measures to reduce greenhouse gases. It will make more sense for them to do so if they are joined by the United States and by developing countries that in the future are likely to suffer the most from global warming and that are already among the large emitters.

The approach of linking the solution of global problems with the 0.7 target for official development assistance is in many ways becoming increasingly strange and obsolete. Strange, because the target seems to apply to the relatively small group of old DAC donors, whereas many other countries have in the meantime acquired an ability to contribute. Obsolete, because many more countries already actually participate in the funding of ventures beyond their borders, towards both development, and regional and global problem solving. There are several reasons for doing so. Modern economic development, for instance, depends on taking part in world trade and adhering to international standards. Moreover, it is in any nation's immediate interest to cooperate with others to stem instability, diseases, financial crises or environmental hazards.

A key conclusion shared by the International Task Force on Global Public Goods is that global concerns should be addressed on their own merits. The most pressing needs and gaps in what is already taken care of should be identified. In doing this, the principle of subsidiarity should be applied. For each issue, an analysis should be made of why action and cooperation is necessary, what inaction will mean to whom and what it will cost. Estimates should also be made of benefits for global and regional collectives as well as for individual nations. Such analyses might show that it is justified to use development cooperation funds in some instances, but they may also convince national governments (and publics) that it makes sense to contribute from other sources, which could include innovative financing schemes under discussion and early implementation.

The international Task Force on Global Public Goods has highlighted five key areas where improvements in the provision of global public goods are urgent. These are peace and security, preventing the spread of infectious diseases, mitigating climate change, financial stability, and a fair and open trading system. In addition, knowledge is singled out as a crosscutting global public good of particular significance. Research and development of knowledge are as important as action to improve the provision of global public goods and should be based on the best possible scientific analyses and evidence. Furthermore, capacity to assess knowledge by all countries and stakeholders is important, not only for development but also to facilitate more equitable participation in international negotiations and decision-making on global issues.

The specific areas have been singled out because of their relevance and because they are interlinked and need to be addressed in any serious effort to enhance more widely-shared human security and prosperity. However the emphasis in the approach of the Task Force is on some necessary reforms and improvements of the way the international cooperation system operates. Analysis of past experience and of what it would take to make progress in the provision of global public goods in the priority areas underpins the structural proposals.

While the observation is made that international organizations already exist for most purposes, they are both individually and as a system performing below potential. Responsible leadership for reform can only come from concerned member states. But as the present governing structures are cumbersome, sector specific, and in some cases not representative enough, inertia, mandate creep, and not so purposeful competition for resources are obstacles to reform. Because of this, the Task Force argues that the G25 of national leaders should be formed. Its role should be to ensure, in a more legitimate yet efficient manner than the G8 (and G20), that the most urgent global issues will be dealt with. The G25 would comprise leading and resourceful countries from all continents that would be expected to spearhead action and commit resources. The role of the G25 would be to be a catalyst for setting priorities for moving issues onto the agendas of international cooperation. For the sake of legitimacy and for reasons of efficiency, decisions would continue to be taken by, and negotiation conducted in, the proper structures of organizations where all countries have their say. As more responsible leadership is exerted, organizations in the system would however be challenged to reform. The Task Force also joins others in a quest for making the Security Council and the Bretton Woods institutions more representative of today's geo-economic and geopolitic realities and also for efficiency reforms of the UN system. The specialized agencies should in their respective fields be hubs of professional networks, and their research departments should endeavour to monitor the state of affairs in key areas and to provide more evidence-based analysis of what needs to be done and what might work. Organizations like the OECD also have a role to play in this regard. If countries, and for that matter the private sector, are to be convinced to commit more resources to international programmes for their roles in the provision of global public goods, accountability most also improve. Evaluations should be used as a tool for continuous efforts to improve effectiveness and efficiency – for staying relevant.

Naturally, the UN system should be expected to set the stage in the pursuit of global public goods. Some of its agencies are doing so in their fields of competence. A good example is WHO, while others fail to focus or refocus their efforts to fully answer to the present global needs. Somebody like the G25 must prioritize issues to tackle, and somebody must underpin proposals to that end through monitoring with comprehensible top quality analysis and advocacy. There must also be accountability for results and use of resources.

These are questions that the International Task Force on Global Public Goods was set up to find some answers to. The analysis and proposals will hopefully inspire reform and concrete action for dealing better with global concerns in the years to come. The findings should be of particular and immediate relevance in ongoing endeavours to revitalize the United Nations development and cooperation system.

Note

1. For information on the International Task Force on Global Public Goods, and its report 'Meeting Global Challenges: International Cooperation in the National Interest' (published 18 September 2006), see http://www. gpgtaskforce.org.

11
Global Governance and the Future of the United Nations[*]

Peter Wallensteen

Global players in global governance

The international system has gone through a series of dramatic changes in the past 20 years, unleashing an unusual set of cross-country connections, cooperative efforts, and forms of integration. The dramas have largely been connected to the field of international peace and security. They stem from the needs for democracy, accountability, welfare, dignity, and sustainability. The results are debatable, and indeed there has been much discussion in international conferences, workshop, journals, and in the streets.[1] Globalization has turned into a catchword, with positive ramifications to some and inherent dangers to others. A central concern is the issue of global governance: who (if any) is to have the most influence on the future of this planet and what (if any) is the role of the United Nations?

There are good reasons to focus on global governance: there is, as of yet, no institutional set-up corresponding to a national or local government for the planet as a whole. Much theorizing assumes that this will emerge. However, the discrepancy between closer international connections (globalization) and the lack of an authoritative decision-making centre (governance) is likely to result in dislocations, increasing inequities, turbulence, tension, and conflict. The lack of governance may in the end bring globalization itself to a halt. There is a need and a potential for institutional innovation, whether in the form of a global regime

* This chapter has benefited from inputs from participants in the workshop in Rio de Janeiro in January 2006, particularly Dan Brändström, Anders Mellbourn and the editor, Björn Hettne. It is part of the United Nations in Armed Conflict project of the Uppsala Conflict Data Program, see www.ucdp. uu.se. The conclusions remain the sole responsibility of the author.

building on shared understanding, or a formal institution with charters and powers.

Such institutions can take many forms and only one is a peaceful world order for all, *Pax Omnium*. This would be a regime created consciously, openly and in representative forms. If this is not the way world order is constructed, alternatives may be those built on separated regional orders, emerging from regional cooperation or regional dominance. There is also an option of a world order structured on the present distribution of global power, *Pax Americana*.

The concept of 'world order' brings to mind matters of security, rather than development or justice. The relationships between these aspects of human life are intricate and not necessarily easy to dissect. It seems that the most intensive form of globalization takes place between areas, players, and states that are at peace with one another. Globalization has been a strong tendency for Western Europe, North America, Pacific Asia, and Oceania. These are areas with fewer wars or serious conflicts at the time of globalization. Peace provides a ground for economic development, trade, and investment. It is also where civil society organizations can develop. It seems clear that 'unpeace' does not create conditions for development: wars and conflict scare most investors away, only attracting profiteers. Thus, development needs peace, but peace will also need development to be sustainable, and, with democratic conditions prevailing, a measure of justice. The creation of peace and security is central for globalization and a primary concern for global governance.

This is also why the United Nations enters the equation. It is the only legal body for global decisions in matters relating to peace and security. Its parallel institutions (UNDP, IMF, World Bank, etc.) are part of the same structure and ambition, although bringing in the development concerns. The UN family constitutes one contender for a role in a future global governance structure, moving world order in the direction of *Pax Omnium*. It may connect to still other possibilities involving states, civil society organizations, and multilateral corporations.

In fact, looking back at the events since the end of the Cold War, it is clear that 'globalization' – seen as a phenomenon where a majority of players are working under the same principles of economy and national governance (a liberal market and/or a liberal democratic state) – intensified at this moment. The seclusion of the countries of the Soviet block ended. This is also when global integration came to involve the People's Republic of China and Vietnam, to name two others that previously had been outside the global parameters, but by now (2007) belong to the winners in globalization.

Following this formative event, other tendencies have served to broaden the scope of players that impact on global affairs. The international organizations (IOs) constitute one distinct group, primarily the ones related to the UN. However, they are composed of states, which thus make up a second type of players, particularly the stronger states. States often demonstrate a traditional agenda of sovereignty underneath a surface of welfare thinking. The quest for democracy has led to a third category of internationally engaged players, a vigorous, diversified, and increasingly significant civil society community (CSOs), particularly with a basis in democratic states and with capacity to influence international organizations. Then there is a fourth set, the players who actually carry economic globalization as part of their daily operations: the large corporations that have become main providers of investment capital around the world (multinational corporations, MNCs). These four categories include many individual players with specific concerns. Still, in a discussion on global governance these four have to be included. This essay asks what is the role of the United Nations in scenarios where these four types of player intersect in different parts of the world?

New features of global governance

The four categories of players combine to affect international affairs and their significance can be studied in issues that require concerted solutions. First, the four players have different standings in formal decision-making. Only the state has the authority to make binding decisions for itself and its citizens.[2] Thus, legally speaking, the state is an unavoidable unit of analysis in matters of global governance. Traditionally CSOs and MNCs have acted to pressure the state to make particular decisions (through lobbying, advertising, public campaigns, etc.). Today, secretariats of international organizations also act in this way. The state has to agree to particular developments and give them direction through its formal decisions.

Second, this does not necessarily mean that the state has originated any ideas or even is a main benefactor of particular decisions. There is a complex interplay. For instance, IOs are composed of states, and thus express state interests, although in a combination with other states. They represent aggregated, reconciled state interests, which may be different from the interests of individual states. Similarly, CSOs and MNCs lobby IOs to take up their issues. Sometimes there can be a close correspondence between particular governments and a CSO or a MNC. The interplay has many facets and is not easy to disentangle. In fact, there is at present no complete understanding of how all these relations inter-act. Most analyses take up one of the relations, e.g. the impact of MNCs on a government (for instance, in studies of oil business), or how a CSO works on particular issues (for instance, Greenpeace). Thus, it is hard to get full insight into decision-making on all the issues that together con-stitute present *de facto* global governance.

Third, in fact, much analysis has a bias, in favour of one or the other of the four categories of players. For some, the corporations are the decisive element (often a view of economists, whether Marxist or not), for others it has to be the state (typical for 'realist' thinking, for instance).[3] These are inbuilt assumptions, with the strength of such points of departures, but often with a limited perspective on the complete picture.

Global analysis finds itself at juncture, where there is only partial insight into crucial aspects of how this planet 'actually' works in the broad set of issues that concern its inhabitants. Here it suffices to make some observations:

– A striking feature of the 1990s is the emergence of international conference diplomacy. The environment issue is a good example. A first occasion was the conference in Rio de Janeiro, Brazil, in 1992, a more recent event the meeting on the Kyoto Protocol in Montreal, Canada, in December 2005. These fora are, theoretically, meetings of member states and signatories to the documents. In reality, there is much more to it. International organizations are present in a formal capacity. Another role is performed by the civil society that takes the opportunity to voice its reactions. In the corridors there are lobbyists of concerned economic interests. The four categories can be seen to operate in the same context. The outcome document will be signed by the states, but most of them are likely to be aware of the concerns of international organizations, CSOs, and business communities. 'Real' decision-making could prob-ably be understood from a close analysis of international conference diplomacy.

– A result of this is that the conference diplomacy becomes increas-ingly complicated. To arrive at agreements entails considerable willing-ness to give and take, including compromises that meet demands only in part; trade-off deals that include one demand, but neglect another; developing plans of action that incorporate contradictory demands by spreading their fulfilment over periods of time, etc. The 1990s witnessed considerable innovation in deal-making. The complexity increases the need for interpretation of what has been achieved. It may make implementation difficult and slow. The more resource-demanding a treaty, the more difficult it will be to gain national support for internationally agreed measures.

– This in turn, increases complexity, as the next conference will have to evaluate what has been implemented as well as suggest measures that further the intentions behind the original agreements. The discussions will easily and necessarily become very detailed, in order to make sure that decisions can be implemented and have the intended results. This makes the conferences realistic and practical. There is, however, also a risk of debates and decisions becoming too technical even for the most concerned citizenry. There is a real danger of creating a backlash in the general public: what is this all about, and why to 'we' have to yield on 'our' demands and even carry out painful changes, when 'others' do not?

There are pluses and minuses in this development. On the one hand, it can be seen to support what David Mitrany once suggested: functionalist cooperation is the wave of the future and that will make issues technical, rather than political (Mitrany 1943, 1975). The 'final' say is left to non-political, technical expertise who knows how to implement the decisions. In Mitrany's scenario, global governance turns into a matter of employing a professional cadre, who can talk to each other, and carry out needed action, without necessarily alerting or informing the political levels of society. Issues, in other words, are de-politicized and manageable. The understanding is that what matters for the citizens is not the decision-making, but the outcome, in terms of better living conditions.

On the other hand, this reduces transparency and might hide politically significant effects of agreements and their implementation: some benefit more than others, there might be drawbacks with some actions that are 'hidden' in technical documents and understood only by a few, etc. If a calamity occurs, such as an accident in a nuclear power plant or a natural disaster that was not foreseen, it is no longer a matter of technical 'fixes', but an important political event that will have repercussions for the state, civil society, and business communities. At that point the functionalist approach may contradict the political understanding of what has been decided and implemented. In the end, the political approach may gain the upper hand, as a form of populist agitation against 'technocrats' and 'distant' decision-making.[4]

A danger is that this complexity results in a reaction that says that 'we' are constantly losing from the arrangement, and thus cooperation is no longer in 'our' interest. Countries might, thus, withdraw from international agreements or refrain from entering treaties. This has also been an element in the post-Cold War period. The United States chose not to become party to the Kyoto Protocol in 2001. The same country, although having signed the agreement creating the International Criminal Court (in 2000), chose not to ratify it in 2001. In 2003, it wanted UN support for unilateral action against Iraq, and went ahead without such an authorization.

Thus, if the leading state in the world can put its own interest first without severe consequences, others may strive to do the same. In 2004, North Korea chose to leave the Non-Proliferation Treaty (NPT), later claiming it possessed its own nuclear weapons and in October 2006 announcing its first nuclear weapons test. The unilateral paths set by these two countries – at contrasting ends of the political spectrum in ideology and global influence – may be followed by others, for instance, Iran with respect to its nuclear programme. The outcome of the latest NPT review conference, when the signatories could not even agree on a substantial final document (May 2005), is ominous. The same is true for the lack of reference to disarmament in the World Summit outcome document (New York, September 2005). These negative results of international conference diplomacy provide arguments for those claiming that 'we are losing' and 'others' benefiting.

This is, however, not a uniform trend. Libya, for instance, chose in 2003 to dismantle its nuclear weapons programme, and instead began to interact more constructively with the international community. To be 'outside' may, in the long run, not be so attractive. In late 2006, the United States preferred diplomacy together with the European Union in dealing the Iranian nuclear issue, and with China in talking to North Korea.

In conference diplomacy it is obvious to experts and leaders, that a given-and-take attitude is necessary and that there are at least two sides to a coin. There is a joint willingness to integrate the interests of opponents (a universalistic attitude). The participation of civil society and business organizations may create a shared interest in particular outcomes, and be a bonus for international agreements and their implementation.

In a national audience, however, this may not necessarily be the way a conference outcome is understood. More particularistic notions may dominate, and the indicator of success is not what 'we and the others' achieved together, but more narrowly 'what's in it for us?'. Political pressure may accumulate from such views. The states are sovereign and may choose not to ratify agreements. For political leaders, the loss in reputation in an international forum might be small compared to the gains in votes on a national arena.[5]

Although the global trends are strong and observable, they do not prevent states from defining issues in particularistic terms, rather than in a universalistic way (Wallensteen 1984). All cooperation requires, in the end, a willingness to see the perspective of the other sides. Democratic processes may, however, generate leaders that base themselves only and exclusively on 'national' interests. This does not necessarily generate war, but may stifle the trend towards stronger non-state players (CSOs, MNCs) and international organizations.

There are such shifts in globalization, perhaps at a rate of one per decade. The Iranian revolution (1979) was a typical event, with considerable regional and global repercussions. The end of the Cold War (dated around 1990) was another, profoundly changing international relations, possibly speeding up globalization. September 11th 2001 is a third example, affecting dramatically the way the US leadership viewed international affairs: globalization implied a threat to its security. It is safe to suggest that such surprises will come in the future as well. Candidates may be a severe economic crisis in China, an unexpected escalation of the conflict in the Middle East, or the break-up of the European Union, but a genuine surprise is harder to suggest.

Still, we can see that global priorities give rise to cooperative efforts, aiming at a regime for the globe, a form of global governance. But we can also witness counter-reactions, a backlash, resulting in particularistic demands. A comprehensive assessment is likely to conclude that the trend is stronger towards global arrangements. That estimate, however, has to incorporate potential challenges and surprises. There are neither linear trends towards uniform globalization, nor only random events in other directions.

The United Nations and global governance

So far, these reflections have concerned very general propositions. The primary interest here is the United Nations as a global expression of international concern for peace and security, but also as an arena where the interests of states, civil society, and corporate power come together. As an embryo for global governance, world order, and *Pax Omnium*, its strengths and weaknesses are important to understand.

The UN mandate is to maintain international peace and security. Over its first 60 years the organization has gradually adapted to new conditions. It has been mandated to take on a large number of smaller and larger wars. The arrangement of having several organs dealing with peace and security (the General Assembly, the Security Council, and the Secretary-General) has been to its advantage. The three bodies have been able to play special roles at special times (Wallensteen 2006). Together with an ability to add new instruments (peacekeeping operations, special representatives, targeted sanctions) and normative developments (going from inter- to intra-state conflict, for instance), the organization remains at the centre of international thinking on peace and security.

Recently, it has been argued that the reduction in armed conflict that is visible in global statistics since the early 1990s correlates with the increase in international commitment to peaceful settlements of disputes (largely, but not only UN activities, Human Security Report 2005). This is to suggest that – although there are some obvious failures in the international response to crisis situations – the global commitment in itself serves to activate social forces in favour of peaceful settlements. Thus, we need to look more closely at the reform initiatives and the role of the UN in different parts of the world, and how this relates to the four sets of players identified here.

Reforming the United Nations

The present process of reforming the United Nations, initiated by the Secretary-General in 2003, and resulting in the thought-provoking and bold report of the High-Level Panel in 2004, gained momentum during 2005 (High-Level Panel 2004, UN Secretary-General 2005). The outcome document of the World Summit in New York in September 2005 was somewhat disappointing (2005 World Summit Outcome). It was left to the General Assembly to deal with the reforms during the 2005–2006 session, the sixtieth of the UN. Particularly significant in the Outcome document was a global commitment to the principle of an international responsibility to protect populations in danger of genocide or similar threats in cases where the governments were not taking appropriate actions. This followed on a normative development that constitutes learning from the failures of the 1990s. It was also referred to by the Security Council in April 2006, thus beginning the implementation of this principle.[6]

On the institutional side, a new body, the Peacebuilding Commission, started its work in 2006. A new Human Rights Council was created and began to operate almost immediately. A challenge was to find an international definition of terrorism and progress on an international strategy was recorded.

This shows that the UN system for international peace and security is gradually reforming itself. The pace is slow, however, and reform appears as an uphill struggle. The reform movement is largely vested in a set of 'like-minded' countries, that is, states that see the UN as important for their own as well as for world security. There is an interest also among civil society organizations, but at the World Summit in New York, September 2005, there was not the same popular participation as has been witnessed in conferences on global economy (for instance at meetings of the G8, the IMF, and the World Bank), or on global environmental issues. The same is true for international business interests. It is noteworthy that the direct security concerns are still largely left to the states, which are also strongly represented in international bodies. The 'supra-national' element in the UN is less than in the EU, for instance. The UN Secretary-General has a smaller and leaner secretariat at his/her disposal than the EU Commission, and in the field of independent collection of information, the Secretariat has very little. The shift in influence from the General Assembly to the Security Council also demonstrates a shift towards certain member states (the five permanent members). The UN remains strongly an inter-state organization. What can be agreed are those matters on which the member states are in agreement.[7] The Secretariat's role in reforming the body rests ultimately on the support that can be generated among member states.

UN attention selectivity

By 2020 the UN will reach its seventy-fifth birthday and more than 30 years will have passed since end of the Cold War. In a 'surprise-free' scenario, it could be said that the four types of players are likely to remain the significant ones. State failure, that is the declining state revenue in some developing countries, may continue to weaken some states, but not the major ones. Terrorism focussing on disrupting international linkages may take new forms (air transport and tourism have already been targeted; the near future may include a focus on Internet, financial transactions, disruption of satellite traffic or other forms of international communication). The unprecedented consensus on combating terrorism is likely to remain. Civil society organizations may become more effective in raising global awareness of threats to human rights, human dignity, peace and justice, as such organizations take root in more repressive societies. Undoubtedly, multinational corporations are strongly entrenched although the dominance of western corporations is likely to be challenged by companies based in other parts of the world.

This suggests a move towards more global participation. Will this also affect the UN? For the first 15 years after the end of the Cold War, the UN attended to some conflicts, but not to all. This can be demonstrated by analysing the Security Council resolutions under Chapter VII of the UN Charter (which are mandatory decisions for all member states, and may involve the authorization of sanctions or the use of force). Since 1946 there has been 254 such resolutions, most of them adopted since 1990 (all but 17). The geographical distribution is highly significant: Africa 34 per cent (dealing with 13 different conflicts), Europe 30 per cent (mostly relating to former Yugoslavia), and the Middle East (that is, West Asia and North Africa) 29 per cent (mostly dealing with Iraq and Afghanistan). The rest of the world accounts for less than ten per cent of all resolutions. For Asia there are only two conflicts that have given rise to mandatory resolutions. These were on the Korean War in 1950 and East Timor almost exactly 50 years later (1999–2002). Asia was the scene of one of the most deadly conflicts since the Second World War, the Vietnam War. It was never brought to the Security Council. Also for the American hemisphere there are only two conflicts that entered the Security Council record with a mandatory decision: the Falklands/ Malvinas War of 1982 and Haiti 1993–1994 (Johansson 2003).

Although the UN is a global organization, there are demonstrable limits to its involvement. Most analysts emphasize that they are set by influential states. When major powers do not want the UN to be involved, they have the power to prevent such action (formally, of course, by using the veto in the Security Council, but politically long before there is a vote). The same is true of regionally strong states that can have support of major powers in the Council (for instance, India could prevent negative decisions on the Kashmir issue; Indonesia could for long bar the East Timor issue) (Wallensteen 2002; Wallensteen and Johansson 2004). These features make clear that conflicts in the Americas today will not be subject to Council decisions, unless the US agrees.[8] The same applies to conflicts in Asia, where the influence of China and India is likely to be as effective an obstacle as any.

Mostly the UN has only attended to conflicts where there has been consensus among major powers for UN action; where significant regional powers are not blocking; and where governments are willing to allow measures even in internal conflicts. In all cases this may be because they hope to benefit from UN action, or are too weak to resist international measures. The net result is revealed in the statistics which were just presented. To put it in concrete terms: since the end of the Cold War the UN has dealt more with conflicts in a typical European space, the regions north, south, and east of an extended Mediterranean basin.[9] Together, more than 90 per cent of all binding Council decisions have concerned conflicts in Europe, the Middle East, and Africa, combining three distinct but interconnected regions. The linkages make this area highly internationalized, even 'globalized': there is a shared history, colonialism, human settlements, raw material exploitation, migration patterns, and development assistance. There is knowledge but also prejudice; there are common interests, but also contradictory ones. The geographical variation in UN interventions corresponds to webs of connections, where not only states are significant players.

To this we need to add that many armed conflicts today have to be understood as 'internationalized' in a malign way. A recent review showed that 80 per cent of the internal conflicts had outside players supporting one or the other side. Furthermore, most typical this was by neighbouring states, not distant major powers (Harbom and Wallensteen 2005). This confirms the need of understanding contemporary conflict patterns not as isolated entities, but in a larger, often regional context. There is selectivity in the way the UN attends to conflict and, thus, in the way global security is provided. Let us pursue this one more step.

UN decision-making and regional security

It has been pointed out that the world since 1989 has taken on a character of *a trifurcated international system* of specific regional concentrations, with the United States as the only player that appears in all three spaces: the European, the Asian, and the American spaces (Wallensteen 2002, 2007). They all carry different traits. The larger European space houses a great organizational infrastructure, not only with the UN but also other international organizations (EU, NATO, CoE, OSCE, AU, ECOWAS, SADC, IGAD, etc.). Asia – containing close to half of humankind – on the other hand has no overarching organizations at all, thus its security is dependent on each country's own sources and the direct engagement of major powers, including the United States (e.g., in dealing with the many issues surrounding North Korea). The third system is the Americas, dominated by a US-South American relationship, with many mixed experiences. There are considerable and strong interconnections, often captured in terms of 'imperialism'. US-based corporations are found all over the region, but very few South American companies operate in the United States. These two spaces are 'under-organized' in peace and security. Thus, we may wonder whether the UN will take on a larger role in these settings or remain confined to the larger European space.

A first point concerns UN decision-making. Leading states may block the UN from action. A reason for doing so is that the UN is seen as an extra-regional organization. The region as such has only limited influence, and thus, regional players may agree to not let the UN enter. The countries in the European space, may, however, be certain that they can 'direct' the organization and thus be less worried about it acting outside their preferred course, in a broader sense. This brings us to one issue of UN reform that has been on the agenda, but without any change so far; the composition of the Security Council. No other structural question has such obvious long-term effect as this one. Including more permanent members would mean a change in the power over the UN. Thus, this reform issue serves as a mirror of the future of the organization. Changes in composition may change the attention of the UN and impact on global priorities. It would make the UN a more truly global body. What would it mean in the longer term for the two 'under-organized' spaces?

Structurally and substantially, the *South American states* would have much to benefit from the UN becoming active in their region. In 2004, Brazil took the lead role for the UN peace operation in Haiti, demonstrating its increased commitment to the organization but also that there are others with peacekeeping capabilities. The only permanent member of the Security Council from this hemisphere is the US and it has often preferred to involve the OAS, other regional groupings, acting bilaterally or even unilaterally. UN attention may affect this pattern.

The question of power over the UN is pertinent. Most structural reform proposals include the idea of at least one more permanent member from this hemisphere, in order to 'balance' the regional considerations, and – in effect – also 'balancing' the United States on hemispheric matters. The chief candidate, Brazil, has recently joined three other contenders to pursue their interest in becoming permanent members, the Group of 4. The bid was unsuccessful in 2005, but Brazil's candidacy is likely to remain. The idea of Brazil 'representing' the entire continent may not be attractive to all South American states. At the same time, the size and significance of Brazil makes it difficult not to have this country on the Council. In the long run, Brazil probably has a good chance of being seated, most likely, however, in a seat that is not eternally permanent, but for a six or ten-year renewable term. Even such a reform of the Council may lead to a change in the way the UN is involved in South America.

Substantially, the serious conflict issues in the Americas have concerned internal wars along a left-right spectrum. Colombia's situation typifies such divisions, Venezuela might be next for such dynamics, as could possibly be the fate also for Cuba (after Castro). Conflict prevention, in other words, would have to deal with deeper democracy, approaching unequal distribution of income and resources, combating corruption, and restricting trade in small arms.

New items are accumulating energy and might lead to international reactions. The CSO community and the multinational business may, in fact, confront each other over issues in South America. A case in point concerns environmental degradation (e.g., in Brazil). Another is the role of the indigenous populations who have become increasingly aware of their human rights (e.g., in Peru, Ecuador, and Bolivia). Ethnic clashes are common elsewhere, and experience shows that they cannot be subsumed under a left-right paradigm. These developments will make the UN framework useful, allowing for learning from other continents. Due to such new security concerns and new connections, participation in international organizations and in global governance can be expected to increase. Changing the composition of the Security Council will serve to strengthen this trend, and make the UN more meaningful to a new group of stakeholders.

The second space that is 'under-organized' in international security is *Asia, primarily East and South Asia.* Typical for both these Asian areas is the strength of the governments and the state apparatus in domestic as well as international affairs (be they one-party states, military regimes, or functioning democracies). In large measure, Asian international relations can be understood in terms of classic Realpolitik. Each state fends for itself, it takes the security actions it sees fit, and neighbours sometimes perceive such measures as threatening and requiring counter-reactions. A traditional security-dilemma is in operation and alliances are formed accordingly: Japan is allied with the United States (as are South Korea, Taiwan, and others) in order to 'balance' China. China is now extending relations to other countries, not the least Russia, possibly as a way of countering the US.

There are two contradictory visions for security in East Asia: a new Cold War (East Asia style) and a democratic security community (East Asia style). They need to be spelled out.

First, there is **the East Asian Cold War scenario**. It predicts stronger rivalry between China and Japan, where China uses its power to prevent Japan from reaching its economic and security goals in the area. This means denying Japan its hotly desired permanent seat of the UN Security Council. This would result in the UN being kept out of East Asia. Disputes would have to be dealt with in an *ad hoc* conflict management mode, just as was the case with European affairs during the European Cold War: conflicts are frozen, partitions are maintained, economic growth is non-integrative, and opposing blocks are constructed. East Asia exhibits some of the same ingredients, for instance, with a divided Korea. It may be even worse as the two Koreas have actually been at war with one another. Even more challenging is that leading states themselves have unsolved territorial issues (China-Taiwan, Japan-Russia, India-China). This scenario expects the civil society to be limited, state-controlled and the business community to 'play by the rules' given to it by state authority. Regional tensions serve to further the preponderance of state players.

A second possibility is **the East Asian Security Community scenario**. It assumes a rapprochement between China and Japan, sees the end to old issues such as textbooks and shrine visits, includes increased economic integration, and reduced emphasis on military spending, in short, more confidence-building. This would amount to an East Asian version of the *Ostpolitik* of Willy Brandt in Germany in the 1970s. It would allow for a *détente*, improved by mutual connections, and friendlier relations. This in turn, as happened from *détente* in Europe, would further democratization, this time in China. Thus, a community of more shared political values would follow. From the point of view of international peace and security, the second vision involves the least risk. Thus, to have Japan in the Security Council would be a good beginning, signalling a more cooperative scenario. China's attitude on this issue is an early indicator of where the region may be heading.

These two scenarios are *complicated by the dynamics of South Asia*. The issue of the UN Security Council seat is again a useful metaphor for the overall relationships. As we have seen, India is another contender for a seat in the Council. Its main antagonists are Pakistan and China. This means that China is in a position to block any other permanent Asian representation in the world organization, and can play one against the other. In terms of history and strategic rivalry, Japan is most important for China. Paradoxically, although Japan has been a contender for the longest time, India may be the first to get a seat, as far as China is concerned. This is further complicated by the India-Pakistan relationship which is largely determined by the Kashmir issue. The peace process underway since 2004 may indicate a chance for change, which the region and the world would welcome.

That is also a point where *a regionally 'external' player, the United States*, enters the question. What happens in South Asia has strategic implications. Pakistan and India both prefer good relations with the United

States. The US in turn needs Pakistan in its global struggle against terrorism, in Afghanistan, and against an Islamist Iran. India, however, is attractive for the international business community, and gets good marks for democratic governance and an active civil society. There is likely to be division in the US administration as to what emphasis US policy should have. A plausible outcome is that the United States will not make a choice, but prefer to support both.[10] This would give the US a strong interest in the two states finding an agreement on Kashmir. Either way, however, a situation of *détente* in South Asia would stimulate *détente* in East Asia. The global issue of the composition of the Security Council serves as an indicator of future relations in Asia.[11] It has obvious regional implications.[12]

For the US, the Korean issue may the central security concern, the substance being more important than the structural dimension of UN reform. North Korea's nuclear weapon programmes, its involvement in nuclear proliferation and its development of ballistic weapons, are among chief worries on the US side. In dealing with North Korea, an understanding between China and Japan is helpful. North Korea has been attempting to play on the China–Japan tension. If that tension can be removed, the US would be in a strong position to achieve change in North Korea. Furthermore, if the issue of Kashmir is solved peacefully, so could the Korean equation. As is the case in South Asia with India and Pakistan, the US has good reasons for choosing both rivals, in this case Japan *and* China, for solving its East Asia problems. This would support the chances of the security community vision being the option that will prevail.[13]

These two scenarios for East Asia, building on a traditional analysis of dominant state players, still suggest that the UN could be useful for Asia as a whole.[14] The UN activities in Cambodia and East Timor should comfort regional leaders that are sensitive on sovereignty issues. Both these missions were completed within short time, and the countries were left to find their own solutions. In this region, UN activities have been short (a few years, at most) or very limited in scope (such as the observers on the lines between India and Pakistan).[15]

The state-centric scenarios that prevail among leaders and analysts are likely to be challenged by the emergence of CSOs and MNCs. There are already active national CSOs in most countries, but their activities have so far seldom gone beyond state boundaries. There might even be prohibitions against this. This is unlikely to remain for a long period of time. Economic trends are likely to spill over into cultural and social connections. Also, MNCs tend to be state-dominated and geared at supplying the 'home' country in an almost colonial way.[16] As companies become richer, have more resources abroad, and learn to operate on the world market, their connections to the state might be reduced. Interestingly, China has recently become a more active member of the UN, where India and Japan already have a record of involvement.

What about *the large space connected to Europe (Balkans, Caucasus, Middle East, Africa)?* To a great extent the UN divide between rich and poor, North and South, is a divide within this space, where 'Europe' also includes the United States. The statistics on Security Council Chapter VII resolutions implies that this is where UN peace missions have been concentrated. It is also the organizationally densest region. Thus, it is appropriate to consider it to be a place where there are international alternatives to the UN. The continuation of armed conflicts is likely to involve more such organizations. The European Union is already developing its own rapid deployment force and has tested its capacities (with strengths and limits) in the Democratic Republic of Congo. NATO is engaged as well, notably in Afghanistan. This diversification of organizational frameworks may become stronger. Much of this, furthermore, might increasingly take place under the authorization of the UN Security Council. This brings us back to the indicator for future change in global governance: the composition of the Security Council. Interestingly, the only explicit contender for a seat in the Security Council from this entire area is Germany, and its quest has met resistance. For the US, Germany has not been such a reliable partner as it may have wanted (i.e. during the Iraqi decisions in early 2003). For others the question is raised, why yet another European state on the Council? The idea of African countries on two permanent seats, furthermore, has less strength, as there is a lack of all-African support of candidate countries.

Furthermore, this is the space where a number of the new concerns of the UN will play themselves out: the ideas of a responsibility to protect exposed populations may largely come to concern African cases (Sudan, and what happens in the Darfur region is frequently mentioned). The campaign on countering terrorism also has a focus here, in particular as it relates to a special strand in Islam. The uses of targeted sanctions have so far been restricted to this geographical space as well (with the exception of Haiti; Staibano 2005). The only case of a unilateral, external military attempt to install democracy since 1945 is also taking place here (Iraq since 2003).

Peace and security are tied to the successful dealing with the crises in Central Africa (a large part of Africa) and Palestine (for the Middle East).

The two players who could play a role in direct negotiations are undoubtedly the US and the UN (with the support of the EU). Any short-term forecast of the Middle East suggests more turbulence rather than less, where a realistic scenario also has to include a popular revolt against the ruling elite in Saudi Arabia, which would affect intra-Arab relations as well as international oil supply, far into the future.

Still, there are lessons to be learned. In the Congo, the UN, European institutions and African neighbours went together to end this war as well as the related ones (Burundi, Sudan, Uganda). A cumbersome process has yielded results: gradually peace talks and peace agreements emerged and agreements were implemented. Such a concerted action is lacking for the Middle East. Instead, outside powers are divided and allowing regional divisions to strengthen themselves.

The United Nations and world order

Clearly, all of the set of players do not have a specific link to the United Nations. The civil society organizations are active in international conference diplomacy, in public diplomacy, media, and popular advocacy. The formal linkages to the UN in general and to the security issues in particular need new organizational expressions. The Cardoso panel had some such suggestions (Cardoso 2004).[17] The new Peacebuilding Commission could be a forum for such proposals.

Also the linkages between the UN and the corporate community remain weak. To big business the UN is probably a strange bird and it does not offer many business opportunities.[18] Through the Global Compact, the Secretary-General has attempted to create bridges, particularly in the field of corporate responsibility. The cooperation of the business community is important, for instance, in the implementation of sanctions or in the provision of investments to support peace processes.

When analysing post-Cold War trends and thinking about the future, the geographical divisions of the world demonstrate significant differences, which are relevant for the UN and its future. The four sets of players are particularly distinct for a geopolitical zone that could be termed the European space (including North America, West and East Europe, West Asia, Africa, and Oceania). This is also the space where the world body, the UN, has been the most active, and where it is likely to face the strongest demands also in the coming years. Many of the new principles exposed in the UN system find their application in this geopolitical configuration. There is a correlation between the density of this network of interconnections and international commitment to dealing with conflict. In this sense, there is already 'globalization' within this space, although governance is insufficient and there is a need for international regulation, including the UN.

The other two spaces, Asia and the Americas, do not exhibit the same characteristics. However, the discussion here makes clear that similar conditions are developing and that they will result in an interest for countries in South America and in Asia to give more of a role to the UN. This points in the direction of not only developing the agenda for action of the UN but also of the need of Security Council reform (Malone 2004).

In the introduction, it was asked who has the most influence on the future of this planet and what the UN role could be. A sceptical reader might object that world order today and in the future depends on power relations in the world as a whole. Furthermore, one form of power is linked to international peace and security, coercive power. In a period over 10 to 15 years, the sceptic might surmise, economic growth or societal stagnation will have profound effects on the regional and global distribution of power. Today there is a focus on the rise of China and India. The emergence of new ideological frameworks may affect popular mobilization (religious systems have had that role for some time, in some regions). The introduction or creation of new weapon systems may affect regional or even global conditions. Scarcities of certain economic assets may stimulate rivalry, but also result in new forms of cooperation. These resource-based and capacity-focussed variables may be stronger determinants of the future than suggested here.

This 'realist' analysis yields different scenarios for the future: there is a possibility of increased major power rivalry and a return to Realpolitik on a global level. This could be in the form of new bipolar constellations, for instance, of the West versus an axis of China, Russia and India; or one of China versus the US with other players floating between. There is also *Pax Americana*, with one country dominating all the others. In these scenarios, IOs, CSOs, and MNCs are reduced to entities that depend on the state and its capacity.

In such pictures, the discrepancy between globalization and global security is dealt with through accumulated power and force. Power defined as preponderance of resources is the decisive element; the size of industrial capacity, military might, ideological coherence, and access to raw materials. This approach would expect negative disruptions from military, revolutionary, or counter-reactionary actions, using coercive strategies to challenge the system. 'Stability' becomes a key word, maintained with overwhelming power.

Without denying the importance of such factors, however, present trends of globalization point to resources that are not accumulated in this simplistic way: smart technologies, quick communication, educated populations, creativity, intellectual power, social visions, and individual entrepreneurship. These are the factors that also drive players, and affect that standing of the states. This 'softer' globalization may reduce the state's ability to fully control developments. It suggests other types of 'disruptions': positive events, social innovations, and political experiments, such as democratization, at unexpected moments in seemingly unlikely places (China, Burma, Iran).

Thus, the United Nations and future global governance will be formed by an interplay of factors and players, including the 'hard' and 'soft' approaches. The former may stem from ambitions to build power globally or regionally for one or a few, the latter from a belief in representation, openness, and transparency. The former may result in attempts at global hegemony (supremacy) or preventing others from gaining pre-eminence (balance of power). Historically such ambitions have been justified as a matter of creating 'lasting peace'. It has been seen as a global solution to the problem of general war among all (*Bellum omnium contra omnes*, Hobbes 1651).

In this contribution it is argued that the debate now has to go beyond states, and incorporate international organizations, civil society, and major corporations as increasingly independent and important players. Peace, furthermore, requires the commitment of all players. The webs created through globalization restrict actions of the states, reduce the space for coercive power, bring forward new interests, and add new competence. This may result in a world order composed of a broad, diverse and difficult-to-govern international society, where a reformed, more representative UN has a leading role. This is the beginning of *Pax Omnium Inter Omnes*, a peace for all among all. It may be a more creative way of solving the discrepancy between globalization and governance.

Notes

1. The debate can be found in a number of leading journals such as *International Security, Security Dialogue, Global Governance, Foreign Affairs* and *Foreign Policy*. It is worth an analysis in itself.
2. The UN Security Council acting under Chapter VII can make binding decisions, for all member states, but also for all IOs, as they are largely constituted

by the same member states. In its use of targeted sanctions, the UN also makes decisions for specified individuals and non-state organizations. The European Union has authority over matters that earlier were the exclusive concerns of the state. Thus, it is debated whether the EU is a regional IO or something beyond the traditional state.

3. This applies also to the present author, who bases this essay on an understanding of international organizations and their role in peace and security, more than any other field.

4. The Swedish referendum on nuclear power in 1980 is seen in this light by opposing sides: the nuclear power industry and nuclear physicists saw the outcome as a vote for preventing advanced technical development. To the environmentalists it was a powerful testimony against a detached, technological establishment. A similar debate unfolded in 2003 over whether Sweden should join the European monetary union and switch to the *euro*, or not. Again the issue was highly technical and much of the public debate instead dealt with a mass-elite dichotomy.

5. An example of the dynamics is when Palestinian leader Yassir Arafat chose in 2000 to say 'no' to a proposed settlement for the Palestinian issue. Historically it was an unprecedented offer, but the Palestinian public was sceptical and Arafat received a heroic reception on his return. An opportunity was lost, however; a second *intifada* began; a hard-line government took over in Israel; later followed by a Hamas government in the Palestinian territories.

6. Security Council Resolution 1674 (2006) reaffirms the relevant paragraphs of the 2005 World Summit Outcome Document.

7. This was demonstrated when four unarmed UN observers were killed by an Israeli bomb in South Lebanon on 25 July 2006. It took the Security Council two days to agree to lamely react to this event, although a citizen of one permanent member (China) and one from the Presidency of the EU (Finland) were killed.

8. The events of September 11th 2001 were condemned the following day, leading to an enlarged definition of what constitutes matters under Chapter VII; international terrorism was added. A new operation was initiated: financial (and related) sanctions as a tool against terrorism with as special, vigorous Counter-Terrorism Committee as lead body (SC resolution 1373, 2001).

9. This, in a way, is the old Roman area of operation, but its reach into Africa did not go beyond the Sahara, while the UN today is heavily involved in sub-Saharan Africa.

10. An indication was the US President George W. Bush's visit in 2006, staying longer in India and signing more agreements there than in Pakistan.

11. The changes proposed by G4 assumes that there is a 'review' in 2020 on the composition of the Council, thus, in theory limiting the permanency for the new permanent members. Thus, when countries take sides on this issue, this may very well be the time perspective they apply. It fits well with the time frame used in this chapter.

12. Other indicators would be the China-Taiwan issue, and democratization of Hong Kong (which by 2020 will have passed half of the stipulated period of a special autonomy within China), and of China itself.

13. This is the case, independent of US administration. Many of the moves made by the Bush government in this region parallel those of the previous Clinton regime.

14. This may have to be demonstrated to Asian leaderships. For China it should be recalled that Dag Hammarskjöld, as UN Secretary-General, helped solve a major problem in China-US relations in 1955, by doing so contributing to a secret link between the two major powers. Having a South Korean, Mr Ban Ki-Moon, as UN Secretary-General improves the prospects of an enlarged UN role in this region.

15. The UN was quick to leave East Timor in 2002 as requested, something many regretted when the country was again hit by conflict in 2006, and when a new operation was put in place.

16. An analysis of, for instance, Chinese companies in Africa is likely to show a preoccupation with raw materials of use for China, even to the point of bringing Chinese workers along. The interest in local development is limited.

17. On 20 September 2005 the Security Council held a special session on the role of civil society in conflict prevention, S/PRST/2005/42.

18. An exception was the Oil-for-Food programme that the UN administered 1996–2003, in total a value of US$ 67 billion. It has resulted in allegations of corruption against some officials and corporations. It demonstrated the weakness of the UN Secretariat in administering large economic transactions; it was not part of the original design for the UN; and it is not an experience likely to be repeated.

References

2005 World Summit Outcome (2005) UN General Assembly, A/60/L.1, 20 September 2005.

Cardoso, F. H. (2004) *We the Peoples: Civil Society, the United Nations and Global Governance*, The High-Level Panel on the relations between the United Nations and Civil Society, New York: the United Nations.

Harbom, L. and Wallensteen, P. (2005) 'Armed Conflict and Its International Dimensions 1946–2004', *Journal of Peace Research* 42: 623–635.

High-Level Panel (2004) *A more secure world: Our shared responsibility*, Report from the Secretary-General's High-Level Panel on Threats, Challenges, and Change, New York: the United Nations.

Hobbes, T. (1651) *The Leviathan*.

Human Security Report 2005. War and Peace in the 21st Century (2005), The Human Security Centre, University of British Columbia, Oxford University Press.

Johansson, P. (2003) *UN Security Council Chapter VII Resolutions, 1946–2002. An Inventory*, Uppsala: Department of Peace and Conflict Research.

Malone, D. (ed) (2004) *The Security Council. From the Cold War to the 21st Century*, Boulder, Co and London: The International Peace Academy and Lynne Rienner.

Mitrany, D. (1943) *A Working Peace System: An Argument for the Functional Development of International Organization*, London: Royal Institute of International Affairs, Chatham House.

Mitrany, D. (1975) *The Functional Theory of Politics*, New York: St. Martin's Press and London School of Economics.

Staibano, C. (2005) 'Trends in UN Sanctions. From ad hoc practice to institutional capacity', pp 31–54 in Wallensteen, P. and Staibano, C. (eds) (2005) *International Sanctions. Between words and wars in the global system*, London: Routledge/Frank Cass.

UN Secretary-General (2005) *In larger freedom: towards development, security and human rights for all*, New York: the United Nations.

Valladão de Carvalho, M. I. e de Castro Santos, M. H. (orgs) (2006) *O Século XXI no Brasil e no Mundo*, São Paulo: EDUSC.

Wallensteen, P. (1984) 'Universalism vs. Particularism. On the Limits of Major Power Order', *Journal of Peace Research*, 21 (3): 243–257.

Wallensteen, P. (2002/2007) *Understanding Conflict Resolution*, London: Sage. Second, revised edition 2007.

Wallensteen, P. (2006) 'UN in armed conflict: Studying its limits and strengths', in Valladão de Carvalho, M. I. e de Castro Santos, M. H. (orgs) (2006) *O Século XXI no Brasil e no Mundo*, São Paulo: EDUSC.

Wallensteen, P. and Johansson, P. (2004) 'Security Council decisions in perspective', pp 17–33 in Malone, D. (ed) (2004) *The Security Council. From the Cold War to the 21st Century*, Boulder, Co and London: The International Peace Academy and Lynne Rienner.

Wallensteen, P. and Staibano, C. (eds) (2005) *International Sanctions. Between words and wars in the global system*, London: Routledge/Frank Cass.

Conclusion

Björn Hettne

This book, focussing on *human values and global governance*, together with a companion volume on *sustainable development in a globalized world*, is the final outcome of six years' work of the 'Sector Committee on Culture, Security and Sustainable Social Development' within Riksbankens Jubileumsfond. The project, described in the preface, is reported in two complementary volumes. This book takes us from the process of development in the global context over the formation of new collective identities to the cultural dynamics of social interaction at different societal levels. This emerging field can be called global studies, and the theoretical approach global social theory. The cultural consequences of globalization manifest themselves in the form of 'multiculturalism'. Multiculturalism means that culture has been separated from geography, i.e. many cultures co-exist in the same place. Multiculturalism is a complex concept informing different perspectives on integration. Here the paradigmatic difference 'before and after globalization' can be illustrated by, on the one hand, immigration as a security policy discourse and, on the other, global migration as the bearer of new transnational structures characterized by cultural hybridization. On the first view (methodological nationalism), continuing 'immigration' constitutes an anomaly, in the sense that it undermines a national identity that has been taken as self-evident; on the other view (cosmopolitanism) global migration (amounting to 100 million people) is a precursor of some kind of post-Westphalian global order, characterized by multicultural metropoles, transnational networks, and diasporas. Multiculturalism is not only a complex but also a controversial concept. It can be defined as the opposite of assimilation, and can also be contrasted with the 'plural society', well-known from a number of colonial contexts, in which different ethnic groups existed side by side without much contact. The management of diversity or *difference* is problematic. Those who support multiculturalism define a multicultural society as a society which is positive towards cultural and ethnic diversity, both because individual cultural identities are respected, and because such a society is culturally richer and more dynamic. Opponents regard multiculturalism as a threat to the national culture. To the extent that multiculturalism is at all accepted, it is regarded as a preliminary stage in the process of assimilation (the melting pot). Similarly, cosmopolitans devoted to universalism are inclined to see multiculturalism as a danger in the form of essentialism, a reifying of cultural differences which locks identities in rigid forms into a kind of 'folk museum'. It thus complicates 'the modern project', universal values and global ethics. The advocates of *hybrid culture*, finally, welcome diversity as a sign of cultural richness and creativity. Multiculturalism can lead to conflict, but of course does not necessarily do so. A common feature in what is known as 'the new conflicts' is none the less the importance attained by the collective cultural identity: everything from 'tribal war' to 'the clash of civilizations'. This is the pessimistic scenario: that cultures or culturally defined groups must necessarily be opposed to one another, which in the light of the weakened nation-state creates an endless future conflict scenario. In the same way, however, stronger cultural identity becomes not only a basis for conflict but also a possible basis for dialogue. An anchorage in a cultural identity is probably a necessary, if not sufficient, basis for dialogue with (segments of) other cultures. Cultural identity can be both a basis for an inclusive dialogue and a point of departure for marking boundaries and exclusivism, leading to conflict. The question is when we will have either the one or the other outcome. The answer cannot be found in the realm of culture. The dialogue will not take place from culture to culture but between cultural segments. It is nevertheless important to view this dialogue from different regional macro-cultural perspectives.

Globalization entails marginalization of social groups which on the basis of ethno-nationalistic arguments (cleansing of 'the others') cling fast to territories ('sons of the soil') and mobilize through 'politics of identity'. Ethnic cleansing, which often reflect a struggle for economic resources, implies collapsing states and 'black holes' ('Chernobyls of culture' is Karl Eric Knutsson's dramatic expression). During the 1990s the global society tried to manage such 'human emergencies' by means of so called humanitarian interventions. To some observers this signalled a new world order. However, after September 11th such interventionism has become more visibly geopolitically motivated, creating doubts about the possibility of a new liberal order.

Discussions on the theme of conflict resolution most frequently deal with different constitutional arrangements to keep the conflict at a manageable level. The question of influence and power is seldom the original occasion for conflict. In the last resort it is a matter of the control of resources and cultural identity, and in a multi-ethnic state these aspects must be built into the development strategy itself. It is a matter of the influence of the development pattern on ethnic relations and of what development principles – if they were applied – would minimize the ethnic conflicts. Conflict management can thus either be 'preventive' – to clear away underlying structural causes of conflict before becoming manifest – or precipitated by an acute conflict. The first option is of course always to be preferred. Failure to prevent will sooner or later raise the issue of intervention.

The phenomenon of intervention in its broad meaning perhaps better than anything else illustrates the globalized, post-Westphalian and post-sovereign condition. The new interventionism constitutes a discourse which would have been unthinkable two decades ago. Cases of intervention (and non-intervention) that have occurred during the 1990s provide material for interesting comparative studies of the implementation of global morality. Nothing shows more clearly the link between the global and the local in the globalized condition, as also the permanent division between the universal and the particular.

Globalization and justice are in the judgement of many not altogether compatible; hence the anti-globalization (or rather alter-globalization) movement. There is a growing need for a common or universal ethics. The Commission report 'Our Creative Diversity', as also earlier the Commission on Global Governance, chaired by Ingvar Carlsson, combined its argumentation for diversity, the right to be different, with the assertion of certain fundamental norms (universal ethics) on which it ought to be able to create a broad unity of opinion.

A dialogue contains elements of consensus and dissent. Universal ethics can be said to take as its starting point what is common to different cultures, while multiculturalism favours cultural diversity, thereby contradicting universalism. It is important to underline that a global ethics which transcends cultures does not presuppose cultural homogenization.

External intervention in acute conflicts is normally followed by a continuing engagement in what is called 'post-conflict reconstruction', where the whole troika of concepts comes into use. From security and back to development. The question of societal reconstruction is highly relevant to security in its broadest sense. This illustrates also the imperative of sustainable social development, since the social development which preceded the conflict was demonstrably unsustainable. Finally, but most important, it illustrates the fundamental importance of the cultural dimension. Social reconstruction, including reconciliation, must take place in such a way that the conflict does not recur. That is brought about by conflict-healing measures and by creating social structures that moderate conflict. Particularly important in this situation are institutions and rules of the game for regime changes that are both democratic and pay regard to the interests of minorities (consociational democracy). Election monitoring with the aid of international observers has become a normal element in healing conflicts and in reconstruction work. But it is not enough. The complex issue of reconciliation and accommodation based on the local understanding of conflict is of the utmost importance, but is in practice neglected.

Now, in the era of post-development, that social engineering is out of fashion as a national policy, it is paradoxically being resurrected in extreme form in societies that are more or less totally destroyed physically, economically, politically, socially, culturally, and morally. The impossibility of imposed nation-building and democratisation underlines the need for civil society to be involved in the work of reconstruction. The problem is, however, that what we count as civil society has also been destroyed, and what remains to build on are 'islands of civility' in a sea of violence, revenge, fear, and suspicion. These gigantic problems lead to major requirements for research concerning culture, security and sustainable social development, boiling down to the very meaning of 'society'.

Index